Peking Diary

January	July
February	August
March	September
April	October
May	November
June	December

Derk Bodde

H E N R Y   S C H U M A N ,   I N C

N E W   Y O R K

Peking Diary

a year of

revolution

to the common people of China,

the *Lao Pai Hsing* or "Old Hundred Names,"
who deserve so much and have ever
received so little.

Contents I

Preface   XV

Prologue: Slow Boat to China   1

August, 1948

AUGUST 29 (SUNDAY) *A Chinese Ducal Palace : Material and Spiritual Impoverishment : Verbalism*   7

September, 1948

SEPTEMBER 12 (SUNDAY) *Campers in the Temple of Heaven : Two Incidents*   12

SEPTEMBER 13 (MONDAY) *Morning Sounds*   16

SEPTEMBER 26 (SUNDAY) *Peking Is a Dream : How the Communists Get Their Arms*   17

SEPTEMBER 27 (MONDAY) *Strike of the Merchants : A Chinese Intellectual Speaks His Mind*   21

October, 1948

OCTOBER 2 (SATURDAY) *A Talk with Our Teacher*   26

OCTOBER 14 (THURSDAY) *"Disasters and Anomalies" : Looking into the Past : Troubles of an Americanized Chinese in China : Inflation Again*   28

OCTOBER 16 (SATURDAY) *The World beyond Our Walls*   33

OCTOBER 27 (WEDNESDAY) *A Meeting with the Madissima :*
War and Food : Disillusionment   34

OCTOBER 30 (SATURDAY) *A Talk with Peita Students*   38

November, 1948

NOVEMBER 1 (MONDAY) *Governmental Criticism from the*
Ta Kung Pao   41

NOVEMBER 2 (TUESDAY) *The Day's News*   42

NOVEMBER 3 (WEDNESDAY) *The Exodus Begins*   43

NOVEMBER 4 (THURSDAY) *The Exodus Grows*   43

NOVEMBER 6 (SATURDAY) *A Coalition Government?*   44

NOVEMBER 7 (SUNDAY) *Anniversary of the Bolshevik Revolu-*
tion   45

NOVEMBER 9 (TUESDAY) *A Marxist View of China*   45

NOVEMBER 10 (WEDNESDAY) *Rice and Riots in Shanghai*   47

NOVEMBER 11 (THURSDAY) *Refugee Students*   48

NOVEMBER 12 (FRIDAY) *The Avalanche*   49

NOVEMBER 13 (SATURDAY) *Two Years behind the Iron*
Curtain?   52

NOVEMBER 14 (SUNDAY) *Glimpses behind the Iron Curtain :*
Our Chinese Boy Cinderella   53

NOVEMBER 21 (SUNDAY) *Emergency Operation : Two Kinds*
of Racket : Two Kinds of Inefficiency : Chairs and
Daggers   55

NOVEMBER 30 (TUESDAY) *Refugees and Relics*   59

NOVEMBER 28 (SUNDAY) *"Strategic Withdrawal"*   60

December, 1948

DECEMBER 4 (SATURDAY) *A Soviet Meeting : Lull before*
the Storm   62

DECEMBER 12 (SUNDAY) *The Tide Draws Nearer*   64

DECEMBER 14 (TUESDAY) *Has the Siege Begun?*   68

DECEMBER 15 (WEDNESDAY) *"Under Fire!"*   69

DECEMBER 16 (THURSDAY) *A Glimpse of Tsinan under the*
Communist : Some Extreme Measures   71

DECEMBER 18 (SATURDAY) *All Quiet*   74

DECEMBER 19 (SUNDAY) *A Visitor from the Other Side : The Tension Grows*   75

DECEMBER 21 (TUESDAY) *Trapped*   78

DECEMBER 24 (FRIDAY) *Christmas Eve*   79

DECEMBER 25 (SATURDAY) *Christmas*   82

DECEMBER 31 (FRIDAY) *New Year's Eve*   83

January, 1949

JANUARY 1 (SATURDAY) *New Year's Day*   85

JANUARY 7 (FRIDAY) *Neither Peace nor War : "White Chinese" : A Report from behind the Iron Curtain*   87

JANUARY 9 (SUNDAY) *How It Feels To Be Rich*   89

JANUARY 15 (SATURDAY) *The Lull Is Broken*   91

JANUARY 17 (MONDAY) *China Then and Now : The Chinese Student*   93

JANUARY 23 (SUNDAY) *Surrender!*   96

JANUARY 26 (WEDNESDAY) *Liberation!*   98

JANUARY 30 (SUNDAY) *No Peace*   99

JANUARY 31 (MONDAY) *Occupation!*   100

February, 1949

FEBRUARY 3 (THURSDAY) *The Changes Begin : Propaganda and Press*   102

FEBRUARY 13 (SUNDAY) *Two Weeks of the People's Government*   107

FEBRUARY 28 (MONDAY) *Landlord and Servant in the New China*   111

March, 1949

MARCH 4 (FRIDAY) *The First Month*   114

MARCH 6 (SUNDAY) *Land : Industry and Commerce : "The Poor Man's Road to New Life" : Intellectuals : Are the Chinese Communists Really Communists*   121

MARCH 17 (THURSDAY) *Barter Trade : A New People's Government : Letters from America : "Jelly Belly, Tailor" : Newspapers : The Police State : Rumors : Prison Reform : Political Revivalism : Spirit of the New China*   128

April, 1949

APRIL 1 (FRIDAY) *Cooperatives : How To Beat the Inflation : Business and Austerity : The New Democracy Youth Corps : Our Shansi Students : Peace Plane from the South : Thought Control : Love in the New China : Foreign Criticism : Politics as a Religion*   137

APRIL 5 (TUESDAY) *Confession and Criticism*   150

APRIL 18 (MONDAY) *We Move House : Foreign Currency : Land Reform : More Rumors : Quick Justice*   150

APRIL 19 (TUESDAY) *Unequal Treaties : Views of a Chinese Liberal*   156

APRIL 22 (FRIDAY) *War : A Communist Compromise : Views of an American*   160

APRIL 24 (SUNDAY) *End of a Dynasty*   164

APRIL 29 (FRIDAY) *The* White-haired Girl   165

May, 1949

MAY 10 (TUESDAY) *Air Raid : Land, Cooperatives and Taxes : Schools and Intellectuals : The Foreigner in China : Group Effort*   170

MAY 20 (FRIDAY) *Food, Prices, and Business : Reform and Reconstruction : The Southern Campaign : Two Art Exhibits : The Old Scholar in the New Society*   176

June, 1949

JUNE 1 (WEDNESDAY) *Shanghai : Relaxation : Culture : Signs of the Times : Self-criticism : Imperialism and "Emperor-countryism"*   185

JUNE 3 (FRIDAY) *Modern Literature* 192

JUNE 10 (FRIDAY) *Beggars and Black Marketeers : The Capitalist in New China : Marriage, New and Old* 193

JUNE 12 (SUNDAY) *The New China and the Soviet Union : The Devil's Tunes* 199

JUNE 26 (SUNDAY) *"Coalition Government" : New Publications : Law : Prices, Cooperatives, and Austerity : The Public Mood* 201

JUNE 30 (THURSDAY) *Unpleasant Intrusion* 206

July, 1949

JULY 4 (MONDAY) *Birthday of the Communist Party : "On the People's Democratic Dictatorship" : "Democratic Dictatorship" in Action : Mass Justice : The Dance as an Instrument of Ideology* 208

JULY 16 (SATURDAY) *Through Train from Shanghai : Business and Taxes : How To Increase Production* 216

JULY 30 (SATURDAY) *The Joys of Travel : Floods, Typhoons, and Prices : Interrogation of Foreigners : Trade and Imperialism : Collectivization : How the Land Program Works : Three Years of War : Culture in the New China—Theory : Culture in the New China: Practice* 217

August, 1949

AUGUST 2 (TUESDAY) Union at the Heavenly River, *Revised* 230

AUGUST 14 (SUNDAY) *Uncertain Exit : Food and Grumbling : Manchuria and the Soviet Union : How To Lose Friends and Antagonize People—Communist Style : How To Lose Friends and Antagonize People—American Style : "All the News That's Fit To Print"* 232

AUGUST 18 (THURSDAY) *Clash of Old and New* 241

AUGUST 22 (MONDAY) *Malthus and Marx : Sudden Conversion : Changes in the Schools : Spare Our "Plowing Friends" : Special Service* 244

Tangku, AUGUST 28 (SUNDAY) *Farewell*   249

At Sea, AUGUST 31 (WEDNESDAY) *Imperialist Blockade*   254

September, 1949

Hong Kong, SEPTEMBER 8 (THURSDAY) *Capitalist Paradise*   256

October, 1949

Philadelphia, OCTOBER 10 (MONDAY) *Home Sweet Home :
The Summing Up*   258

Epilogue: A Plea and a Warning   267

Appendix: Price Fluctuations in Tientsin, August 24, 1948-
August 23, 1949   275

Index   283

Illustrations

following page 104

1   Poster prepared by university students reading: "Expel American imperialism from China!"

2   Poster showing a Communist soldier reaching over Nanking's city wall to seize Chiang Kai-shek.

3   Poster showing a People's Army soldier thrusting back a ship carrying a Japanese admiral and General MacArthur, coming to rescue Chiang Kai-shek.

4   Poster showing an industrial worker and a farm girl, and saying: "Strike down the reactionaries and build a new China."

5   Poster reading: "Plant the victorious banner throughout China!"

6   Poster showing a student, worker, and farmer, and calling upon the intellectual to unite with labor and agriculture to build a new China.

7   Poster showing Chiang Kai-shek shrinking back before an avenging fist.

8   Poster portraying the mass meeting that was held in celebration of the "liberation" of Peking.

9   Altar of Heaven, showing sleeping quarters of refugee students.

10   Laborers constructing an emergency airfield in Peking during the siege.

11   Parading students performing a peasant "planting song" dance.

12   Another folk dance performed by students dressed in proletarian garb.

13   Students, workers, and other groups participating in the great parade celebrating the "liberation" of Peking.

14   Close-up of poster portraits of Mao Tse-tung and Chu Teh.

15   Infantry approaching the northwest gate of the city of Peking.

16   First infantry detachment to enter the city.

17   Truckloads of soliders.

18   Trucks carrying troops and pulling guns toward the main south city gate.

19   Cavalry approaching the main south city gate.

20   Soldiers saluting a congratulatory banner which reads: "In a hundred battles a hundred victories."

21   Armored cars moving toward main south city gate.

22   Gun, with main south city gate in background.

23   Truck float showing portraits of Mao Tse-tung and Chu Teh.

24   Band marching up Hatamen Street.

25   The author, in Chinese costume.

26   The author, his wife and son, in Chinese costume.

27   Path from the front entrance leading toward the rear courtyard of the author's home.

28   Chinese servants in the author's household.

Preface

"As regards the size of this city you must know that it has a compass of 24 miles, for each side of it hath a length of 6 miles, and it is four-square. And it is all walled round with walls of earth which have a thickness of full ten paces at bottom, and a height of more than 10 paces. . . . And they are provided throughout with loop-holed battlements. . . . There are 12 gates and over each gate there is a great and handsome palace. . . . In those palaces are vast halls in which are kept the arms of the city garrison.

"The streets are so straight and wide that you can see right along them from end to end and from one gate to the other. And up and down the city there are beautiful palaces, and many great and fine hostelries, and fine houses in great numbers. All the plots of ground on which the houses of the city are built are four-square, and laid out with straight lines; all the plots being occupied by great and spacious palaces, with courts and gardens of proportionate size. . . . Each square plot is encompassed by handsome streets for traffic; and thus the whole city is arranged in squares just like a chess-board, and disposed in a manner so perfect and masterly that it is impossible to give a description that should do it justice. . . ."

This is how Marco Polo describes Peking* as it was between

* Peking ("Northern Capital") was the city's name during the period from 1421 to 1928, when it was China's capital, and this name was officially resumed on October 1, 1949, when it became the capital of the new Central People's Republic of China instituted by the Chinese Communists. From 1368 to 1420 the city was known as

the years 1275 and 1295. In many ways it has changed remarkably little in subsequent centuries. With its walls and gates, its intersecting avenues and triumphal arches, its palaces and parks, its temples and houses, each structure built around an inner courtyard and orientated to face the south, Peking to this day remains a supreme example of city planning and architectural magnificence. For ten months of the year an unclouded sun shines upon the innumerable trees of its parks and courtyards and upon the vast glittering array of its yellow-tiled palace roofs. Its lakes and moats, sheathed in ice for three months of that time, are transformed in summer into a green carpet of lotus leaves. A few miles away the Western Hills raise their graceful contours above the rim of the great North China plain. Between them and the city walls stretch the closely tilled fields of rural China—gray, barren wastes in winter, lush masses of undulating grain in summer.

Yet Peking is much more than an architectural marvel. With its scholars and artists, its book shops and curio stores, its universities, libraries, and museums, its restaurants, theaters, and handicrafts, Peking has long been the cultural center of China. Its street cries, its marriage and funeral processions, its open markets and temple festivals, have for many years made it one of the most colorful cities of Asia. During the past seven centuries it has variously been ruled by Chinese emperors, warlords, and republicans, by Mongol, Manchu, and Japanese conquerors. Whether known as Peking, "the Northern Capital," or Peiping, "Northern Peace," it was during most of these centuries the political center of China. Peking, in short, has been and is today the heart of the Chinese people.

During the six years of 1931-37 I had the good fortune to live in Peking—then Peiping; my wife Galia has known the city even longer. Thus it was with a feeling of returning to an old home that we, with our eight-year-old son Theo, started our journey to

---

Peiping ("Northern Peace"), and under the Kuomintang government (1928-1949) Peiping again became its official name. Old-time residents, however, as well as all who loved the city continued to refer to it as Peking during the Kuomintang period. For this reason, and for the sake of simplicity, the name of Peking has been used throughout this book, except for cases where "Peiping" appears in quoted statements or in certain proper names.

Peking in the summer of 1948. What we found there was in many ways a much sadder and more impoverished city than the one we had left eleven years before. What it had lost in ancient charm and grace, however, it made up for in the accelerated interest of day-to-day political events.

Our return had been made possible by the Fulbright Program, under which many Americans are being sent to teach, do research, or study in the countries that were America's wartime allies. China was the first such country to join the program, and I was the first Fulbright Fellow to be sent to China. My project—that of translating a history of Chinese philosophy written by a Chinese professor who taught at one of Peking's many universities—was arduous, and its completion within the year allotted required intense concentration. Often it provided a curious backdrop to the drama of inflation, siege, Communist occupation, and numberless other events connected with our daily life in Peking.

Particularly do I remember the dark days of December 1948 and January 1949, when the city, almost entirely cut off by siege from the outer world, lacked electricity and running water and had but little food. In the evenings, while our family of three sat huddled around a primitive oil lamp, with shell explosions and machine-gun fire rattling our windows, I was struggling to render into understandable English the terms for the eight forms of consciousness discussed in a particularly abstruse seventh-century school of Chinese Buddhism.

We had left America that summer fully convinced that our year in Peking would see changes of epoch-making importance not only for China but for the world. In this we were certainly not disappointed. Two days before we arrived (August 21, 1948), the Nationalist (Kuomintang) government launched its final major economic effort to stave off impending disaster, instituting for this purpose a new gold yuan currency and proclaiming "permanent" price ceilings on all important commodities. During the five and more months that followed, we witnessed the collapse of this government and with it the disintegration of a whole ancient way of life. The prevailing mood during this time was one of gloom, tension, and uncertainty. In November, when crisis became imminent, an exodus of most of the foreign colony, especially Americans, swelled the steady southward flow of well-to-do and politically prominent Chinese that had already begun previously.

This period culminated in six weeks of siege, ending with the peaceful entry of the Communists. From then until our departure almost seven months later (August 24, 1949), we watched the introduction and growth of the new ideas in urban China, and their spread southward until they had encompassed most of the country. During this period the mood of most, though naturally far from all, Peking Chinese seemed one of renewed hope and optimism.

As far as we ourselves were concerned, our entire year in China, with the exception of the siege, was physically comfortable as well as intellectually exciting.

For our son the year was as successful as for ourselves. Not only did he learn quite a bit of spoken Chinese and a fair number of the written characters, but he also received excellent preparation for life in a world in which international relations have became of paramount importance. The Peking American School which he attended, and which had opened in the fall with an enrollment of 160, dwindled sharply during the weeks of exodus and closed entirely during the siege. Only through the heroic efforts of its excellent American lady principal did it reopen in January in a private house, with an enrollment of forty for all its ten classes. Three of these, including Theo's third grade, were housed in a single room and taught by a Swiss lady married to a Chinese. The one girl and twelve boy pupils in these three classes included seven different nationalities: American, English, French, German, Russian, Greek, and Chinese. The combination, in which there was only one other American boy besides Theo, worked out beautifully.

In keeping the diary which follows, familiarity with the Chinese past and the old pre-war Peking life stood me in good stead, as did contact with a wide range of Peking's population—Chinese and foreign, intellectuals and coolies, missionaries and business-men, officials and diplomats, rich and poor, radicals and reac-tionaries. The one important group, in fact, with whom we, like virtually all other foreigners, were unable to make personal con-tact was that of the Chinese Communists themselves. Our view of the Communists, therefore, had to be from the outside. It was clarified to some extent by contacts with non-Communist Chinese intellectuals sympathetic to the new regime, as well as with a very few non-Chinese in its service.

Most important of all, however, was the ability to hear and read what the Chinese were saying in their own language, with-out dependence on translation. In every country, but perhaps in China more than most, the native often becomes a very changed personality when he talks a language not his own for the benefit of the foreign visitor. Chinese was the medium in which many of the conversations and most of the written materials recorded in these pages were spoken and read.

A good deal of personal or inconsequential material has been discarded from this diary, and names of most persons mentioned in it have been changed. Other than this, it records events as they happened, or my comments on them, irrespective of their later confirmation or denial by subsequent events.

One charge to which the record is open is that of inconsistency. In some places it praises what in others it condemns; sometimes it is hopeful, at other times gloomy. If this be so, it is because history in the making is itself often inconsistent, and because it is almost impossible to watch a revolution from day to day without being seized by conflicting emotions. Only later when the his-torian sifts the significant from the trivial, examines his data for their basic tendencies, and then fits them into seemingly neat categories, do they begin to assume purpose and meaning.

Every writer, furthermore, is the victim of certain prejudices and predilections. Within these inevitable limitations, however, I have tried to report as objectively as possible what I saw and heard, the good and bad alike. In general, my attempt has been to see events not only from the viewpoint of the handful of for-eigners residing in China, but also in the light of the significance they may have for the Chinese people themselves—especially the great mass of common people, the *lao pai hsing* or "old hundred names," who have been both victims and heroes of the struggle taking place.

It is very important, I feel, for us Americans to know—on the basis of observation rather than assumption—just what happens when Communism comes to a vast country like China with a strikingly different history and traditions. It is also important for us to understand something of the background that has made possible the seemingly sudden emergence of this movement from the Chinese countryside into the great cities. This diary, then, is offered in the hope that it may have some historical value as a fragmentary record of a crucial year in Chinese history, seen from the city which became the focus of events during this year. So far as I know, no other foreigner kept a similar record while I was in Peking, the more so as the news activities of all foreign correspondents were halted by the Communists less than a month after their arrival.

In conclusion I wish to express deep gratitude to the organizers of the Fulbright Program who appointed me a Fellow, and above all, to its administrators in China, who, under extraordinarily difficult conditions, made it financially possible for myself and seven other Fulbright Fellows to continue working in Peking throughout 1948-49 despite political change. It is a tragedy that this program has now been forced to cease in China, after only one year of very successful operation. The views expressed in these pages are, of course, entirely my own. In no way do they represent those of the Fulbright Program or of any other official agency, American or Chinese.

I am also grateful to the University of Pennsylvania for granting the year's leave of absence which made it possible for me to go to China. To my mother, who read these pages while in illness, and to my father and wife, especially the latter, I give thanks for the stylistic improvements they have offered and their suggestions for the retention or omission of various passages.

To Mr. Edgar Snow I am particularly grateful for having brought me in contact with the publisher of this book, Mr.

Henry Schuman. To the American Institute of Pacific Relations I am indebted for permission to reprint a few of the pages near the end, which originally appeared in the Institute's *Far Eastern Survey.*

DERK BODDE

April 10, 1950
Philadelphia, Pa.

Peking Diary

Prologue:

Slow Boat to China

One morning in March 1948 the telephone rang in my home in Philadelphia. It was a call from Washington. "Would you be prepared to go to China as a Fulbright Fellow?" the voice asked. "We would like an immediate decision, if possible, so that we can make a press release today to say that the Fulbright Program has been started." I swallowed my surprise, remembering from wartime experience in Washington that when things happen there, they usually do so explosively. "I'll be tremendously happy to go," I replied. "Please tell me the details."

It was in November 1947, shortly after reading of the signing of the Fulbright agreement by China and the United States, that I had written to Washington, outlining a project for which I should like to be sent to Peking. Some time later a reply came, stating that the Program's board was "much interested" in my project and that formal application blanks would be sent as soon as printed. Many weeks passed and nothing happened. Then came the Washington phone call. It was only afterward that the forms were finally sent me. Such was the unorthodox beginning to an unorthodox journey which was to culminate in a decidedly unorthodox year in China. We were offered accommodation on a fast 13,000-ton British freighter about to start her maiden round-the-world voyage from New York, via the West Coast, Manila, Hong Kong, Shanghai, and Tientsin. We leaped at the opportunity and decided to cross the continent by rail and board her in Los Angeles. Only afterward did we learn that she was really not a new ship at all, having been built in Seattle in 1944 as an aircraft carrier for the British Navy, sold after the war to a British shipping company with headquarters in Hong Kong, and just now converted into a freighter in a Norfolk, Virginia, shipyard.

The first unexpected incident in our journey was a two-week wait in Los Angeles, caused by engine trouble suffered by our ship while we had been crossing the continent. It was with great relief that we finally boarded her and sailed from Los Angeles on July 7.

Our two cabins were large and comfortable, the food good, and the run to San Francisco as fast as one could wish. A routine check after docking, however, revealed that somehow the engine had burned out a bearing. As a result, it was not until the evening of July 14, one day less than a month since our departure from Philadelphia, that we finally steamed out through the Golden Gate and saw the lights of San Francisco gradually drop below the horizon.

One night four days later, I was suddenly awakened by a violent nudge from Galia and her exclamation, "The engine is dying!" She snapped on the light just in time to see it gradually fade into blackness. The whole ship was dark, and the former hum of the engine made its present utter stillness all the more oppressive. Presently the silence was broken by steps running past our cabin, then the urgent cry, "Electrician! Electrician!" Then again silence. We pulled on our bathrobes and stumbled through the inner blackness to the comparative light of the deck outside. In the flare of my cigarette lighter I looked at my watch. It was 4:15 A.M. The ship was now completely motionless save for the slight peculiar roll characteristic of a vessel no longer under way. It was awesome to feel, as we did at that moment, that the ship which was the center of our life had suddenly become a dead thing, and that we were more than a thousand miles from nearest land.

Presently voices could be heard from the depths of the engine room. At the same time a couple of sailors climbed to the topmost deck carrying two large red oil lanterns, which they hoisted one above the other on a rope—the signal that our ship was out of control. It seemed a futile and pathetic thing to do with the realization that probably for hundreds of miles around there was no other ship to see.

As we walked up and down the deck, we talked in low voices (and it is strange how sudden silence causes one to do this) about the chances of repair and the probability that tugs would have to come to tow us to Hawaii. As dawn broke, the red lanterns— the only lights visible on our ship—were replaced by two large black balls made of wooden frames covered with canvas. Near our ship we could see groups of great seabirds that had hitherto been flying vigorously behind us since San Francisco. Now they bobbed gently up and down on the almost waveless sea. They too must have been puzzled by this sudden halt.

After a delay of four hours, the engine was somehow made to run and we got under way once more. Then, within an hour, it stopped again but this time took only an hour to repair. During the following days, as we moved across the Pacific, four or five similar breakdowns occurred. Fortunately the sea was always calm. No one ever seemed to know *why* these troubles occurred, because each time they had a different origin. Once it would be the generator, another time the fuel pump, still another a bursting steam pipe. Our British officers cursed freely at the shoddy work done by an American shipyard. We countered by asking how any reputable British steamship company could have accepted such work.

As we entered the tropics, the engine room became almost unbearably hot. From it the heat seeped through the ship, making our cabin floors so hot we could hardly touch them with bare feet. Already in San Francisco we had noticed that for some incredible reason the main ventilator shaft to the engine room had been built aft instead of forward of the engine-room skylights opening on the top deck. This meant that all hot air escaping from these skylights was immediately drawn into the ventilator and thence returned to the engine room in a closed circuit. Worst of all was the complete cessation of lighting and ventilating systems whenever the engine stopped functioning. On such occasions the heat in the engine room soared to as much as 160 degrees, and then it was a race between it and the endurance of human beings, working in relays with flashlights, to get the engine moving again before they themselves were prostrated.

To add to the general woe, the refrigeration system failed us a few days before Manila when a broken pipe allowed the freezing fluid to leak out. Thus as we entered the hottest stretch, we were faced with the unpleasant realization that the ship's frozen meat was gradually thawing. Not only this, but ice was no longer available for the drinks which by this time we and officers alike were consuming in increasing quantities.

The only other passengers aboard were a kindly and oldish grocery store proprietor and his wife from a tiny town in northern Michigan. They were true innocents abroad who never before had visited any city larger than a few thousand people. But because their son had been a college friend of one of the ship owners, this trip had been given them as a way to see the world. As day by day we moved across the Pacific, the husband became progressively more gloomy and depressed. "So much water!" he exclaimed at almost every meal. "Not a ship! Not even a plane!" But when the refrigeration system broke down, he came into his own. With professional pride he paid daily visits to the freezing locker and gave instructions as to what meat and vegetables must be thrown overboard and what could still be used.

On arriving in Manila on August 1, we were disappointed to learn that thorough-going repairs on the refrigeration system must wait until Hong Kong, as it would be cheaper to buy new freezing fluid there than in the Philippines. Five days later, as we left Manila, our engine again went dead. For four hours we floated helplessly upon the waters of Manila Bay while several other steamers sailed grandly past us. As we learned afterward, the boilers had run dry and, if the engine had not been turned off immediately, a disastrous explosion would have followed. By this time morale was so poor that the engineer considered to be the particular expert on this aspect of the engine refused to go below because he happened to be off duty.

At Hong Kong, where we arrived August 7, our ship was moved as soon as possible into a large shipyard owned by the company. Our memories of the following days are chiefly of heat, thirst, and noise. Night and day, the temperature in our cabin never dropped below 95 or 96 degrees. Part of the time the repair work stopped the flow of all washing water, part of the time buckets were needed to flush the toilet, and none of the time did we have any ice. From our own ship and others nearby came a deafening din of hammering and welding, seldom lessening day or night. Yet to find accommodation ashore would not only have been expensive but extremely difficult, for already at that time Hong Kong was being flooded with refugees from the mainland.

On August 14 our ship finally set sail once more, having lain idle an extra day, apparently to avoid departing on Friday the thirteenth. But as we headed out to sea, the engine again made its all too familiar unnatural whine and then stopped dead. Another bearing had burned out as the result of a clogged feed pipe. We dropped anchor in the bay and twenty-four hours later were pulled back by three tugs to the hated shipyard. No one knew how long the delay would be this time—at least a week, perhaps a fortnight. To make this particular repair, it was necessary to cut a hole through a bulkhead so that part of the engine could be lifted ashore.

By now we had reached the limit of endurance. Upon our vigorous protests, the company reluctantly agreed to furnish us plane passage for the last leg of our journey to Peking. On August 19 we said goodbye to the ship, leaving our trunks aboard to follow when they could. On the morning of the 21st, after an intervening day in Shanghai, our plane dropped us onto the dusty Peking airport, nestling at the foot of the hills a few miles west of the city. From the muggy heat of the South we emerged into the crystalline blue atmosphere of North China. Two months and six days had passed since our departure from Philadelphia.

As we learned much later, the ship broke down yet again on her second attempt to leave Hong Kong and had to be towed back for further overhauling. It was only on the third trial that she succeeded in getting away. Our baggage, as a result, did not reach us in Peking until the night of October 9.

Despite all the delay and discomfort, we would not have missed this voyage for the world. It was a unique way to travel and a fitting prologue to an eventful year in China. But one year

later, when on the point of returning to America, we learned
that this very same ship, by some strange quirk of fate, was about
to arrive again at Tientsin. Ships to North China were few at the
time, owing to the Kuomintang naval blockade, and as we ourselves intended to fly from Hong Kong, it was necessary to send
our heavy baggage as separate sea freight. "Why not try this
steamer?" suggested our shipping agent. Is it surprising that we
answered with a resounding "no"?

August 1948

August 29 (Sunday)

A Chinese Ducal Palace

We arrived in Peking one week ago yesterday and are still staying in the College of Chinese Studies—an American missionary institution better known to Peking's foreign colony as the Language School. Though grateful to have this temporary roof over our heads, we shall not be sorry to move on September 1 into the privacy of the charming Chinese house which we have rented. It lies not far south of here, and also not far from the Peking American School which Theo is to attend. Its *hutung*—as Peking's innumerable smaller streets and lanes are called—bears the impressive name of Fang Chia Yuan or "Garden of Fragrant Excellence." At the moment we are busy buying furniture.

Our future home, like most houses in Peking, is a low one-story structure, surmounted by an overhanging roof of gray Chinese tiles, and facing south upon a small garden protected from the outside world by high surrounding walls. In a more elaborate establishment the courtyard would be flanked by three or four semi-detached narrow buildings. Ours, however, is faced only by the single northern structure, divided from east to west into a series of rooms. Chief among these is a large *k'o-t'ing* (guest hall), the noble proportions of which are enhanced by its roughly hewn horizontal roof beams, from which rise the rafters of the exposed roof. The entire southern face of the room is pierced by windows designed to catch the maximum of Peking's bountiful sun. On one side of it lies what is to be my study, on the other side two bedrooms. These subsidiary rooms are separated from the guest hall only by silk partitions rising as high as the horizontal roof beams. This arrangement will make it possible, we hope, to heat most of these rooms by a single large coal stove, which, when winter comes, we shall have to install in the guest hall. The eastern extremity of the building includes a kitchen which faces upon a small courtyard of its own. This in turn is connected with the larger garden by a "moon gate"—a picturesque circular gateway piercing an intervening whitewashed brick wall.

Actually, what we have rented is only one small cell in a much grander establishment—one that in the nineteenth century was a ducal palace, inhabited, I believe, by a brother of Tz'u Hsi, the famous Manchu empress dowager. Our home-to-be had once been the carriage building. To enter the Hsia Kung Fu or Palace of Duke Hsia, as the whole place is still called, one steps from the unpaved outside *hutung* through a gate wide enough to admit a good-sized truck, then walks past a gateman's lodge, and thus descends a slight ramp into a large brick-paved courtyard crowned by a towering tree and flanked by servants' quarters. From this front courtyard several passageways lead to a series of separately contained gardens, courts and buildings (enough to supply generous living space for six or more families). At the very rear, farthest from the street, lives the landlady, Mrs. Sung, a vivacious middle-aged lady with five children and a Western education. Between her and the small northern windows of our own house stretches an extensive garden, filled with flowers, bushes, and persimmon and other fruit trees.

Material and Spiritual Impoverishment

Though we are impatient to move into our modest wing of this impressive establishment, we nevertheless find the Language School a good place in which to begin life in Peking. Through conversations with the missionaries who come here from many parts of China, as well as through personal observation, we are gradually building up impressions. These add up to the fact that Peking has changed greatly in the eleven years since we were last here, and mostly for the worse, even though at first sight the city looks much the same.

Impoverishment is the aspect that becomes most evident as the days pass by—an impoverishment both spiritual and physical. Physically, to be sure, most of the major streets have been paved, so that there is considerably less dust than before. Beggers, too, are not too much in evidence. One of the greatest changes from the past is the replacement of the old hand-drawn rickshaws by a new vehicle known to foreigners as the pedicab and to Chinese as the *san lun ch'e* ("three-wheeler"). This curious hybrid between a bicycle and a rickshaw resembles a bicycle in front (where the operator peddles) and a rickshaw behind (where the passenger sits). Following its introduction during the Japanese occupation, it has made the rickshaw virtually obsolete.

In former times many gates of Peking's houses were painted a brilliant red and studded with gleaming brass knockers. But today most buildings—including, especially in our part of the city, a good many monstrosities from the Japanese regime—look drab, gray, and unpainted. Traffic on the streets seems slow and thin compared with former days, and business appears to be in a somnolent state. Goods in the shops are in general meager in quantity and variety, high in price, and poor in quality.

There are obvious reasons for this situation. In the first place, Peking has become increasingly isolated from the outside world by the civil war; hence it no longer receives the products which once reached it in abundance. We are told, for example, that the Peking glass industry is now a thing of the past, the reason being that the needed raw materials, formerly brought from Shantung, no longer come in. In the second place, many of the rich families have liquidated their property and gone south. Formosa seems to be especially popular as the new Promised Land. And finally, much of Peking's former prosperity depended upon its large foreign colony and many foreign tourists. Now the colony has dwindled and the tourists for the most part no longer come.

This physical decline is paralleled by a spiritual impoverishment which, if not so immediately apparent, is equally pervasive. In part, of course, the two are interlinked. It is obvious that a city which for more than ten years has been struggling to keep its belly full, first under alien occupation and then civil war, cannot divert much energy to the "higher" things of life. The prevailing poor quality and bad taste of so many of the things on sale are undoubted reflections of this fact.

Actually, however, the decline in taste has far deeper roots. Long before the Sino-Japanese War it was evident that the Chinese were losing their old artistic standards, while failing to understand those of the West whose material gadgets they seized so eagerly. This was less apparent in pre-1937 Peking than elsewhere, largely owing to the foreign patronage which helped keep the old handicrafts alive. (Many of these same handicrafts were looked down upon by the Chinese themselves as quaint and old-fashioned.) But foreigners are few, and the handicrafts die. I doubt whether they will ever be revived. It is more profitable, less arduous, and more obviously useful to be a car mechanic than a jade cutter. Today we are observing the disintegration of an ancient civilization, of which Peking has long been one of the last remaining citadels. It is impossible to believe that the vitality which made this civilization great has expended itself, but it seems unlikely that what will take its place will assume definite form in the near future.

Verbalism

Peking's spiritual impoverishment, however, has more than purely material roots. It springs, too, from the intellectual straitjacket imposed by the Chinese government. There is something terribly sterile in the effort of a government to retain its grip upon a people whose confidence it no longer enjoys. One manifestation of this sterility is what may be called "verbalism." Verbalism is nothing new in China. All too often the Chinese, with their almost mystical respect for the written word, have been content to allow the word to stand for the deed. Again and again we read in the dynastic histories that such-and-such a law was promulgated or such-and-such a mandate decreed. By the traditional Chinese scholar it has been too commonly assumed that these laws and mandates actually achieved their purpose. But did they? In many instances the histories fail to tell us. In others, however, scattered hints indicate that words and deeds did not always correspond.

This discrepancy becomes particularly apparent in times of political disintegration. As a government becomes increasingly unwilling or unable to act concretely, it relies increasingly upon empty slogans and exhortations—slogans which accomplish nothing and which everyone knows can accomplish nothing, but which are nevertheless written and recited so that the proper forms may be observed. This is the stage now reached here in China. Its symbols are the huge characters, written above the city gates and in other public places, exhorting the people to "Eradicate sin, unify the country," "Get rid of disorder, achieve local self-government," and practice the virtues of the New Life Movement.

September 1948

September 12 (Sunday)

Campers in the Temple of Heaven

This morning we made a trip to the Temple of Heaven. Our anticipation was keen as we neared this magnificent architectural monument, situated within a "sacred grove" of ancient cypresses that covers hundreds of acres in Peking's South City. Here the emperor used to kneel, once a year, on a three-tiered, open-air marble altar, to worship Heaven on behalf of himself and his people.

When we arrived, the outer grounds looked much as we remembered them, but inside, what a depressing spectacle! All the buildings, including the Temple of Heaven itself and the approaching gateways, are filled with hundreds of young men (also, in certain quarters, girls). They are wartime student refugees from Shansi, some of whom seem hardly older than twelve or thirteen. Most of the stone terraces outside, as well as the floors of the temple itself, are covered with their thin sleeping pads and meager possessions, leaving only narrow passages for the occasional tourist. The marble balustrades of the Altar of Heaven are festooned with bedding drying in the sun. A few students sleep under small mat coverings erected on the altar, while dozens more occupy military tents pitched within the surrounding enclosure. The columns of the great temple and adjoining buildings, much faded from their former brilliant red, are covered with ugly written notices, and dust and debris lie everywhere on the once gleaming marble. As one mounts the steps toward places once reserved for the emperor and his followers alone at the most solemn of religious ceremonies, one can but turn from this scene of human misery and degradation to look at the unchanging Western Hills on the horizon.

Most depressing, however, is the demoralization of the young students themselves. Now and again can be heard the sounds of a flute or *hu ch'in* (Chinese violin); two students can be seen playing a game of Chinese chess; still others move about or are engaged in conversation. But the greater number lie inert on their bedding and do or say nothing. Nowhere do we see books that might keep them intellectually alive, or signs of organized physical activity. The reason, perhaps, is the traditional belief that work with one's hands is beneath the dignity of the educated man.

As a result the mental condition of these boys is far worse than that of the poorest coolie. There is no trace of leadership or organization. Portions of the courtyard, and even of the lower tiers of the Altar of Heaven itself, are littered with their half-dried excrement. One might think that a minimum of leadership could have organized squads to dig latrines in the extensive grounds outside. Such leadership is apparently not forthcoming—either from the students themselves, or from Peking's many universities (which might have arranged lectures and other activities to keep them occupied), or from the government. Perhaps it is too much to expect from these young men themselves, uprooted from their homes, many perhaps orphans, and all, no doubt, underfed. But what about the authorities who shipped them to Peking as a "cultural center," rather than to Tientsin, where many non-student refugees have been sent? One may say that the demoralization of these boys is really the demoralization of their government. One wonders if students could have been treated so indifferently in the days of China's "united front," ten years ago.

They have been here, so I am told, since June of this year. And not only here, but in many other of Peking's most famous buildings and parks: the Chung Hai and Nan Hai,* the T'ai Miao,† the

---

* Pei Hai, Chung Hai, and Nan Hai (Northern, Central, and Southern "Seas"). Three beautiful park enclosures dating from imperial times, grouped around a series of lakes extending through the city.

† T'ai Miao ("Great Temple"). Ancestral temple of the Manchu rulers of the Ch'ing dynasty (1644-1911), southeast of the Forbidden City.

Temple of Confucius,[1] the Hall of Classics,[2] the Lama Temple,[3] and many lesser edifices—almost everywhere, in fact, except in the Central Park,[4] the Pei Hai,[5] and the Forbidden City.[6] What will be their fate two months from now when the winter cold comes? Or two or five years hence? How many will still be alive, and what will they be doing?

Two Incidents

Last Monday when Galia was taking Theo to school for the first time, she passed a young man lying prone on the street. When she returned he was still there. Stepping from her pedicab, she made inquiries of the crowd which had by now gathered. "He is very sick," someone said. "He must have been sick a long time and apparently has no family." The cause, they thought, was lack of food.

On returning home she asked our cook what could be done. He suggested the police. She made a trip to the nearest police station, but on explaining the situation as best she could, was told that such a matter does not fall within their province and that she should go to another organization (perhaps the Bureau of Social Affairs?) some distance away. This meant a long extra trip, and by now it was time for her to go back to school to pick up Theo. On the way she again saw the man and stopped. She offered money to a pedicabber if he would take the man to a hospital. "Hospitals won't accept cases who have no family," was the reply.

While she was talking, a Chinese in Western dress appeared,

[1] Temple of Confucius. Temple and enclosure in the northeast of Peking.
[2] Hall of Classics. A building and enclosure adjoining the Temple of Confucius, so named because the emperors used to expound the classics there.
[3] Lama Temple. Large lamasery for Mongol and Tibetan monks in the northeast of Peking.
[4] Central Park. A popular park southwest of the Forbidden City, containing the Altar of the Soil of imperial times.
[5] See footnote on Pei Hai, Chung Hai, and Nan Hai on preceding page.
[6] Forbidden City. An almost mile-square moated and walled enclosure in the center of Peking, containing hundreds of palace buildings, courtyards, and gardens of the former Manchu dynasty.

who turned out to be a doctor on his way to a patient. Using a stethoscope, he decided the man was not ill but suffering from starvation. "Hospitals won't take such a man unless he is ill," the doctor declared. He tried to talk to the man but received only incoherent mumbles in reply. By then he had to proceed on his call, leaving Galia alone to cope with the problem. She got the crowd to lift the man to the side of the road and persuaded a woman to bring tea and gruel from her house some distance away. Part of this the man managed to swallow, but the rest was spilled on his trousers. Galia then gave the man three dollars, which a pedicabber put into the man's pocket for her. With this she hoped he could be taken somewhere for food and sleep. But by now she herself had to leave. Later, when she passed by the same place again, the man was no longer there. Next day, however, she again saw him lying as before, though this time in another *hutung*. Whether his money had been taken from him or not she did not know. At any rate, he himself was too weak to make use of it.

When she told the story that day to an English friend, Fitz-hugh, by whom we were entertained for lunch, he said that the Salvation Army—which in Peking functions under British auspices—was the only organization to handle such a case. The next day, when Galia again passed through that *hutung*, the man had disappeared and hasn't been seen since. Probably he died.

Galia was much upset by this incident and we talked about its causes. No doubt these are both economic and social. Economically, the struggle for life is so keen in China that it leaves scant surplus for help to any individual unfortunate enough to become separated from his own social group. Socially, the cohesion of the family is such that it gives a man strong claim upon his relatives and immediate friends, but very little upon society as a whole. Therefore, many functions which in Western society are performed by the government are left to family and friends. In structure, moreover, the government is like a magnified family in which each unit has its own status and functions, distinct from those of every other unit. That is why the police will not pick up a starving man, nor a hospital accept him.

The familial structure of Chinese government and society also brings with it the concept of personal and group responsibility. Since each family is responsible for its own members, anyone outside the family who accepts that responsibility is held accountable for whatever happens when he has thus overstepped the bounds imposed by his social status. Nobody in the crowd to whom Galia spoke dared to assume care of the starving man because each knew that by so doing he would be held responsible for expenses in case of death.

The other incident is briefer but makes a neat corollary to the preceding. On the same day that Galia vainly tried to get the police to help the dying man, her pedicab operator, newly engaged on a monthly basis the day before and given an advance payment of $20,* failed to show up. Finally, to our relief, he appeared in the middle of the afternoon. The reason for his tardiness? On leaving his house early that morning, he had forgotten to take his jacket bearing the license number issued to each pedicab operator by the municipal government. He was therefore picked up by the police, fined one dollar, and not released until the afternoon. The reason for such diligence on the part of the police, our cook told us, is that twenty cents out of every dollar of fines goes to the policeman making the arrest.

September 13 (Monday)

Morning Sounds

Every morning we are aroused by a succession of early sounds. The process begins shortly after six A.M., when regularly, while the sky is still black, we hear the roar of airplanes overhead. How many they are and where they are going we do not know, but we believe they must be bound on military missions. Galia thinks they go from east to west; Theo and I, that they move

* Here and elsewhere money references are to Chinese currency, unless otherwise specified. At the time of this entry, Chinese $20 was equal to U.S. $5.

southward. Each day I am determined that next time I will run out into the courtyard to see, but when next morning comes, I am too sleepy to do so.

Following the planes, we hear, south of us, the call of bugles. Later, this in turn is followed by the unmistakable sound of soldiers singing in unison. It is only after such evidences of military activity have thoroughly aroused us that the sounds of ordinary civilian life begin: first the characteristic Peking hum of a flock of pigeons wheeling in the now light sky—a sound caused by the tiny bamboo whistles fastened to the tails of these birds by their owners; then the cries of early morning peddlers from the *hutungs*. By this time one's mind is so full of thoughts that sleep is no longer possible.

During the daytime, evidence of military activity is much less striking. It is true that many military trucks are to be seen on the streets; that the streetcars are covered with clinging soldiers who in this way move about the city free of charge; that, when I go to the Central Bank, I see many soldiers waiting there to cash their pay checks; and that war casualties hobbling on crutches are a fairly frequent sight. Nevertheless, Peking by day seems a curiously quiet backwater, and it is hard to believe that not so far beyond its walls civil war is in full swing. Despite the considerable traffic on its streets, the place seems dead. The body remains, but it is only half-alive. One senses the same thing when one goes into the shops.

September 26 (Sunday)

Peking Is a Dream

There is a curious dreamlike quality to our life in Peking. For one thing, it is so seemingly like and yet so fundamentally unlike the Peking we knew eleven years ago. Many of the people we knew then are still here, but how different is their present life. At that time not a few enjoyed a measure of comfort and economic well-

being. Now they are impoverished and deeply worried about the
future. Eleven years of Japanese occupation and civil war have
made them older and grayer.

It is sad enough to see the plight of the Chinese. Professors live
cramped together in crowded compounds, almost penniless, too
proud to speak of their destitution to the outer world. They sup-
plement their scanty university earnings with various kinds of
part-time work, including the anonymous writing of popular trash
which they despise but send to the newspapers. Yet without the
meager food allowance provided by the government, it is doubtful if this and other activities would keep them going.

Even more pathetic, however, is the plight of those non-
American foreigners—Russians, French, Germans, and others—
who still remain. For the Chinese, at least, impoverished though
they are, a possibility exists of doing some kind of work to keep
alive. But for many of these foreigners there is nothing. Those
who could, have already gone elsewhere. Those who remain do so
simply because there is nowhere else to go. Many have lived here
for decades. Now they have almost nothing, and before them lies
the prospect of even less.

Yesterday I visited the National Library, the finest library in
China. The buildings are intact, and within them the movements
of life continue, but I had the impression of an almost lifeless
shell. I was told that the Library's monthly operating budget,
exclusive of salaries, comes to the equivalent of US$190, and that
the director, who was absent, had had to borrow money for a trip
to Nanking to beg additional funds from the government. Here
and everywhere in Peking people seem to be struggling in a bot-
tomless morass from which there is no escape, while pretending to
themselves and others that their movements are the ordinary ones
of a man walking on firm ground. It is only when one enters the
parks and the Summer Palace * that the illusion of the old Peking
momentarily returns, and even there the large number of soldiers
soon reminds one that things are no longer the same.

The changed economic situation is reflected in the greatly reduced tempo of social life. Before the war it was possible for even
"little people" to entertain and be entertained from time to time.

* Imperial palace enclosure, 7 miles northwest of Peking.

Though much of Peking's social life was undoubtedly shallow and vapid, it also had considerable gaiety and charm. But now, whatever large-scale entertaining there is, is usually limited to dull official functions attended by endless Chinese generals and officials. Or it centers around the activities of the predominantly American diplomatic crowd, who live a life of their own, curiously oblivious to the facts of life outside, delighted with the picturesqueness and "cheapness" of Peking, and rather incredulous when one tries to tell them of the changes that have taken place. Whatever evidences of prosperity there are these days usually turn out to be attached to a string of American dollars. The same phenomenon, of course, is found all over the world, and it makes one wonder why to a few fortunate Americans should be given so much, and to so many other less favored people so little.

I myself feel this keenly when I contrast our simple but charming house and our economic security with the privation, uncertainty, and fear that beset so many here. When, for example, I enter the dark and rather shabby home of Professor Muller, a graying and otherworldly German scholar, I notice the torn paper fluttering from the latticework of his door while hearing him explain in a rather tired voice that he was teaching last year but has no classes now, and that he would like to go to America but at his age it is difficult to get established there.

What makes this life perhaps most unreal is that we have no part in it ourselves. We come here as outsiders, we know that a year hence we shall have returned to our very different life in America, and above all, we have the blessed power to move elsewhere at any time, if necessary, which these people lack. We might, in fact, almost be observers from another planet. But when I try to explain these feelings to other Americans who, like ourselves, are here as visitors but, unlike ourselves, did not know the prewar Peking, it is hard to put into words what I feel.

How the Communists Get Their Arms

I have written earlier that Peking is a quiet island, curiously immune to the disturbances that wrack the countryside. A week or ten days ago, however, the Communists began their fall campaign with simultaneous attacks at many points, and these are causing inevitable ripples to lap their way into our city. Every time I go on the streets, soldiers seem to be everywhere, on foot, in jeeps, or driving carts loaded with supplies.

One thing we no longer hear is the predawn foray of planes that used to wake us every morning. Perhaps the intensified fighting has drawn them from their regular schedule, for at other hours they are frequent, sometimes flying very low. About four nights ago, perhaps around three A.M., I suddenly awoke and was conscious of a low and distant rumbling, apparently southeast of the city. Thunder! was my first thought, but then I realized it could not possibly be thunder at this time of year. There is no doubt that it was distant artillery fire.

From today's papers it is evident that the fall of Tsinan (capital of Shantung province) is imminent. Street fighting is in progress, and half the city is already reported in Communist hands. In this struggle, judging from the pro-Kuomintang newspapers, the defenders, though holding an advantage in arms and equipment, are pitted against a foe who enjoys superiority in numbers and, above all, in morale. Indicative of the latter is the defection of a defending divisional commander to the Communist side. Another indication concerns the source of Communist arms. How do they get these arms? They possess few arsenals, and it seems agreed here that Russian help has been insignificant, save perhaps in Manchuria at the end of the war, where the Soviets allowed surrendered Japanese arms to pass into Communist hands.

Much Communist equipment has undoubtedly been captured from the Nationalists. But there is another explanation as well: they sometimes actually *buy* arms from the Nationalists. This was pointed out by Professor Chang, when he called on me this morning. A friend of his was present at Shih-ching-shan (some ten miles west of Peking) during the fighting there this summer. The Communists were in the hills and the Nationalists on the plain, but when the Communists came down and drove the Nationalists away, this friend had a chance to talk to several of them. He was assured that many of their arms used in this engagement had been bought from Kuomintang troops.

The assault on Tsinan represents a new phase in Communist strategy. Heretofore they attacked only isolated points and scrupulously avoided the larger cities where they would be outnumbered. Now, however, they are ready to mass large forces against such centers, the capture of which will confront them with new and difficult problems. This changing situation has resulted in a curious Communist-Kuomintang shift in propaganda. While the Communists now tell the urban populations that they have nothing to fear under Communist rule, that private small business is necessary and will be encouraged, and that they (the Communists) wish only to destroy the bureaucratic capitalists and corrupt officials, the Kuomintang talks increasingly about the need for agrarian reform and for protecting the people's livelihood against big business and officialdom. This propaganda shift parallels that in military strategy: whereas the Communists are now beginning large-scale positional warfare, the National government talks more and more about developing a local people's militia and mobile guerrilla tactics.

September 27 (Monday)

Strike of the Merchants

Many people feel that the future of the government hinges upon the fate of its new currency, the gold yuan, which was introduced August 19 in place of the inflated fa pi dollars, at the rate of GY\$1:FP\$3,000,000. But how can even a well-backed currency—and this one is gold only in name—remain stable when the demand for goods outstrips the supply and 80-90 per cent of the national budget goes into war? After remaining fairly stable the first month, the gold yuan began rising sharply this past week. The day before yesterday, for example, our cook announced that he had had to pay GY\$1.50 for a pound of pork, the official ceiling price of which is \$0.70. To do so, he had had to buy the meat surreptitiously from under the counter, and since then even this illicit supply has dried up.

What is happening is that the merchants are conducting a strike against the government's ceiling prices. This is true not only of food stores; in the Tung An market—a huge covered arcade with hundreds of stalls and shops—many other stores are temporarily closed. I have no doubt the merchants will win their strike; several days ago the authorities already announced the possibility of price adjustments for certain commodities.

There are some grain shops in the city, their windows covered by heavy steel bars, where holders of ration cards may periodically buy flour (mostly of E.C.A. origin) at low government-controlled rates. These shops may be spotted from afar by the crowds struggling to get inside. As one approaches and studies the intent faces of these jostling figures, it is easy to imagine how quickly they might become a mob of rioters were any breakdown of authority to occur.

A Chinese Intellectual Speaks His Mind

The past year has seen university circles in a constant uproar over the government's frequent arrests and shootings of what it chooses to call "subversive" or "Communist" students. On July 5, for example, some 1,500 student refugees from Manchuria, having staged a parade before the house of the chairman of the municipal council, were fired upon by gendarmes just as they were dispersing. More than twelve deaths resulted. Cause of the demonstration was the rumor that they were to be drafted for the civil war. These students, whatever else they may have been, were not Communists. Many had walked long distances to reach Peking through Communist territory, refusing Communist invitations to remain with them. The latest incident is that of August 19, when the government arrested, or tried to arrest, hundreds of students all over the country, including some 250 in Peking alone.

Students here seem to be rather solidly united against the government. Faculty opposition, too, is large and growing, though there are a fair number of government supporters in strategic administrative posts. Among the students there is a percentage of

Kuomintang "special service" spies and informers, whose presence in the universities, I am told, often results from the Ministry of Education's insistence that certain individuals be admitted without entrance examination. For the great bulk of students, however, these examinations continue to operate with scrupulous fairness. In them, in fact, the same procedure is followed as under the old imperial civil service system. That is to say, the names written by candidates on their examination books are pasted over with numbered slips so that the identity of these candidates remains unknown to their examiners.

Ten days ago, three or four of us Americans rode out to Tsinghua University, the famous government institution which lies six miles northwest of Peking. There we had a long and frank conversation with a distinguished group of Chinese liberal professors. In the course of it one of my companions said in essence:

"Many Americans, including government officials, wonder why Chinese intellectuals are anti-American and pro-Russian. How would you explain this situation?"

There was a moment of silence, during which the Chinese looked expectantly at one of their number, a distinguished-looking man with graying hair and short-clipped mustache—a former member of the Kuomintang, long noted as one of China's outstanding liberal thinkers. His reply, in carefully phrased English, ran something like this:

"Most Chinese intellectuals would prefer not to bother about politics. But while they have heard the government repeatedly proclaim its intention of bringing democracy and honest administration to China, they have seen these protestations repeatedly flouted in actual fact. Indeed, far from improving, the government becomes steadily worse, so that today few thinking people hold much hope for its reform. That is why we intellectuals have gone through three phases in our thinking. At first, most of us supported the government, recognizing its many faults, but hoping it would reform. Then we became increasingly discouraged with reform prospects, but saw no feasible alternative. Though the present government, we felt, was bad, what might take its place would be even worse. During this second phase, intellectuals were uncertain and bewildered. Then came the present, third phase. We have become so completely convinced of the hopelessness of the existing government that we feel the sooner it is removed the better. Since the Chinese Communists are obviously the only force capable of making this change, we are now willing to support them as the lesser of two evils. We ourselves would prefer a middle course, but this is no longer possible.

"But while we Chinese have thus been forced more and more toward the left, we have seen a countermovement at work in America. At one time it apparently wanted a genuinely progressive government in China. During the past two or three years, however, it has seemed to be interested less and less in liberalism and more and more in anything, no matter how reactionary, that might be a bulwark between it and communism. This change has coincided with growing reaction within the Chinese government itself. The result is an American government which talks constantly about democratic rights yet continues to aid a Chinese government increasingly mindless of these rights. That is why we Chinese have become anti-American—we are not against the American people but against the American government.

"That we are anti-American, however, doesn't mean we are pro-Russian. The very fact that Americans automatically regard anyone who opposes their policies as pro-Russian in itself indicates the prejudice with which they view the whole Chinese situation. Normally we would prefer America to Russia. But today the Communists are China's only hope. Besides, we are not convinced, as are Americans, that they are merely tools of Russian communism. After all, the Chinese Communists are Chinese as well as Communist, and conditions in China are different from those in Russia. Therefore it is doubtful if communism of the Russian type can be successfully transplanted to China."

The discussion then turned to the cultural influence of various Western countries on modern China, and I was surprised by the rather airy way in which these Chinese dismissed the American impact as relatively insignificant. Very little American literature, they say, has been translated into Chinese, and what translations exist have had little influence. English, French, and Russian literary influences, on the contrary, have been considerable. Proust, who was translated fairly recently, has enjoyed quite a vogue, and the popularity of Russian literature antedates both the Chinese and Russian revolutions. It was added that the Chinese feel a certain psychological kinship with Russia—both revolutionary and prerevolutionary—which they do not feel toward America, perhaps because China and Russia have both been backward agrarian countries.

These Chinese professors, of course, were speaking only of in fluences on a high cultural level; not of technology or such in fluences as the movies.

October 1948

October 2 (Saturday)

A Talk with Our Teacher

Three times a week Mr. Ma comes to our house to give Galia and Theo their Chinese lesson. He is a man in his late fifties or early sixties, with an eager, high-pitched voice, vigorous gestures, and eyes that peer keenly forth from behind thick-lensed spectacles. His entire life has been spent in Peking, and he knows everything worth knowing about the city, both past and present. Whenever he comes, he always has something new and interesting to tell, expressing himself forcefully and graphically in his resonant Chinese.

Three days ago, as he was taking his leave from Galia, I joined them for a moment of conversation. He immediately launched into a heated tirade on the current situation. Beginning with the meat shortage, he observed that pigs, for example, are no longer being brought into the city. The reason, at least in part, he said, is that the farmers prefer to barter them for products coming from Communist territories.

As he continued, his voice filled with bitterness and passion. There are too many poor people in China, he said, and not enough rich. When all the money falls into the hands of a privileged few, trouble is inevitable. How can people continue living under present circumstances? If the lack of foodstuffs continues, there may be mob violence. People like us or himself may perhaps have cause to fear the Communists, but that is not true of people who have nothing at all. He makes a point these days to listen to what is being said on the streets, and what he hears is that it will be good if the Communists come soon. It is not only foods that are lacking in the shops; the same is true of all other daily commodities. When he telephones the coal shops, for example, he is told they have no coal, but when he goes in person he sees their yards full. Then he is told that this coal has already been sold to army officers, to the American Consulate, or to other large organizations.

The great trouble is that the government only cracks down on the little businessman but not on the really big people. In Shanghai, for example, where there has been so much commotion over hoarders and speculators, the net result has been the execution of one lesser man and sentencing of a few bigger people to six or eight months of imprisonment. How can this be expected to have any effect?

The government also acts stupidly toward the educated classes. It arrests non-Communist students because they oppose the government, thereby driving them inevitably into the Communist camp. On the military front it is equally blind. Having lost Tsinan, War Minister Ho Ying-ch'in announces that this loss has no strategic importance, instead of honestly admitting that the situation is serious and needs drastic action.

The Kuomintang itself is riddled with cliques, each with its own publication in which it attacks the others. By the time one has finished reading all of them, one reaches the conclusion that all are equally bad.

This and much more Ma poured out in a talk of more than half an hour. What was interesting was not so much *what* he said as that *he* should say it, for he is an unusually intelligent, but nevertheless traditional, scholar of the old school, without Western education or knowledge of foreign languages, and hardly a man who could be accused of radical tendencies.

October 14 (Thursday)

"Disasters and Anomalies"

The weather these weeks has been unusual for Peking—hazy, warm, and quite unlike the crystal-clear atmosphere one expects at this time of year. About a week ago the warmth culminated one evening in a thunderstorm, at first very distant, yet so powerful that our house literally shook under the thunderclaps. Later in the night the storm returned with even greater violence, accompanied by torrential rain—a most unusual occurrence in October. It forcibly reminded us of the ancient Chinese theory that Heaven shows its displeasure over human wickedness by sending down "disasters and anomalies"; by superstitious Chinese it could certainly be taken as a sign that the world is out of joint.

One or two days later, about the middle of the morning, we heard very clearly the sound of "human thunder." It lasted perhaps half an hour and was obviously cannon fire from the south, considerably louder than that which we had heard once before very late at night.

Looking into the Past

Our lives here are a succession of pulls from the maelstrom of current events into the quiet backwaters of the dying past, and then back again into the present. Most of the time it is the present that holds us, with its nervous tenseness and feeling of impending cataclysm. Every once in a while, however, a little scene or episode momentarily takes us back into the China that was, and these are the most poignant and nostalgic moments of all, because in them we are aware of that gentler and easier way of life that has now gone never to return.

One of these moments came on the afternoon of October 6, when I visited the Ethnographic Museum at Fu Jen (Catholic)

University. It is situated in an old and run-down, but still lovely rock garden— a quiet spot seemingly aloof from the trouble and bustle of the present world. There for a couple of hours the single Chinese in charge showed me with enthusiasm through a fascinating collection of shadow-play figures, painted theatrical masks, grave figurines, door gods, models of Peking street vendors, scissor cut-outs from red and white paper, peasant pottery and textiles, kites, and countless other forms of popular art. Again and again he remarked with sadness that this or that object is now no longer made in Peking, or can be obtained only with great difficulty and of far poorer quality than the examples exhibited in the museum; that whereas six types of a certain kind of street vendor once existed, only two survive, and so on. Most of these changes have taken place in the short space of eleven years since I was last in Peking. It is fortunate that the Catholic fathers of Fu Jen have assembled this unique collection of objects, because, not falling into the category of formal art, they would otherwise soon be gone forever. But when a culture reaches the stage in which museums must be built for its preservation, it is an infallable indication that that culture is dead or dying and giving way to something new.

Troubles of an Americanized Chinese in China

Another impressive glimpse of China's artistic past, on a more sophisticated level, came on October 10, when I visited a one-day exhibition of Chinese paintings at Tsinghua University. They are the property of a private collector who, it is said, has been known to sell a house in order to acquire a single painting. The long series of horizontal scrolls, beginning with one attributed to the Sui dynasty (590-618) and running through the Ch'ing (1644-1911), is probably better than any comparable collection on public view in China today. Some of the Sung and Yuan examples were breathtaking in their universality and deep penetration into life's mystery, and a few of the Ming works were almost equally fine. It was sad, however, to see in the Ch'ing paintings the unmistakable hardening, stereotyping, and loss of philosophical insight which set in at that time. Artistically, there is no doubt that the really creative phase of Chinese civilization came to an end centuries ago, though, by way of compensation, much development took place thereafter in certain "uncreative" aspects, notably historical and textual criticism, philology, and other fields of humanistic scholarship.

Two days before, I had attended a preview of an exhibition of Peking handicrafts (cloissoné, brass work, Peking glass, rugs, embroideries, etc.), held in one of Peking's national museums. A tea accompanied by endless speeches left only little time to examine the display itself in the gathering twilight. What we saw, however, was another commentary on the Peking of today. The objects were few in number and disappointing in quality; many of the best were not contemporary products at all but loans from private individuals who had acquired them years ago. A theme constantly reiterated in the speeches was that Peking's handicrafts have declined sadly during the past decade or so; that the causes are lack of good materials, high labor costs, loss of markets, and other factors connected with war and economic instability; and that every effort must be made to preserve and revive these handicrafts for which Peking is famous.

All true, no doubt. Yet the most important factor, I still maintain, is that internal artistic decay which I have already previously observed. This is particularly apparent in the rugs, embroideries, and other articles commonly bought by foreigners, in which the breakdown of the old standards has been accompanied by infiltration of non-Chinese motifs of Western origin. Other articles more uniquely Chinese in function, such as the carved bamboo armrests used for writing calligraphy, avoid the alien motifs and therefore retain the old standards more successfully. Even in these, however, the results are imitative rather than creative. Once the spiritual essence of an art has been lost, it is hopeless to look for any genuine artistic "revival," regardless of how much financial or material aid may be forthcoming.

Riding the bus to see the paintings at Tsinghua, I happened to share a seat with the museum director who had arranged the handicraft exhibit. He is a dynamic, outspoken Chinese only recently returned from a long term of museum service in America, and as we bumped along, he poured out the story of the troubles he has encountered since coming back to China. One of the foremost, of course, has been financial. For the operation of his museum he has received, aside from salaries, only a few million fa pi dollars per month (about US$2.00 at current exchange rates). Money for his handicraft exhibit had to be raised in driblets of GY$10 or so from a bank and a few other sponsoring institutions, so that he himself had to contribute from his own pocket. He was forced to write ironclad guarantees for the safe return of all objects before many of the handicraft producers could be induced to loan a few of their wares. Even then, as I have remarked, many of the best objects came from private collectors.

Worse than the financial difficulties have been the indifference and passive opposition he encountered every time he tried to make any innovation. On assuming his post, he was confronted by a group of employees, many of whom were not even graduates of middle schools (equivalent of the American high school). For years they had apparently felt that the only thing needed to earn their salaries was to appear at the museum during hours and there read their papers, chat, or simply do nothing. These salaries, he pointed out, are not too bad as things go today in China. Any request for action on his part would be met by assent, but on returning next day he would find that nothing had been done. Finally he was forced to make several dismissals—always a dangerous step in China, but one he took successfully by pensioning some of the dismissed men, partially out of his own pocket. In their place he introduced a younger and better-educated group, including one of his own museum-trained students. Among these men, one can double as a carpenter and thus make some badly needed repairs; another knows how to make rubbings of the objects on display. In this way something is beginning to be done.

With some bitterness, my friend also recounted his experience as adviser to another of Peking's museums. Taking his duties seriously, he started by trying to make a complete inventory of the contents, for which purpose he asked to be shown the objects in storage. This request met with a blank refusal. No person, he was informed, except the director himself, could have access to objects not on public display. On complaining about this treatment, he was told cynically: "Don't be a damn fool. You have been away from China so long you have become just like a foreigner who only wants to stir up trouble. Don't you know that when they made you adviser they didn't really expect you to do anything but only wanted to use your name?" My friend compared this incident with his experience as a visitor to the Fogg Museum at Harvard, where, upon request, he was handed the keys to the storage room and allowed to enter it freely for an entire week without any supervision. He is now trying to instill in his students a similar concept of the museum as an organ of public welfare rather than a preserve of private interest.

Inflation Again

By now there can be no doubt of the collapse of the new currency, despite deceptive statements from Finance Minister Wong Yun-wu, at present in America, that the gold yuan has been a brilliant success. We thought prices astronomical a couple of weeks ago; in comparison with today's they seem reasonable. Prices of most everyday products have tripled, quadrupled, or even quintupled since mid-September, and most of this rise has taken place in the last ten days. Despite this phenomenon, the government clings to its artificial exchange rate of US$1:GY$4.

After personally seeing what has happened, it is fantastic to read yesterday's interview with Chiang Kai-shek in the government's English-language paper, *Peiping Chronicle*. "Press reports of recent price increases and rush purchases were 'greatly exaggerated,' " he is quoted as having said, "and did not give a true picture of conditions. He said that during his personal inspection of Peiping, Tientsin and Mukden, he saw nothing to support these allegations." The rest of the interview runs in similar vein, blaming the people in general and intellectuals in particular for allowing themselves to be "bewitched" by Communist propaganda, and frowning upon the "overcritical attitude" of legislators and Control Yuan members toward the government. In place of this, Chiang urges "a cooperative stand to assist the government in achieving unity of purpose and action."

The same mentality characterizes a new flock of wall slogans that have appeared since Chiang's Peking visit: "Purge away the bandit plots," "Unite the city to exterminate the bandits," and the like. By appeals such as these the government hopes to put down a revolution.

October 16 (Saturday)

The World beyond Our Walls

Yesterday, from an American engineer who has traveled widely as an adviser to the National government, I received some scraps of information about what is happening outside our city:

Mukden: Conditions were terrible when he was there recently. Half a million people have left, either for Communist areas or as refugees to North China. Industrial production is down to almost nothing. A primary factor is lack of food, caused by the siege. Rationed food lasts a worker only ten days out of every month. Many people are forced to live on the large Manchurian soybean cakes, ordinarily used only for cattle and fertilizer. These, probably because of vitamin deficiency, eventually produce night blindness among adults and permanent blindness among children—in some cases even actual disintegration of the eyeballs. Lack of food results in lowered coal output, which cuts electric power, which in turn leads to flooding of coal mines. Production appears to be coming to a complete standstill. This coming winter there will surely be starvation. Conditions in Changchun are, if anything, worse.

Tsinan: Yesterday this engineer talked to a mill owner outside Peking, who in turn had seen a man just arrived from Tsinan. This man reports that, following Communist occupation, schools there reopened October 6, food was shipped into the city, and no one was arrested save a few top officials. The man himself was readily allowed to go to Peking when he asked permission to see his family. At the same time he was assured by the Communists that he would be free to return whenever he wished. My engineer informant compared this treatment of educational institutions with the depressing conditions here at the Temple of Heaven, where the refugee students receive two meals of corn bread a day, and recently, because of price rises, even had this meager ration suspended for two days.

October 27 (Wednesday)

A Meeting with the Madissima

Two days ago Galia found our landlady in a state of considerable exhilaration, having just returned from a luncheon given by Mme. Chiang Kai-shek at her Peking residence. Only six or seven other public-spirited Chinese ladies were invited to the meeting, the purpose of which was to organize a drive for relief funds. Mme. Chiang, according to our landlady, spoke very frankly and was as charming as usual. She said she was fully aware of the economic situation in North China. (One wonders why, in that case, she has been unable to convey this information to her husband.) What particularly impressed our landlady was her simplicity of living. The Chinese meal consisted of only four courses, and when these appeared the madame remarked that ordinarily her husband and herself would make that number do for two meals. A little later she stressed the need for economy in present-day China and, by way of illustration, told her *amah* (maid) to bring forth her dressing gown, once lovely, but now badly patched. This, she remarked, she had been wearing for ten years past, despite her *amah*'s urging to throw it away.

War and Food

Within the last two or three days the government has had a great victory (duly celebrated in the headlines of the *Peiping Chronicle*) in the recapture of Yingkow; it has also (and for this one has to dig deeply into the Reuter dispatch following Central News under these same headlines) lost Kaifeng, Chengchow, and Paotow. The loss of Chinhsien and Changchun (the latter not yet officially admitted) occurred some time ago. Fighting around Taiyuan apparently grows in intensity. A special ship is said to be coming to Tientsin within a month to evacuate the heavy baggage of Americans—and, if need be, Americans themselves. The local packing firms are flooded with orders.

Economically, for unexplained reasons, there has been a temporary easing of the situation. Perhaps Chiang's visit? At any rate, a 44-pound bag of flour, costing GY$120 a couple of weeks ago, has now dropped to half that price. But the economic pinch is still severe, especially for the salaried class. When I saw Martin at Tsinghua three days ago, he said he had been spending much time in town in a vain effort to raise money for needy Chinese colleagues. Eighty-seven professors of Peita University * have issued a manifesto demanding a doubling of salary and threatening a three-day strike if it is not forthcoming. They have been joined by professors at Tsinghua, the Normal College, and other institutions.

Disillusionment

While writing these pages and thinking back over my impressions since arriving here, I am struck by the critical spirit with which I now view China. How different it all is from the days in Peking fifteen years ago, when with youthful enthusiasm I steeped myself in Chinese philosophy, joyfully witnessed the picturesque festivals which then took place, regarded Chinese scholarship as the fountainhead of all wisdom about China, and

* Peita is the Chinese abbreviation for Peking National University, one of the two or three most famous universities in China.

looked upon the Chinese themselves as the most well-balanced and happy people in the world. I remember my doubt when an American friend, also a student of things Chinese, explained his attitude on a certain point by saying that he was, after all, a Westerner and on the whole preferred having been born as such rather than as a Chinese. At the time I regarded this as chauvinism, but today I think I appreciate what he meant. For Western civilization, despite all its harshness and its stress on personal advancement, and despite the two wars with which it has laid waste the world within the space of thirty years, still offers, it seems to me, the greatest hope for improvement because of the place laboriously won in it for individual expression outside of prevailing orthodoxies. In other words, the very element of struggle which has loomed so darkly in our Western world, destructive though it often is, is what has given it its possibility for evolution and ultimate advancement.*

In China, on the contrary, this element has been largely lacking. Chinese society has been based on the ideal of a static "harmony," insured by the rigid subordination of one social group to another—a society in which individual differences are discouraged and the interests of family or friends are commonly emphasized at the expense of general public welfare. In China there has been little social consciousness and no proletarian philosophy of the sort that, despite suppressive efforts, has forced its way to the surface in the West during the last few centuries. What "social consciousness" does exist in China is usually of the benevolently paternalistic type, operating from superior to inferior, symbolized by Madame Chiang's philanthropic activities. In reading Chinese philosophy, one is struck by its class basis. Even in the highest moral flights of the most eminent thinkers, unconscious prejudices and assumptions of the social *status quo* are almost always apparent. There is no Locke, Rousseau, or Marx in Chinese thought. Such individuals were impossible in a society, the orthodox ideology of which was Confucianism, and which Taoism and Buddhism, though opposed to

---

* With the growing East-West tension and the prospect of a new hydrogen bomb, it has become harder, since returning to America, to remain as optimistic as when these words were written.

Confucianism on many points, did little to alter, owing to the retreat of the one into nature, and the search of the other for a salvation outside our existing world.

In ancient China the man who most nearly broke through the social straitjacket seems to have been Mo Tzu, the non-Confucian philosopher of the fifth century B.C. who preached "universal love" and opposed aggressive warfare. It is also he who today seems the most "Western" and least "Chinese" of Chinese thinkers. He commands respect despite the humorless puritanism, asceticism, and matter-of-factness which caused him to be discarded. In later Confucian China, perhaps the nearest approach is the idealist philosopher Wang Shou-jen (1472-1528), whose unorthodox attitude to life is reflected in his own remarkably successful official career. Yet even he never reached the point of questioning the basic assumptions on which Confucian society was founded.

All these impressions, of which I began to be clearly conscious during my years of wartime work, are confirmed by the little incidents I observe in Peking today: the starving man whom Galia saw lying untended on the street; the experiences of my museum friend in organizing Chinese museums; the indictment I have heard several times of students and intellectuals generally for their failure to make contact with other social classes and hence be spokesmen for other than their own small group. (When I mentioned this latter criticism the other night to a very intelligent university student, he admitted its validity. At the same time he quite justly pointed out that China's industrial backwardness makes it difficult for students to have much contact with labor groups, and that, being mostly concentrated in a few large cities, their contacts with the peasantry are necessarily limited.)

The latest incident of this kind is that of our exceptionally gifted cook, who unexpectedly left us a few days ago, on the eve of an important lunch we were giving for several Chinese friends. He had been given a few days leave to settle some family affair and had left a substitute in his place. When the allotted time passed and he failed to reappear, we sent our pedicab man to summon him. It was then that our cook told us that he had no intention of coming back. His reasons were dissatisfaction with present wages in view of rising prices and the fact that he had found a job elsewhere.

When we upbraided him for his lack of frankness and reliability, he replied that it would have been *pu hao k'an* (bad form) to express open dissatisfaction about his wages, that he actually did have private business to attend to when he departed, and that anyway he had left a reliable substitute in his place. (Previously he had told us that this man was inferior to himself in cooking Chinese food.) No amount of argument could convince him that his leaving us unexpectedly in this way was much more *pu hao k'an*—for him toward us and for us toward our coming guests—and that it would have been better for him to have told us frankly of his difficulties. We are very sorry to lose him as the result of this difference between Chinese and Western ideas of "face."

That China needs to escape from her age-old framework, and that this can be achieved only through the impact of intellectual forces originally alien to her traditional civilization, has long been evident. Today the Chinese Communists seem the only group likely to supply these forces. Regardless of their own ultimate fate, it is hard to believe that if and when they leave, China can ever revert to what she was before their coming.

October 30 (Saturday)

A Talk with Peita Students

Last night I discussed American politics with a group of about ten Peita students. The room—one of Peita's reception halls— was magnificent (Chinese style, newly painted), but large, cold, and cheerless (the weather these days is becoming rather wintry). I arrived with a half-hour's delay caused by trouble with my bicycle. Nevertheless the students were attentive and apparently interested, and their reactions to America were instructive.

The topics we spent most time on were: (1) The Negro problem. (2) The concept of states' rights, especially in the South. (3) The status of the American Indian (an outgrowth of the Negro discussion). (4) The role in politics of American and Chinese students respectively. (5) The relative intellectual maturity of American and European labor. (6) Henry Wallace's attitude toward China. (7) American policy toward China in the event of a Republican victory. (8) The role of the various departments of the government (State, Defense, etc.) in determining American foreign policy. (9) Why didn't Americans such as myself in China tell the American government what its policy in China ought to be? (10) The difference in attitude between Chinese and Americans toward Chinese communism (that of the Chinese: it is an internal problem we must settle ourselves; that of Americans: it is simply part of the world-wide struggle between democracy and communism and must be treated as such). (11) Is America a democracy?

The responses of the students illustrate the truths and half-truths they have about America, the dangerous oversimplifications with which they approach the complexities of American thought and life, and the difficulties that any American educational program among them has to face. (It is obvious to me that a program conducted along official lines, like that of the U. S. Information Service, can have little effect upon students such as these; much more could be done through small informal discussions conducted by open-minded Americans with whom the students could speak frankly.)

Judging from the discussion, their two obsessions would appear to be that America is ridden with racial prejudice (the status of Negroes and other minority groups), and that it is controlled by a small and vicious oligarchy of capitalists.

Toward the end, one of the students asked me whether or not I regarded America as the most undemocratic country in the world today. My answer was that politically it is more democratic than most (free elections, free speech, no concentration camps); that socially it is also democratic (the slavish subservience, in certain European countries, of the "lower classes" toward their "superiors," as observed by me in 1938, contrasting with the free and easy behavior of the average American); but that economically its thinking has in some ways failed to keep pace with what is happening in other parts of the world.

One of the tragedies of our time is that a nation which today holds so much political and economic power fails to realize the inexorable forces that are working to shape the world in ways which, though often different from the traditional American "way of life," cannot be permanently stopped, simply because the economic conditions of most modern countries make some form of government planning the only alternative to complete chaos. In my discussion I tried as much as possible to explain the historical background from which the American ethos has sprung, and, without blinking at the unpleasant sides of the American scene, to point to ways in which evolution and improvement have been taking place (Supreme Court decisions on Negro rights, etc.). Through what I said I hope I at least convinced some of the students that the true picture of America is a good deal more complex and less one-sided than they had supposed.

November 1948

November 1 (Monday)

Governmental Criticism from the Ta Kung Pao

Yesterday's *Ta Kung Pao** contains an editorial, "The Government Ought To Realize Its Responsibility," which is more bitterly critical than anything I have yet seen outside of such intellectual periodicals as the *Observer (Kuan Ch'a)* and *China Reconstruction (Chung Chien)*. It paints a merciless picture of the effects of currency reform to date: The rich remain as powerful as before. The middle and lower bourgeoisie, having turned in their silver and foreign currency, are still waiting for the August 19 price ceilings then guaranteed them by the government. The great masses of poor are undergoing unprecedented sufferings. In Shanghai, for example, many pedicab operators refuse to take passengers, complaining that they are too hungry to pull. The Chinese term for "republic" literally means "people's country." In present-day China, however, the "people" have become divorced from the "country," and the latter has been subsumed under the term "government," with its many officials, decrees, and compulsions. When the "service" ostensibly being rendered by this government to its people results in such suffering and uncertainty, is it not time for it to recognize its real responsibility?

* A Tientsin daily long known for its high journalistic standards. Before the Communists took Tientsin, it was part of a chain of Chinese newspapers bearing this name that were published in several major cities.

November 2 (Tuesday)

The Day's News

It was an unpleasant surprise to learn yesterday that the new monthly subscription to the *Ta Kung Pao* will cost GY$21 (US $5.25), as compared with last month's rate of about GY$3 (US $0.75). However, even this sum will seem well spent if it brings us many more headlines like yesterday's, which reads (in Chinese):

GETTING FOOD TO EAT IS NOT EASY
BUT GOING TO THE TOILET IS ALSO DIFFICULT

The story that follows vividly describes the troubles of people trying to buy everyday necessities in Shanghai. Barter is widespread, and one must wait in line even to buy toilet paper, sales of which are limited to ten sheets per customer.

Another potpourri of economic items from Kwangtung and Kweichow is headlined:

WHEN BUYING OIL TODAY, HOW DARE
ONE ASK THE PRICE? WHEN MONTHLY
WAGES ARE $2, HOW CAN ONE FOSTER
HONESTY?

This story describes how at a town near the Canton-Hong Kong Railroad, people no longer dare ask the price of peanut oil, since they know full well that no merchant will sell it at the August 19 price ceiling. All they can do is to hold out a dollar and a bottle, and ask the clerk to pour as much oil into the bottle as the dollar will buy. In Kweichow, the story continues, county magistrates now receive less than $10 per month. How, it concludes bitterly, is honesty to be expected under such circumstances?

Other items from the same paper: Tientsin telegraph operators go on hunger strike; employees of the Hopei Medical College in Tientsin "request leave of absence"; during a brief stopover of his plane in Tsingtao, Premier Wong Wen-hao listens to tales of people in distress; professors at Peita and other Peking universities resume classes, but middle and primary school teachers continue their strike; a three-day strike of Yunnan University professors begins today; rice famine continues unabated at Hankow, where teachers have appealed in vain for help.

In other words, the economic distress is not restricted merely to North China where the "Communist bandits" might be held directly responsible. A primary factor is the government's admission, made around mid-October, that the original note issue of GY$2,000,000,000 has already been increased to over GY$9,000,-000,000. The resulting pressure on the August 19 price ceilings has proved irresistible. Now, as of November 1, the government has officially removed these ceilings and approved other measures which mean the tacit abandonment of its promised August 19 objectives.

November 3 (Wednesday)

The Exodus Begins

A circular we received from the American Consulate two days ago urges Americans, in view of the worsening military situation, to "consider the desirability of evacuation at this time while normal transportation facilities are still available." Special shipping may be provided if enough Americans signify their intention of leaving.

November 4 (Thursday)

The Exodus Grows

During the last twenty-four hours something approaching hysteria has gripped large numbers of Americans, especially in places like the Language School, where every opportunity exists to exchange rumors. Most of its students are apparently leaving, so that it looks as if the school may soon close. Several missions boards have also ordered the complete evacuation of personnel. The American Consulate, on the other hand, is laying in large stocks of food, and all but one of us fifteen Fulbright Fellows have decided to remain.

This morning our landlady, Mrs. Sung, proclaimed to Galia that she had no intention of leaving, quoting the remark of a certain Chinese doctor: "Whatever happens, I don't want to become a refugee. If I have to die, I want to die in my own house." On the other hand, the Chinese aviator who only two weeks ago brought his family here from Nanking and rented the largest house in our compound is now leaving. And well he might, for if anyone is hated by the Communists, it is the Kuomintang fliers. The evacuation of his family is being made at government orders—a significant fact, because it indicates that the government no longer expects to hold out here, whereas only two weeks ago it did.

November 6 (Saturday)

A Coalition Government?

This afternoon, from a Russian businessman from Tientsin and an American Lutheran missionary, Galia garnered two rumors: (1) The Communists have offered a coalition government, to comprise approximately fifty per cent Communists, forty per cent Nationalists, and ten per cent neutrals. (2) Five northern Kuomintang generals, having just held a meeting here, have declared to Nanking that they will not be responsible for the morale of their troops if resistance is continued. They urge Nanking to offer a coalition government to the Communists. The second story sounds more probable than the first, but the interesting thing is the similarity between the two, despite their widely different origins.

November 7 (Sunday)

Anniversary of the Bolshevik Revolution

The Bolshevik revolution took place thirty-one years ago today, and in the Soviet Consulate a reception was held this morning to celebrate the occasion. A good part of Peking, Chinese and foreign, seemed to be present, irrespective of political coloration. The great hall was packed with people, and the roar of conversation almost drowned out the strains of a band. Cocktails flowed freely, and the *piroshki* were excellent. The consul and his wife received near the door, the former resplendent in a blue diplomatic uniform. Chief topic of conversation among the several hundred guests seemed to be whether or not to leave Peking. Most have apparently decided in the negative, and several instructed us as to what we should do: begin laying in supplies now, not only of foodstuffs, but also of kerosene and water (for use when the utilities go).

November 9 (Tuesday)

A Marxist View of China

I have just finished reading an article by a well-known Peita economist on "The Meaning of the Chinese Renaissance," appearing in the November 5 issue of *China Reconstruction*.* This intellectual and social movement, the author argues, has failed, despite a history of thirty years, to realize its potentialities, primarily because it has failed to take four necessary steps: (1) Rejection of Chinese traditional philosophy, with its overemphasis of mind and underemphasis of environment as the two determining factors in human conduct. Tolstoy, who continued

* A fortnightly liberal magazine edited by a group of Peking intellectuals.

living on his estate despite his social theories, is cited by the author as support for his thesis that the outlook of the average capitalist or landlord is, in general, limited by his economic status. (2) Rejection of the theoretical concept of liberty, which, while adequate for economically and socially advanced countries like England and the United States, becomes meaningless in the case of a backward country like China, and, indeed, even acts as a check upon the gaining of liberty in the true sense. (3) Acceptance of the Marxist materialistic conception of history, according to which man's thinking is determined by his existence, and not his existence by his thinking. America is cited as a prime example: "American capitalists act in order to protect their financial interests and capitalist gains; only then are they ready to utter nice-sounding words [about democracy, etc.]." (4) Giving of political and social leadership to the long oppressed peasantry and proletariat.

Application of these principles, the author continues, will result in a new kind of society—a real heaven on earth, created as if by God himself. Science and industry will flourish; men will need to work only four hours a day; everyone will be freed from superstition and fear. All activities will be based on the principle of cooperation: studies will be pursued in common, as will recreation, agriculture, and industry. The joys or sorrows of a single man will be those of ten thousand. Nor will this society need to publicize itself, because neighboring peoples will of themselves all come to observe it; it will not need to export itself, because neighboring peoples will of themselves all feel obliged to study and imitate it. So widespread will be its influence that perhaps within fifty years all countries on earth will transform themselves into similar societies.

The naïve thinking of this article is disappointing in a magazine which aspires to be *The Nation* of China. It lends substance to a view I have already heard expressed, namely that the present-day Chinese "liberal" can sometimes be as dogmatic and closed in his thinking as his scholarly forebears, even though his approach is apt to be Marxist, while theirs was Confucian. Particularly striking are the closing paragraphs, with their Marxist parody of the Confucian utopias described in such classics as the *Book of*

Rites. Even the Confucian doctrine of peaceful conquest through virtue is not lacking; for just as, in ancient China, the virtue of the sage rulers Yao and Shun was so efficacious that all people, far and near, voluntarily submitted to them, so too, in modern China, the influence of the new Marxist society will, within half a century, and without any specific action on its own part, cause all countries of the world voluntarily to model themselves on its pattern.

November 10 (Wednesday)

Rice and Riots in Shanghai

We have thought inflation was bad in Peking. But under a large headline: "Shanghai Market shaken by Fierce Billows," here is what, according to yesterday's *Ta Kung Pao,* happened in Shanghai on the eighth:

The price of rice rose from GY$300 per picul (133 lbs.) in the morning, to $1000 by noon, $1400 by afternoon, and that evening there were cases of persons buying at $1800. Other prices followed suit. At the Navy Y.M.C.A., for example, an order of pork chops rose successively from GY$7 at 11 A.M., to $12 at noon and $24 by 2 P.M. Commodity prices as a whole had by November 8 risen twenty times over what they had been on August 19, when the gold yuan was introduced.

The story goes on to describe eight cases of rice rioting and pilfering during the same day. Typical is that of a rice shop before which several thousand prospective purchasers of ration rice were already waiting when it opened its doors that morning. Suddenly one man shouted: "Grab! Grab!" Everyone at once surged forward and began seizing what he could. The police made twenty-nine arrests, but losses have not yet been calculated.

Why, one wonders, does anyone want to flee south under such conditions? Yesterday Dr. Andrews told us a story which, after all, is perhaps more than just a story. It seems that a Peking

Chinese recently decided it would be a good thing to move to Shanghai. Just as he was about to leave, imagine his surprise at running into a Shanghai friend of his on the streets of Peking. On asking his friend what he was doing here, the latter replied that, in view of the economic difficulties in the south, he had decided it would be a good idea to move north. Having recovered from their initial astonishment, the friends came to an agreement highly advantageous to both: the Peking man is to take over his friend's house in Shanghai, and the Shanghai man is to take over that of his friend in Peking!

November 11 (Thursday)

Refugee Students

It has grown quite cold the last few days, and a thin coat of ice and snow still remains from an unexpected snowfall the day before yesterday. While basking in the warmth of our large stove or lying snugly in bed at night, I have often wondered about those unhappy refugee students whom we saw two months ago at the Temple of Heaven. Yesterday we learned the answer. As Galia was coming home in her pedicab, she saw trucks containing hundreds of young men and women drawing up before three adjoining houses on Nei-wu Pu Chieh (Avenue of the Ministry of Internal Affairs), which is only a few blocks from where we live. These, she quickly discovered, are the former Temple of Heaven refugees, and they seemed happy indeed over their new quarters, even though the houses do not look too large and have no heat. Overcrowding, of course, will be intense, and sanitary conditions no doubt terrible.

November 12 (Friday)

The Avalanche

As I begin writing this evening, I still feel breathless from today's events. Almost forgotten in the rush is the early morning news that the exchange for the American dollar has been officially raised from 4:1 to 20:1.

It was a solemn group of Fulbright Fellows that assembled in the U.S. Information Service auditorium at 10:30 this morning in response to the summons sent out the day before. Vice-Consul M. silently distributed a notice stating that a chartered plane will be provided on November 15 for all Fulbrighters deciding to leave here for Nanking, that we must give our decision by 3 P.M. today, and that no further stipend payments can be guaranteed for those who remain.

All this has left us very much up in the air. At last report more than half of the fifteen or so Fulbrighters had elected to go.* We ourselves, after some soul searching, have decided to stay and are trying hard to convert what money we have either into American greenbacks or the old Chinese silver dollars. Meanwhile Galia is going job hunting.

On returning home from the U.S.I.S. meeting, I noticed that the main gate of our large compound was ajar. Scarcely had I entered our house when I noticed that three or four young fellows had wandered from the general compound into our private courtyard and were peering into our windows. On seeing me, they slipped away without answering my shouted demand as to their business. Hearing a hubbub outside, I went to the outer compound and there found an avalanche of humanity pouring in through the front gate. It turned out to be those same student refugees whom Galia had seen moving into the Nei-wu Pu Chieh houses the day before yesterday. From the main court they were fanning out in all directions, some invading our landlady's garden, others the front building recently vacated by the air pilot.

* Eight was the number that eventually remained.

Many carried piles of bedding and other belongings. All attempts to argue with them fell on deaf ears. They had spent the last couple of nights in the open courtyards of the Nei-wu Pu Chieh houses; now they had found an empty building and most definitely were going to occupy it. It was an amorphous horde, with no apparent leader with whom to talk. While I tried to stop some, the others continued pouring in.

Our landlady, Mrs. Sung, who arrived at this juncture with no previous inkling of what had been happening, quickly sized up the situation and in honeyed tones explained that though the main building was at the moment unoccupied, rent had been paid on it for six months in advance and the belongings of its tenant were still there. Her words were equally ineffective. As she talked, dozens of students stripped her trees bare of their *hai-t'ang* (crab apples), which they began munching, while some ensconced themselves in the air pilot's chairs. Still others carried their belongings to Mrs. Sung's pride of prides—the terrace of her great *k'o-t'ing* at the rear of the garden, a museumlike hall filled with valuable Chinese furniture acquired over the years by her husband (now in the United States). Her greatest fear was that the students would despoil this hall.

It was useless to talk further. Some of the students (mostly young fellows in their teens) seemed amenable to reason, but others assumed a belligerent air. They were here, and here they were going to stay. Mrs. Sung began phoning her various contacts but at first could get no one, this being the anniversary of Sun Yat-sen's death and therefore a holiday. Finally she reached a friend of the air pilot, himself an aviator, who arrived shortly afterward with three soldiers. They mounted guard at the entrance to Mrs. Sung's private court, bayonets drawn and cartridges slipped into their rifles, and for a moment I was afraid there might be trouble. After vainly arguing for some time, however, the aviator withdrew in defeat, taking with him his soldiers. Later in the afternoon three other pilots arrived, finally followed by Mrs. Sung's pilot tenant himself (who had just flown in from Nanking). He too, however, was unsuccessful and finally decided that the only thing to do was to salvage what he could of his furniture by moving it out as soon as possible. Very late in the afternoon a fairly high police official put in an appearance, only to announce solemnly to Mrs. Sung—in the hearing of many of the students— that under the circumstances he was powerless to remove them but would be willing to act as a go-between.

These students, as a consequence, have been left in complete possession. They not only occupy the pilot's house but also the smaller building behind, as well as Mrs. Sung's great hall, from which they have helped her to remove the furniture. Coming home in the late afternoon from an attempt to exchange money, I found streams of students passing through the front gate, bringing with them their daily fare of steamed corn bread (provided, I learn, by the Bureau of Social Welfare). For a while after dinner we heard a flute being played, but now all is quiet. We discovered not long ago, however, that a narrow passageway directly behind the rear window of our kitchen is being used as an open-air toilet. Thus all the filth which shocked us at the Temple of Heaven is now being brought directly before our eyes. Fortunately the weather is cold, so that there are no flies to spread disease.

By piecing together scraps of information, I have been able to reconstruct the events leading up to the present situation. These students, all from Taiyuan middle schools, were evacuated months ago by plane to Peking, where they were dumped in the Temple of Heaven. After first enduring rains and then the recent cold weather, they finally decided they could stand no more and moved en masse into the T'ai Miao (ancestral temple of the former Manchu emperors). Before long, however, they were ejected at the orders of Fu Tso-yi (Kuomintang commander in North China), and removed to the Tung Yüeh Miao, a large Taoist temple outside the east gate of the city.

Finding this too small, some of them then appealed to Fu Tso-yi and the municipal government for additional quarters. The reply they received was that the municipality itself was helpless to do anything, since no house owner would voluntarily accept refugees like themselves. However, *the municipal authorities would agree to raise no obstacles if they, the refugees themselves, would invade the city and commandeer whatever empty places they might find available.* This they accordingly did, and the outcome was the move to Nei-wu Pu Chieh, where they found three rather large houses, vacant save for their landlord and some furniture (straightway removed by its owners). These houses, however, being still insufficient for the almost two thousand refugees, scouting parties were then sent about the neighborhood to look for other possibilities. A group of seven or eight came here yesterday afternoon, were carelessly admitted by our compound's not overly intelligent gate keeper, and today's descent is the result.

All this, heaped on our other worries, made today the most depressing one since we have arrived in Peking, and gives an unpleasant foretaste of what may happen if things really get out of hand. Our young refugees, though cold and underfed, are at the moment comparatively docile. But what may they become if there is complete breakdown of authority and their meager food rations are interrupted?

November 13 (Saturday)

Two Years behind the Iron Curtain?

Another hectic day, though less nerve-racking than yesterday. Yesterday we made our decision to stay. Today we are preparing to meet the situation accordingly.

In the morning I requested that a telegram be sent to Nanking asking for as large a lump-sum payment on my stipend as possible. Peters of U.S.I.S. is doubtful that anything can be done. His view is that China may be isolated from the outside world for as much as two years before diplomatic recognition may make a resumption of normal contacts possible. Hence the Consulate has been accumulating a year's supply of foodstuffs from Tsingtao, for which its members have individually contributed a considerable sum.

I myself withdrew all except GY$20 from the bank this morning and spent the greater part of the day on the black market converting it into solid currency. The major transaction—conducted in

the rear, windowless room of a small tailor shop—was at the rate
of 29:1. Yesterday I could have had it at 22. My tremendous pile
of fresh gold yuan has thus shrunk into a tiny folder of well-worn
greenbacks. Prices have jumped proportionately.

November 14 (Sunday)

Glimpses behind the Iron Curtain

This afternoon, at a tea given by Forke to look at his many interesting Han rubbings, I met a number of Peking's sinologically-
minded Catholic fathers. Before looking at the rubbings, the
conversation inevitably turned to politics, and I heard something
of life behind the iron curtain. Only a week ago Father Eimer
received news about Harbin from an Austrian dentist recently
arrived from that city. Food there is abundant, he says, and life
goes smoothly, though it took the Communists a year to get the
city administration into good working order. Most startling is the
claim that one can live adequately on US$5 per month! Father
Hals also retailed reports of what he has heard from the Catholic
missionaries in Tsinan. They have been left unmolested and allowed so far to conduct their school as usual. In fact they were
even given rice by the Communists when the latter first came
in, and persons who wish to leave the city have been allowed to do
so without trouble.

Our Chinese Boy Cinderella

Our pedicab boy, Chin, deserves a few words of praise in this
record for the way in which he serves us. He is a rare example of
unspoiled simplicity and honesty combined with a native intelligence that might take him far did he have the benefit of a decent
education. His life, though he is only twenty-three, has not been
particularly easy. As the youngest in his family, he has been a

true boy Cinderella, the object of constant abuse from his elder brother, who operates a beauty parlor. In his early teens, before finishing primary school, he was apprenticed to a shoemaker, for whom he had to toil from six in the morning until late at night. Small wonder that he sometimes nodded over his work, on which occasions he would be beaten by his master. Once he was punished so severely that he fled home and refused to return until forced to do so by his elder brother. Finally he ran away to Fengtai and succeeded in getting a job on the railroad. It was several months before the family saw him again, and since then he has lived independently, eventually becoming a pedicab operator.

Today he is not merely Galia's pedicab man but our houseboy as well. He shows remarkable talent for everything mechanical, especially electricity, about which he has picked up considerable knowledge. On his own initiative he installed a complex system of electric bells, linking us with the kitchen, the front gate, and our landlady's quarters. He also manufactured skeleton keys for the broken lock to our gate, wired an electric lamp for his pedicab, and is skilled as a repairer of pedicabs and bicycles. Around the house he makes himself useful at all sorts of jobs. When sent on errands he always gets us the best bargain possible without pocketing a commission for himself. Being the youngest son, he is the sole support of his widowed mother and grandmother, for whom his elder married brother does nothing. Yet this brother often berates him for being no good, though recently, needing to install some electrical equipment in his new beauty parlor, he called on Chin to do the job. Incidentally, Chin's most devoted admirer is our Theo, who follows and "assists" him in his work and, I have no doubt, has learned more Chinese from him than from Mr. Ma, his regular language teacher.

Mr. Ma is another man for whom we have high regard. Though getting on in years, he is alert, widely interested in many subjects, and active both physically and intellectually. He rides a bicycle which he prides himself on keeping in excellent repair with his own hands—a rather unusual accomplishment for an elderly Chinese gentleman of the scholar class who, among other things, has written an unpublished history of the Chinese shadow drama.

November 21 (Sunday)

Emergency Operation

It is fortunate that we did not try to take the Fulbright evacuation plane, which finally left on the sixteenth, a day later than originally scheduled. It is also fortunate that Peking possesses such a fine institution as the famous Rockefeller-endowed Peiping Union Medical College (P.U.M.C.), and such an excellent surgeon as Dr. Loucks, who is attached to that institution. Otherwise there is no doubt that Theo would no longer be living today. On Sunday the fourteenth he began complaining of severe abdominal pains, which during the next twenty-four hours reached almost unbearable intensity. The doctor whom we summoned seemed unable to diagnose it, so on the evening of the fifteenth we finally appealed to Dr. Loucks. The result was that Theo was rushed immediately to the hospital and operated on late that night. What was supposed to be appendicitis turned out to be a case of intus-susception (rolling up of one intestine within the other). But Theo is now well on the way to recovery and expected home within two days.

Two Kinds of Racket

Although the new 20:1 exchange rate was announced in all the papers on the twelfth, we were told on the sixteenth that the P.U.M.C. was still being forced by the local branch of the Central Bank to convert its American funds at the old 4:1 rate. The ostensible reason was that the bank had not yet received official confirmation from Nanking of the change in rate. Two days later I heard this story repeated by Mr. James, a curious old gentleman, apparently an ex-missionary, whom I have seen wandering around the P.U.M.C. grounds—usually wearing a Chinese gown—where he holds some sort of glorified janitorial position. According to him, the Central Bank even offered to help the P.U.M.C. out, if it were temporarily short of funds, with a loan at thirty per cent interest! *

The local authorities, it seems, are now endeavoring to arouse Peking's residents from their lethargy concerning the Red menace. Their aim, in the words of the *Peiping Chronicle,* is to make the people realize that "the present war is not a civil war but a campaign to eliminate the enemy of democracy, peace, and freedom." For this purpose they have organized a city defense training program into which they eventually hope to draw some 300,000 able-bodied civilians between the ages of 18 and 45. Women as well as men, according to the same news story, are expected to do their bit. Training under "specifically designated women disciplinarians" is to be given to a curious conglomeration of "245 actresses, 343 nuns, 193 usheresses, and 1,233 prostitutes." From our Chin we learn that all gainfully employed persons will be graciously permitted to undergo this training between 6 and 7 A.M. daily—a time selected in the hope that it will least interfere with their own work.

In addition, the authorities plan to conscript a further 10,000 men in Peking, aged 21 to 28, for actual military service in the Communist Suppression Campaign. All the trappings of democracy are being invoked for this scheme. Each section of the city is being asked to supply a certain quota, to be selected by drawing the names of prospective conscripts from an urn. At this point, however, the resemblance to democratic procedure ceases. On the one hand, no exemption is apparently provided for draftees with dependents; on the other, it is possible for any individual possessing the necessary wherewithal to "buy" another man in his place and thus escape the drawing process entirely. The procedure does remain "democratic," however, to the extent that the "contributions" thus demanded vary according to the economic status of the donor. In the case of our Chin, for example (who is strong and twenty-three, and therefore eminently eligible, despite the fact that he has a mother and grandmother to support), he was told yesterday that a GY$60 contribution would be enough to keep his name out of the fateful urn. Through hard bargaining, moreover,

* This situation continued until some days after the 21st, when this entry was written.

he succeeded in reducing this sum to $30. In fact, he is even hopeful that further bargaining may bring it down to $20. Very reluctantly, therefore, we have advanced him this amount, devoutly hoping it will achieve its purpose.

The authorities are also approaching the general populace for donations to "comfort" the families of those 10,000 men (presumably too poor to buy themselves out) who are actually conscripted. Our landlady, for example, was asked for $500, which she succeeded in reducing to $50. According to yesterday's *World Daily News* (*Shih-chieh Jih-pao*), Dr. Hu Shih * was provoked by a similar request for $400 into writing a letter of protest to the mayor. No doubt this letter was effective as far as Dr. Hu himself is concerned. The question remains whether it will stop further demands from being made upon the innumerable little people who lack Dr. Hu's influence.

Two Kinds of Inefficiency

The past few days have seen long lines of people waiting at the banks to change their remaining fa pi dollars—officially slated to be withdrawn from circulation today—into gold yuan notes. As on some previous occasions, however, the authorities do not seem to have anticipated what would happen when they promulgated this measure. In the present case they forgot that a supply of small change in the new currency (ten- and twenty-cent notes) would be needed to replace the fa pi, which, since August 19, has been functioning as a small change auxiliary to the gold yuan. The result, according to the papers, is that many petty street vendors have been forced to suspend business lately, owing to their inability to supply change for the single dollar bills which are the lowest denomination generally available in the new currency. Yesterday, suddenly awakening, it seems, to the situation, the authorities extended the deadline for the fa pi conversion another fifteen days (by which time inflation will probably have solved the difficulty).

* Chinese scholar famous as the founder of the Chinese literary renaissance thirty years ago and as China's wartime ambassador to the United States. After the war, until the Communist occupation of Peking, he was president of Peking National University.

Aside from the crowded banks, one of the few places where fa pi may still be conveniently disposed of is the post office. Here again confusion reigns, however, owing to two or three successive increases in postal rates during the past few weeks, while few if any stamps corresponding to the new rates have yet been printed. Because of these frequent changes, it is safer to go to the post office oneself before putting stamps on any letter. Even then, considerable ingenuity is necessary to find out, first, what the new rates (quoted in gold yuan) correspond to in fa pi (in which the stamps are printed), and secondly, to be able to combine these stamps in such a way as to approximate the amount required. By the time this process is completed, one's letter has usually become so covered with stamps as to leave almost no place for the address.

Chairs and Daggers

Our students, though giving no personal trouble, are beginning to show signs of unruliness. Two nights ago our *amah*, whose room is located beside the entrance to the outer compound, complained that they kept her awake the whole night with their comings and goings. The next day we heard loud banging in the garden behind our house, and, on looking out, saw whole tables and chairs being smashed to bits. The pieces were then hidden in various out-of-the-way places, including the narrow passageway behind our kitchen, formerly used as a toilet. (I am glad to say that this particular use of it has been discontinued since Mrs. Sung's servants—not the students themselves—dug latrines in other parts of the compound.) At the time we were puzzled by this seemingly senseless destruction, but a story in yesterday's *Ta Kung Pao* explains the mystery.

It seems that the previous day the authorities made a city-wide registration of all refugee students in the course of which they discovered and confiscated, among other objects, several daggers and a number of Buddhist images and sacred texts. (This confirms a story in the *Chronicle* several weeks ago, according to which the monks of the Lama Temple complained that many sacred objects had been stolen by refugee students housed in that temple.) At the Tung Yüeh Miao,* where some of our Shansi students still remain, the discovery of one such dagger led to a fracas in which one official of the Bureau of Education was wounded and seven students arrested. Though the registration officials also visited our students' Nei-wu Pu Chieh headquarters, they neglected for some reason to come here. Thus they failed to discover the tables and chairs which the students had carried from Nei-wu Pu Chieh during the night, then destroyed and hid in our compound. Probably these had been originally looted from the Temple of Heaven.

November 28 (Sunday)

"Strategic Withdrawal"

Paoting, provincial capital of Hopei, has been lost. The military spokesman's rationalization is amusing: After driving the enemy more than 33 miles from the city, the National troops voluntarily decided to evacuate it in order to spare its inhabitants hunger and suffering, as well as to retain their own mobility. They plan to remain close at hand, however, ready at any time to return to the city when asked to do so by the inhabitants.

Over sixty per cent of the Americans in North China have left, or are planning to: in the Peking consular district, 355 gone and 48 scheduled to go, out of a total of 674; in the Tientsin consular district, 55 gone out of an estimated total of 177. Most are missionaries. Many Tientsin businessmen, however, seem prepared to wait and see if they can do business with the Communists.

Prices have jumped again during the past week.

Nothing has yet been done for our student guests, nor is anything expected to be done in the immediate future. According to today's *Chronicle,* the Bureau of Education is "straining every effort to seek for big houses in the city to accommodate those student refugees who occupied empty houses without the permission

* "Temple of the Eastern Peak"—large Taoist temple, not far outside of Peking's main east city gate.

of the owners." This face-saving statement apparently means that all plans for positive action have been dropped. Meanwhile more than two thousand new student refugees have arrived from Paoting. They are to be housed in the Wo Fo Ssu and Pi Yün Ssu, lovely Buddhist temples in the Western Hills.

A few days ago several of us Americans visited a group of Chinese intellectuals, including the fairy godfather of the magazine *China Reconstruction*—a thin, pale-faced young man from Shanghai who speaks almost no English and whose Mandarin is suffused with an atrocious Shanghai accent. Also present was a Peita economist who is one of the magazine's chief contributors—a plump, round-faced, genial man who speaks English slowly and incorrectly but with fair ease. Most of the conversation turned to rather idle speculation and gave the impression that these intellectuals know little more about the situation than do we foreigners. Toward the end, however, as we sat in darkness after the electricity had gone off—a frequent occurrence lately, usually lasting anywhere from one to three hours after 5 P.M.—the question was raised what we Americans would do when the change came. We replied that we would like to stay, provided we could continue to receive funds, would be unmolested in our work, and would have fair assurance of being able to leave after one year's time. The economist replied that it might be possible for him to sound out the proper quarters as to their attitude, and that he would endeavor to have an answer for us as soon as possible. None of us ventured to ask how this might be done.*

November 30 (Tuesday)

Refugees and Relics

Yesterday, with Theo on the rear of my bicycle, I visited the Temple of Confucius and the Hall of Classics. Both places were swarming with refugees: Manchurian students in the one, civilian

* As a matter of fact, it never was done. At least we were never given an answer.

families in the other. The total impression was not quite as devastating as that of the Temple of Heaven, however, because, in the first place, some attempt had been made to construct toilet facilities, and in the second, some families seemed to be engaged in gainful occupations, such as spinning. Nevertheless, I found it actually difficult to recognize these places, so changed were they from the quiet, dignified spots I had once known. All the side buildings, with their stone-tablet inscriptions of the thirteen classics, are now occupied by families. Their lattice windows and doors are pasted across with old newspapers or covered with mats donated by philanthropic organizations. In one corner of the Temple of Confucius lies a great heap of half-smashed furniture, cleared from its original buildings to make way for human habitation. The marvelous tiled archway near the entrance of the Hall of Classics is plastered with posters, among them, ironically enough, U.S. Information Service pictures of New York skyscrapers. Perhaps U.S.I.S. placed them there in the hope of raising refugee morale! Few people, aside from the refugees themselves, come any more. The gatekeeper told me that he sells only ten odd tickets a day.

This visit is another vivid symbol of the breakup of the old China. As the gatekeeper commented, some of the relics within these walls, including the magnificent cypresses, have been standing here ever since the Mongol dynasty (thirteenth and fourteenth centuries). And now in the twinkling of an eye, historically speaking, they are being blotted out. Though this has often happened before in Chinese history, what saved the situation then was that the destruction of one monument was usually followed by the building of another. In this way China's cultural continuity was maintained. But today this no longer happens. What now disappears will never be replaced.

December 1948

December 4 (Saturday)

A Soviet Meeting

The day before yesterday we had a lengthy conversation with S., a well-known Soviet citizen. The conversation—heated but friendly —inevitably turned to politics and brought forth some rather frank remarks on both sides. S. is scornful of the accomplishments of Socialist Britain. The English are too slow, too gradual, he exclaimed. Moreover, Britain is not really democratic because the men who sit in Parliament are not truly representative of the people as a whole. Even the members of the Labor government do not really represent labor, because, while they may have been union leaders once upon a time, they gave this up years ago to become lawyers or politicians. For real democracy, one must go to Eastern Europe. There all working groups (laborers, farmers, white-collar workers, etc.) are represented in the government according to their actual ratio in the population as a whole. Furthermore, these delegates remain really representative of their own class because, when not in session, they continue to do their ordinary work as laborers, farmers, etc. To our objection that the people cannot be really and adequately represented by men who merely attend one gala parliamentary meeting a year, S. made no satisfactory answer. But here in a nutshell lies one important difference between Western and Soviet concepts of democracy.

On Russia we spoke very openly. Granted, we said, that misrepresentation and misconceptions about the U.S.S.R. exist in the West, this could be mitigated to some extent by allowing journalists and others free access to all parts of that country and its population. To this S. replied that: (1) In the prewar years much freedom had been allowed, but the present campaign of vilification in the Western press now made this impossible. (2) Even so, freedom had been granted many people. Henry Wallace, for example, was allowed to travel in parts of Siberia "which had never been seen by outsiders before." (To which I rejoined that this proved precisely that such freedom was not customary.) (3) Secrecy was necessary as long as Russia remained industrially inferior to the United States. All she wanted was a chance to be left alone to build up her industries to the point where she could show them with pride to the rest of the world. When electric refrigerators, for example, would be found in private homes throughout the Soviet Union, she would then be glad to have other people come and see. Even at the end of the present Five Year Plan, in fact, he concluded, we shall see that much of the present stringency will be relaxed.

Lull Before the Storm

The spectacular price rise of the early part of the week has begun to subside, and the U.S. dollar, which reached 55 to 1, has gone back to 45. Hence I am in no hurry to exchange my new remittance from Nanking, which finally arrived yesterday. The exchange, both of Chinese silver dollars and American greenbacks, is now being done openly throughout the city. A few days ago, for the first time, I heard hawkers clinking silver dollars on the streets. Though food and other necessities are high, the general exodus (Chinese as well as foreign) has left many luxury goods a drug on the market. The *Chronicle,* for example, reports that electric refrigerators can be bought in Shanghai for a quarter of their original value, and that apartments formerly requiring thousands of dollars in "key money" now go begging. Here in Peking, it claims, one can buy a 1941 Ford for as little as GY$1000 (slightly over US$20 at present exchange). The corollary is that gasoline has gone up to over GY$42 per gallon.

Despite the military quiescence immediately around the city, the forced conscription of soldiers continues. Ma, poor man, suffered this week from a combination of a bad cold and financial difficulties. He is much worried lest his son be conscripted, and we have loaned him $100 to buy an exemption. (The orginal sum demanded was $400.) He is full of bitterness toward the *pao* chiefs in charge of conscription.* People who refuse to pay, he says, are spirited away in the middle of the night to no one knows where. This happened to a man he knew who had been only recently married. Furthermore, Ma has been approached for "repair money" to renovate the city wall for defense purposes. This is the third such demand made of him since the summer.

The very day before Mr. Ma told us these troubles, General Fu Tso-yi made a statement in the *Chronicle* promising strong action against a large number of abuses, notably corruption in the recruiting of soldiers, and the illegal occupation by force of empty houses!

Our students, incidentally, still remain, though there are rumors of corrective steps "within the next few days." Most of the Language School—largely depopulated as the result of the American exodus—has been voluntarily turned over by its director to some four hundred refugee students from Paoting. Unlike ours, they are accompanied by their teachers, attend classes, and are reportedly well disciplined. Probably he has done well to accept them now, instead of leaving the buildings to a possibly much worse fate later on.

December 12 (Sunday)

The Tide Draws Nearer

So quietly and gently that one is hardly aware of it, yet inexorably, the "red tide" draws nearer. Indeed, at the moment it seems as if it may reach Peking sooner than Nanking and the South. Twice

* A *pao* is an ancient administrative unit, theoretically consisting of 10 *chia*, each of which in turn consists of 10 households. It was revived by the Kuomintang, both in the countryside and in the cities, as a means of maintaining close supervision over the people and was often used as an instrument for "squeeze" and oppression by unscrupulous local *pao* leaders.

this week my subscription to the *Ta Kung Pao* has failed to come through from Tientsin, owing to cutting of the railroad. A day or so ago a station twenty-five kilometers south of us on the Peking-Hankow line was destroyed in fighting, and though the "bandits" were driven off, they are apparently in firm control of Liu-li-ho, only a little farther south. The Communists also move steadily down the Peking-Jehol line, on which they have reached a point some twenty-five kilometers northeast of the city. At Tungchow (ten miles east of Peking), the papers report, some thousand houses and many fine old trees have been razed around the city wall to strip the terrain of all protective cover.

All this heightens speculation about the intentions of General Fu Tso-yi, Kuomintang commander here. Will he fight or not? Some say he will, others that he has already made a deal. My own hunch is that he has been negotiating, but unsuccessfully so far, and will skip out at the last minute, perhaps to join Ma Hung-kuei in the Northwest.

Within the city conditions remain quiet, despite (or because of?) increasingly strict police measures against all possible subversive elements. Visitors from Tsinghua today reported that a close examination is being made of all persons entering the city gates. They themselves were forced to dismount from the Tsinghua bus and then were frisked from head to foot by plain-clothes men. As of this writing, we in Peking are forbidden to listen to enemy broadcasts, to assemble large groups in our home, to open our doors to unknown persons at night, or to do any other of a total of some thirteen items. We are also warned to be prepared for indefinite suspension of electricity and water.

Whatever else may be lacking here these days, there is certainly no absence of activity. Aside from military movements, this is largely caused by two crosscurrents: Peking residents desperately trying to flee southward, and refugees from outer areas flooding into the city. House moving is a common sight on the streets, and a couple of evenings ago I saw a line of carts proceeding down Morrison Street, filled with civilians (obviously refugees, perhaps from Tungchow) perched high atop their piled-up belongings. Economically, the result is curious and tragic. On the one hand, the past week has been marked by the sharpest collapse yet of the gold yuan. Though the American dollar has risen to over 70 to 1, the Chinese silver dollar has gone up even more sharply, so that yesterday it is said to have topped the American dollar for the first time. This remarkable phenomenon apparently reflects the greater Chinese confidence in times of change in the worth of their traditional silver currency. As one enters the Tung-tan open-air market, it is literally difficult to push one's way through the crowds of exchangers who stand on the street clinking their silver dollars.

But side by side with the hectic buying and speculation is the sadder picture of those pinched by inflation or unemployment who sell their belongings in order to keep alive. At the Tung-tan market, for example, in addition to the usual merchants and the new influx of silver exchangers, one now sees little knots of people, men, women, and children—apparently entire families—selling clothing, furniture, and other personal belongings spread before them on the ground. The market is also flooded with the possessions of people fleeing south—among them some extraordinarily cheap bargains for anyone fortunate enough to have cash during these difficult times.

Last Monday, the sixth, at 8 P.M., we thought for a moment that the great change was here when, within a few seconds of each other, we heard two muffled but obviously powerful distant explosions. The second, indeed, was so strong that it forced our southern entrance door to swing inward. Then silence until 10 P.M., when two even louder explosions caused me to rush outside. As I stood there, peering into the blackness of the night, a third explosion, the strongest of all, not only blew open our door but several of the windows as well. It was followed by an intense red glow which lighted the entire southern sector of the sky for several seconds; then again all was still and dark. The next morning we heard that a gasoline tank and ammunition dump had successively blown up at Nan Yuan,* whether through carelessness or sabotage we do not know. It is rumored there were some forty casualties.

At 11 A.M. today, while walking with Theo in the T'ai Miao, I heard very clearly a new series of explosions, obviously gunfire

* Peking's southern airport, used primarily by the military. The city's western airport, Hsi Yuan, was used for civilian planes.

north of the city. The rumble went on almost continuously for perhaps five minutes.

A disturbing recent development has been the large-scale release of prisoners from jail, reportedly to save food and heat. Seventy-seven were let out yesterday. Economic conditions being what they are these days, it is said that some were reluctant to accept their new-found "freedom" and had to be ejected at bayonet point. About eighty per cent, according to the *Ta Kung Pao*, are former collaborators under the Japanese; the rest mostly dope addicts, plus a scattering of robbers. The collaborators include men of considerable note: the Japanese-appointed puppet mayors of Tientsin, Tatung, and other cities; the puppet president of Peiping Normal College; leaders of the Japanese-sponsored Hsin Min Hui (New People's Party), and so on. One wonders how they will be received by the Communists.

Partially balancing this act, however, is the release in Tientsin of a dozen of the students who were arrested there on August 19 and have been held ever since without trial. Other student releases, both in Tientsin and Peking, are expected shortly. The reason is rumored to be that, as the Communists draw nearer, the authorities are beginning to worry about reprisals against themselves.

Meanwhile the conscription racket continues. Today a big celebration, replete with speeches and sound trucks, was held in the Throne Hall of the Forbidden City. Its purpose was to honor the 8,000 recruits (the original quota was 10,000) who, unable to "hire" other men in their place, have been inducted into the army. This ceremony has not stopped the continuing demands for "soldier hire" money from the rest of the population. Our Chin, though possessing a receipt for the GY$20 he has already paid, has been approached, together with the other young men in his section, for an additional donation of three bags of flour each (over $700 at present prices). This demand they rejected, but they have now been dunned for $100 each, which most of them have already paid, some by selling furniture and other personal effects. Chin came to us today for a "loan" for this amount, which we refused to give until he receives assurance that this will end the matter.

One hardly envies the men who are finally inducted as the result of all this hocus-pocus. According to one Chinese friend, Fu Tso-yi's soldiers receive the munificent wage of GY$6 per month for fighting for their country (about enough to buy two packs of the cheapest cigarettes at present prices). This, however, is only the theory. In actual fact deductions made for towels and other articles supplied for their personal "comfort" bring this sum down to about $2.50.

December 14 (Tuesday)

Has the Siege Begun?

Yesterday it seemed for a while that the end might be here. The cannonade, beginning in the late forenoon, continued throughout the afternoon on a wide sector north and west of the city and was obviously nearer than anything we have heard hitherto. As the afternoon wore on, visibility became greatly reduced by a raging dust storm, but the explosions continued with increasing intensity until they were shaking our windowpanes. By the time darkness fell (accompanied by a strict curfew after eight o'clock), it seemed not unlikely that by next morning the city might be in Communist hands. Toward midnight, however, the firing gradually died down, and today all has been quiet save for a few scattered reverberations in the early morning.

What caused all this excitement, according to the papers, was the appearance of about a thousand "bandits" around Tsing-ho (two or three miles from Tsinghua University). Of course (according to these same reports) they were triumphantly driven off. What most disturbs us is that Fu Tso-yi perhaps really intends to make a fight of it. A statement issued yesterday designated both Peking and Tientsin as vital centers, to be defended at all costs even though this may mean distress to their populations. According to rumor, Fu has boasted that if Yen Hsi-shan has been able to hold out all these months in Taiyuan, there is no reason why he, Fu, cannot do the same here.

The ominous tone of these statements is strengthened by what I saw on a bicycle tour of the city this afternoon. Never has Peking been so full of soldiers. Fu is obviously packing them into the city, and outwardly, at least, intends to keep them here for some time. The streets are filled with marching squadrons, roaring military trucks, and long lines of two-wheeled horse carts packed with straw for the animals, and bedding and other equipment for the men. One poignant scene was that of two wounded soldiers being carried on stretchers down one of the largest streets.

Hoping to get a distant view of the fighting, I made a trip to Coal Hill—the artificial hill which stands just north of the imperial palaces near the center of the city—but discovered that the enclosure is filled with soldiers and no longer open to the public. The same is true of the other parks and palace enclosures: the Forbidden City, the T'ai Miao, and the Pei Hai, Chung Hai, and Nan Hai. Only Central Park presented its normal appearance, with a small band of skaters looking curiously incongruous in the midst of all this military activity as they glided over the frozen moat which separates the park from the wall of the Forbidden City. Most disturbing of all was the sight of soldiers stringing military telephone wires between their various encampments. These spectacles create visions of a repetition of the horrible sieges endured by Changchun and Mukden in the past and Taiyuan today, with all the starvation and suffering that this entails.

December 15 (Wednesday)

"Under Fire!"

The ancient city of Peking is now being shelled by Communist guns! So says a San Francisco broadcast picked up here on shortwave today. I can imagine the excitement this is causing at home. Actually it is all nonsense. Firing, most of it southwest of the city

(Shih-ching-shan, Marco Polo Bridge, etc.), has been going on
the greater part of the day, and around supper time became
quite intense—enough to rattle our windows—while for the first
time I hear the heavy booms clearly punctuated by the rat-tat-tat
of machine guns. But so far as I know, no shots whatever have
been directed into the city itself. Moreover, I suspect that ninety
per cent of the firing is the work of the Nationalist soldiers, who
today are packing the city more than ever, and probably expend
their ammunition so recklessly in the hope of scaring their enemies and encouraging themselves. During the last several minutes (it is now eight P.M.) there has been almost no firing.

I write by oil lamp, our electricity having stopped at 10.30 this
morning. The water has also been off during most of the day,
though a thin trickle began a short time ago and we are hasten-
ing to fill the bath tub. Probably there will be no regular electricity or water again for some time to come, but fortunately
there is a pump in our compound which should supply us. The
fact that much of Peking's population still depends on well
water makes a stoppage of running water less serious here than
in a more modern city.

Aside from the radio, I believe we are now completely isolated
from the outside world. Telephone communication no longer
exists with Tientsin. In fact it does not even extend as far as
Tsinghua and Yenching Universities, which, if not already in
Communist hands, may well have been engulfed in the fighting.
The railroad to Tientsin is still cut.

Worst of all is the fact that we are now cut off by air. Yesterday's rumor that the airfields were abandoned has proved correct,
and further rumor has it that Fu Tso-yi's troops destroyed the
control tower of the former before retreating—rather senseless
in view of the fact that the Communists themselves possess no
planes. But it is no more senseless than some other things being
done these days, such as the reported mounting of guns on the
city walls. One wonders if Fu Tso-yi realizes that he is no longer
living in the Middle Ages, and that walled cities are useless as
protection unless bolstered by outlying defenses.

Despite the loss of the fields, today has seen much air activity.
Numerous small fighter planes, perhaps from Tientsin, have

swept at high speed over the city and onward to the north and west, probably for reconnaissance. And both yesterday and today a large civilian plane circled for many minutes very low over the city itself. It wanted to land on the Tung-tan glacis,* but was warned not to do so because of the softness of the ground. The authorities, however, plan to convert the glacis into an emergency airfield.

December 16 (Thursday)

A Glimpse of Tsinan under the Communists

Peculiarly appropriate for these troubled days is a Chinese article, "Tsinan Since Its Loss," contributed to the December 5 issue of *China Reconstruction* by an anonymous Tsinan middle-school teacher recently arrived in Tientsin. After fighting had stopped, the writer narrates, the first act of the Communists was to distribute rice to all volunteers who would clear dead bodies from the streets and stack up the abandoned rifles. Discipline in the (Communist) Eighth Route Army was strict. Personal property that had been stolen by Nationalist soldiers from the American dean of Cheeloo University was promptly returned to him by the Communists. "During my thirty years in China I have never seen such troops as these," he is reported to have said.

Communist field troops were evacuated soon after the fighting was over, but during the interval between their departure and the arrival of military police, there was a wave of looting. Two or three people had to be executed in order to restore order. Soon afterward the writer remarked sarcastically to a Communist officer, "Others say you are the destiny of the poor. Why, then, don't you let these poor people loot? Out in the countryside

* A broad, open field surrounding three sides of the Legation Quarter. After the siege of the legations during the Boxer uprising of 1900, the Chinese houses surrounding the legations, from which many attacks had been launched, were razed to the ground at the demand of the foreign powers.

don't you work at stirring up conflict?" To this the officer replied, "In the country it is necessary to destroy feudalism in
order to increase production, but to do this in the cities it is necessary to protect industry and commerce. Looting is no solution
to the problem of poverty. The impoverishment which has been
created over many years by the ruling class can only be solved
through systematized productivity. It is not something that can
be solved in a single morning."

After occupation, the article continues, the Communists maintained strict discipline over their men and ordered any cases of
oppression to be promptly reported. Two Communist soldiers,
in fact, were executed as a result of such reports. Some of these
Communists had never seen a large city before; they did not even
know how to turn off the electric lights or what a camera was for.

The schools were rapidly reopened. Within half a month virtually all public schools had resumed classes, and not a single
middle-school head, to the writer's knowledge, was removed.
Private schools opened somewhat more slowly. All educated
elements were urged to stay with the Communists, but those who
wished to leave the city were allowed to do so. The troops of
General Wu Hua-wen, whose defection to the Communists had
paved the way for the city's loss, were converted into the "Thirty-
fifth People's Liberation Army," and General Wu himself was
retained as their commander, despite his record under the
Japanese as a puppet general who had fought the Communists.

Some Extreme Measures

Intermittent firing has gone on throughout the day, though less
intense than yesterday. Last night I was awakened two or three
times by sudden bursts, so strong they seemed to come from
within the city itself. Today's triumphant headline in the
Chronicle is: "Red Bands Driven Off from Peiping Suburbs,"
and the text below recounts the usual story of Communist
"heavy losses" and "fierce Government counterattacks." The
grapevine has it, however, that they now control both of the
nearby towns, Fengtai and Tungchow.

A tour of the city reveals military activity everywhere: a long file of soldiers marching south on Nan Ch'ih Tzu, bending under heavy guns, bedding, flour bags, and other supplies, and many of them, despite the cold, sweaty as if they had been marching a long way; an equally endless line of empty military trucks roaring north from the South City through the Ch'ien Men (gate); a big Red Cross van on Morrison Street; half a dozen tanks on Hatamen Street; and so it goes everywhere.

Most frenzied of all is the scene at the Tung-tan glacis, now dotted with several thousand men hard at work converting it into an emergency airfield. Bands of workers are digging out its flanking trees by the roots, snipping off the neighboring telephone lines, and hacking down telephone poles. The streets skirting the glacis are covered with a maze of fallen wires and branches, and the large avenue immediately to the north has been closed to traffic, creating tremendous congestion in the *hutungs* still farther north. If a defense of Peking was really seriously considered, why was not all this done weeks ago?

However, we are not quite so cut off from the outside world as I thought yesterday. A few phone calls are still coming through from Tientsin, though not, for some reason, going the other way. All railroads are cut, and the western airfield, as I thought, is no longer available, but the southern field, contrary to yesterday's rumors, continues in limited use, with four planes expected to arrive today.

In contrast to the activity on the streets, quite a number of shops are closed, reportedly on police orders. The military have published six offenses punishable by immediate execution; they include looting, rumor spreading, harboring subversive elements, and raping. The street cars are no longer running, and electricity, though it came on late last night, is off again today. Water, however, has been flowing sporadically and at the moment is good.

The closing of the city gates is causing a rapid rise in food prices. Today's *Chronicle* reports that "to prevent lawless elements from infiltrating into the city," all refugees are being detained at the gates, where they are crowded into temples and the "half-tumbled-down Japanese factories and buildings." It adds that owing to military operations, "the relief of these refugees has been impeded." One can imagine the pandemonium and misery that prevails on the outer side of the walls, only a mile or two from us.

December 18 (Saturday)

All Quiet

Yesterday firing was at a minimum, and last night, for the first time in several days, there was complete silence. The day before, fighting had raged around the Wan Shou Ssu ("Temple of Ten Thousand Years of Longevity"), only a couple of miles outside the west wall. The Communists apparently control the region beyond, including Tsinghua and Yenching Universities, with which there is no communication.

In the city, too, things are quiet. The work of converting the glacis into an airfield continues, and this morning the first plane succeeded in landing. The press reports that another much larger field is being prepared in the Temple of Heaven enclosure. One wonders how many of the irreplaceable, centuries-old cypresses are to be sacrificed for this purpose.

Meanwhile, the southern field outside the city continues in use. No less than nine planes arrived there the day before yesterday. That afternoon, however, just after two had landed, the Communists started shelling. The result. an eyewitness reports, was pandemonium. Many important personages were on the field at the time, ready to be evacuated. Some jumped into the planes, which immediately roared off, but others ran for cover. The baggage which they left strewn over the ground was promptly looted by the soldiers on guard. Family members became separated during the excitement, some succeeding in boarding the planes, but others (including one small baby) being left behind on the ground.*

* As it turned out, this was the last time the Nan Yuan was used. Since then it, like the Hsi Yuan, remained in the hands of the Communists.

On going to the Peking Hotel yesterday for a haircut, I found all windows being taped over with strips of paper as protection against bombing. What alarms most people, however, is the possibility of looting once food begins to run short. The announcement that 355 prisoners have now been released from the jails hardly allays anxiety. The authorities are trying to raise morale by sending sound trucks around the streets to broadcast news and good cheer to all willing to stop and listen.

There are now some 200,000 soldiers in the city, bivouacked everywhere in private homes. Our Chin has no less than eighteen in his small two-room house. He reports that they are well behaved and polite and supply their own food, but use his fire and coal for cooking. At any rate, this military concentration ends the fear of conscription for him and others like him.

Today we no longer have electricity, though water still operates. Many persons have been killed in accidents involving military trucks. Poor *amah*! For her it is certainly true that "disasters never come singly." Only a few weeks ago she lost her sister and went out to the Jade Fountain on a bitterly cold day to see her buried. Today she learned that her nephew—a young boy who was her sister's son and but recently married—had been run over by a military truck. He died some hours later. The lack of electricity prevented an immediate operation.

December 19 (Sunday)

A Visitor from the Other Side

This morning, about 10:30, there was a knock at our gate, and going out, there on his bicycle was Dick, one of the Fulbright students who studies and teaches at Tsinghua. A man from another world! He had cycled in from Tsinghua that morning with Loehr and another foreigner, hardly expecting to get as far as the city, and much surprised when they succeeded. They pedaled across the fields (the main road would have been impassable), meeting Nationalist soldiers only when fairly near the city gate. They succeeded in passing them by producing documents indicating their Tsinghua connections and explaining that they were merely poor teachers anxious to reach town, one to get some money, another to buy a pound of butter! The only major physical obstacles they encountered were several hastily erected embankments, over which they had to carry their bicycles. They hope to return to Tsinghua tomorrow.

Hardly had Dick sat down in our house when two foreign correspondents appeared on the scene, eager for an interview with this man from the other side. Conditions are quiet both at Tsinghua and at American-operated Yenching University, Dick told them, and one would hardly imagine a war to be in progress not far away, were it not for the wounded soldiers from both sides— some badly shot up—in the infirmaries of the two universities. Classes at Tsinghua will be resumed tomorrow. The turnover came without actual fighting on the campuses, though there was considerable firing at the old Summer Palace near by. On the night of the thirteenth the Tsinghua people were much alarmed when Nationalists installed four large howitzers on the grounds near the observatory. Tsinghua's president, however, who was in the city at the time, was notified by phone, got in touch with the military authorities here, and within three hours the guns were moved away. As Dick remarked, such a thing could happen only in China!

Dick and other Tsinghua and Yenching foreigners have cycled as far as the Summer Palace and Jade Fountain,* which are both in Communist hands. At the Jade Fountain, the Nationalists (who had maintained an observation post in the pagoda) had apparently departed very hurriedly, leaving their belongings strewn in utter confusion.

The Communist Eighth Route Army is made up mostly of young fellows, red-cheeked, cheerful, and friendly. Aside from their tall fur caps and absence of Kuomintang button, their uniform is much like that of the Nationalists. One American who went to look at them at the Summer Palace was greeted with the

* Jade Fountain. A park located northwest of Peking, at the foot of the Western Hills. It is famed for its spring water.

words: "Don't be afraid because you are an American. We know that there are different kinds of Americans; some of them don't like us but others do." To which he replied that he was not at all afraid, and began handing out cigarettes which he happened to have with him.

The Tension Grows

Meanwhile there is little to report within the city. The military are constructing a road which will circumscribe the city, going just within the walls. They are also clearing away all buildings and other cover outside the walls. All this means that they have had to destroy a great many private houses.

I saw four planes on the glacis yesterday, including one big passenger transport, which, however, had burst a tire upon landing. Everyone passing the north side of the glacis is forced to detour through the narrow *hutungs*. As I was doing so today, a truck towing a large disabled tank happened to meet another truck coming out of a *hutung*. This caused considerable excitement, and the several soldiers directing traffic were very busy. Suddenly one of them, I don't know why, jumped upon a civilian (perhaps because he had not moved out of the way quickly enough) and began beating him furiously on the face with his fists. The soldier, beside himself with rage, pursued the unfortunate offender through the crowd, striking again and again with all his force and yelling: "You *Pa Lu Chün!* You *Pa Lu Chün!*"— a popular name for the Communists. With a final explosion of fury he kicked the man's cap high in the air onto the street. The man, who looked as if he might be a student, dodged the blows as best he could, though in a moment his face was badly bruised and blood flowed freely. Throughout, with typical Chinese restraint, he neither raised a fist nor uttered a word. Had he done so, he might well have been shot on the spot. When the storm was over, he stood perfectly still for several minutes, seemingly dazed, then moved slowly away.

The Chinese papers announce that all prisoners with less than twenty-year sentences have now been released. Seven hundred broke out of one of the prisons outside the northwest city gate but are said to have been foiled in trying to sneak into the city. All this hardly eases the general tenseness.

December 21 (Tuesday)

Trapped

Many people who fear the Communists are no doubt given a comforting illusion of security by the thought that a stout city wall separates them from the dreaded "bandits" outside. To me, however, this wall makes of Peking nothing but a gigantic potential deathtrap. On the one hand it means that no one can leave the city without the permission of the defenders, and on the other that no food can be brought in without the permission of the attackers. It also means that these attackers are in no hurry to storm the city, since such tactics would be costly, and that therefore they are naturally committed to starving it out. In other words, it makes a prolonged siege almost inevitable as long as Fu Tso-yi decides to stick it out. A city like Tientsin, on the other hand, which has no wall, will probably fall well before Peking.

The aspect of the city as one goes out on the streets these days is pretty grim. Shops close up fairly early in the afternoon, and the lack of electricity makes a place like the Tung An market particularly depressing on these short winter afternoons. We have definitely entered a siege economy. A 44-pound bag of flour, which cost GY$250 the day before yesterday, shot up to $350 yesterday and $500 or more today. Inflation is helped by the fact that those people who do have money are engaged in a wild buying spree. Though the authorities cheerfully announce that food supplies are enough for three months, this means little in the virtual absence of any organized distribution system.

No doubt one factor that encourages Fu to fight on is his continuing air contact with the outside world, made possible by the reconversion of the Tung-tan glacis. I saw eight planes there this morning looming indistinctly through the fog, though the softness of the ground and the small space make it extremely difficult for big planes to land there. But with the completion of the Temple of Heaven field (to have an air strip three times the size of that on the glacis), the resumption of commercial flights is promised. Even this, however, will obviously not solve the problem of feeding a city like Peking (which with soldiers and refugees must now have a population of well over two million). And when all these people, by the hundreds of thousands, begin to get hungry, what then? The only hope is a speedy settlement in Nanking, but news from there is almost nil these days.

December 24 (Friday)

Christmas Eve

Theo has gone to bed after singing carols, and Galia is wrapping up the few meager presents which we have been able to buy for him in this beleaguered city. The tree, a very attractive little potted fir, has been decorated with the stars and other things which Theo (together with the *amah*) has been cutting out of paper the last couple of days.

As we approach this Christmas, so different from any experienced before, the prevailing mood is one of dullness and boredom. We have passed through the first stage of siege, that in which everything happened at once, and have reached the second, that of patiently waiting for something conclusive to happen. The curfew, the billeting of soldiers in almost all of Peking's parks and beauty spots, the exodus of so many friends for the South, the cessation of letters from the outside world, the scantiness of news in our single-sheet newspapers, the lack of water and electricity, the desperate struggle for existence of so many poor people, the hectic military movement on the streets which makes one want to stay at home as much as possible, and the almost complete curtailment of social activities—all these make of this once lovely city a place unrecognizably drab and dreary. At any moment, of course, the lull may be broken by a new wave of violent and possibly terrifying activity. But for the moment one must sit and wait and fall back upon one's own resources.

A few planes continue to use the Tung-tan glacis, but aside from these and the radio, we remain isolated from the outside world. The Temple of Heaven airfield, which was to have been finished yesterday, will probably not be ready before next week, owing to lack of water with which to make the ground hard. We in this eastern quarter of the city are fortunate to have a tiny trickle of water during the night, for elsewhere there is none. Though it usually drips from one faucet only, it is enough, after several hours, to fill our bathtub with the water we use during the day.

On the streets, long lines of civilians, equipped with shovels, being marched off for forced labor on fortifications and the like, are a common sight these days. Yesterday our Chin and all the men of his neighborhood were impressed for several hours of such work, for which, of course, they received no compensation. In the city streets, pill boxes, barbed wire barricades, and the like, become more prevalent; but most work, aside from that on the emergency airfields, seems to be concentrated upon clearing away the thousands of houses that line the outside perimeter of the city wall. According to yesterday's *Chronicle,* the residents of these homes are being compensated with GY$300 each in the case of adults, and GY$150 for each child *over* twelve years of age. (Apparently no compensation is given for those under twelve.) What this means in purchasing power is indicated by the fact that yesterday I paid $10 for one pack of *ten* Hatamen cigarettes. (American cigarettes cost several times that amount.) After the houses of these unfortunates have been destroyed, it is hours and sometimes even days before they are allowed to enter the city gates and thus swell Peking's population of homeless refugees.

A serious problem confronting the city is the removal of night soil. In normal times the large cities of China, being largely lacking in modern sewage-disposal methods, are linked with the surrounding countryside in a complementary and continuing rhythm: the countryside sends its food into the cities to feed the city populations, and the cities send their night soil into the countryside to fertilize the fields on which the food is grown. Now the siege has broken this rhythm, so that not only does little food come into Peking, but few of the little green carts with their odoriferous contents wend their usual way through the gates into the suburbs. Furthermore, the situation has been aggravated by the fear of some night-soil collectors of being impressed into the forced-labor battalions, and the resulting cessation of their humble but highly necessary rounds of house-to-house collection within the city itself. Fortunately the weather is cold.

Our students have now gained possession of the last of the hitherto unoccupied servant quarters in our compound, though for a while it was a question whether they or a detachment of soldiers would get them first. It seemed as if the soldiers would win—until the teacher who is now in charge of the students found that he was personally acquainted with the commanding officer and after long discussion persuaded him to take his soldiers elsewhere.

This morning I was told, by a man who had himself seen aerial photographs of the results, that on the nineteenth no less than five bombs were dropped on the Tsinghua campus. Fortunately there were no casualties, as the bombs fell on open ground, but one building was damaged by concussion. These bombs were not dropped by Communists, who have no planes and already control the Tsinghua area. They were dropped by *Nationalists,* apparently in the hope of thus scaring many students into the city and in this way preventing the next day's scheduled resumption of classes. A good many of us have not forgotten how less than ten years ago this same Nationalist government was bitterly protesting the bombing and destruction of its universities and other cultural institutions by the invading Japanese. Not a word of this as yet in the papers.

December 25 (Saturday)

Christmas

A really lovely day, quiet and with a genuine Christmas feeling.
We awoke to find snow on the ground and some still falling—a
rare and propitious event in Peking, where the winters, though
cold, are too dry to see more than a few snowfalls a year.

Today's *Hua-pei Jih-pao* (*North China Daily News*) mentions
the Tsinghua bombing for the first time. It refers to the bombs
as "shells" and carefully avoids stating their origin, but the use of
this word naturally gives uninformed readers the impression that
they were "fired" by the Communists. (Had this really been the
case, there is little doubt that this organ of the Kuomintang Ministry of Information would have said as much.)

The same paper announces a successful trial landing yesterday
at the Temple of Heaven airfield, and, incidentally, answers my
question about the number of trees which had to be removed to
make this possible. The reply is 400 (mostly ancient cypresses)
having trunks of one to three meters in diameter, and no less
than 20,000 trees and shrubs of lesser size. Many of the trees belonging to this "sacred grove," once one of the most holy and impressive spots in China, were planted centuries ago. Their destruction is the price paid by humanity to enable a vainglorious
general (Fu Tso-yi) to endure a siege for a few days (possibly even
a few weeks) longer than he might otherwise have done. The
paper praises the authorities (for which read: unpaid labor) for
the speed with which the difficult task of uprooting trees has
been accomplished. The trees themselves are to be used (probably mostly as firewood) by the military.

December 31 (Friday)

New Year's Eve

It is now 10:30 as I sit down to write these words. This New Year's Eve is being spent by us solitarily at home (Galia playing Chopin on the piano a moment ago), with the streets outside as dark and deserted as they have been for two weeks past. And yet several events have occurred since last I wrote to give an illusion, at least, of a partial return to normalcy. One is the reopening yesterday of the southern half of the Pei Hai, which, when we visited it this afternoon, was crowded with skaters. Another is the resumption, during certain hours of the day, of the water supply (made possible by the installation of new generators within the city). A third is the very welcome arrival by plane, a few hours ago, of letters from America—the first since before the siege started. And still a fourth is the extraordinary item in yesterday's *Chronicle* describing the "reopening" of the Peking-Tientsin highway (now running almost entirely through Communist territory) and announcing that "buses are available, taking two days to travel from Peiping to Tientsin." This is one of those incredible things which makes one wonder whether what we have is really a siege or something else.*

Aside from these developments, the political and military conferences now taking place in Nanking have given rise to flocks of peace rumors. Today's *Shih-chieh Jih-pao* (*World Daily News*) has an editorial which is remarkable considering that this paper is an organ of the CC Clique.† Entitled "There Must Be Change," it points out that though for twenty years "the people have longed for reform and the government has advocated reform in words, in actual fact the government officials have never shown the slightest sincerity toward reform, and have simply made a plaything of

* It was one of the last items from this often unconsciously humorous little English sheet. On New Year's Day the *Chronicle* announced that it was temporarily suspending publication "during the New Year holidays." It never reopened.

† The two Ch'en brothers, Ch'en Li-fu and Ch'en Kuo-fu, notorious reactionaries in the Kuomintang.

political power. The people's livelihood has been led down a road
of increasing starvation, while the powerful and influential have
continued their profligate extravagance without measure. . . .
Today is no longer the time for high flown words or for talk in
the style of 'eight-legged essays'! We hope that the meeting now
being held in Nanking will for once be one at which the truth is
spoken."

What this paper is saying undoubtedly expresses what most
people are thinking, but that it should say it at all is a striking
admission of the military and moral depths to which the Kuomintang has sunk. Whatever the Communists choose to do, it seems
evident, as I close these pages for 1948, that the Kuomintang is
entering its death agonies and that the future will see the coming of events which may, I hope from the bottom of my heart,
bring peace to the Chinese people for the first time in almost
forty years.

January 1949

January 1 (Saturday)

New Year's Day

As if to celebrate the New Year, the electricity unexpectedly came on about an hour ago. And what electricity! Brighter than it has been on many occasions in the past. How and where it comes from we can't imagine, for the main plant, at Shih-ching-shan, has long been in Communist hands. One of the jokes going the rounds the past week is that the Communists phoned several times from Shih-ching-shan, politely offering electricity to the citizens of Peking, but that these offers were all sternly rejected by Fu Tso-yi for reasons of face.

Another event that has tremendously cheered us personally is the news, learned as we were returning from this morning's New Year reception at the American Consulate, that steps are almost completed which will assure me and the other Fulbright Fellows in Peking of absolute financial security during the remainder of our stay here.*

By way of contrast, our refugee students have been treating us the past two days to a very unpleasant spectacle of mass savagery. Yesterday morning, shortly after breakfast, we suddenly heard a wild barking near the entrance to the main compound, accompanied by equally wild human cries. On going out to investigate, I saw a ring of some fifteen students intently watching half a dozen of their comrades who, armed with sticks and large stones,

* How this was done is a complex story that cannot be narrated here, other than to say that it reflects the highest credit upon the administrators of the Fulbright fund in Nanking. Our New Year hope became an actuality one week later.

were approaching the mat shelter partially screening one of their open-air toilets in the corner of the court. Behind this mat crouched a dog which had been lured into the courtyard from the street outside. Having cornered the animal, the students were about to beat it to death. The purpose, as we soon learned, was to vary their monotonous diet of *wo-t'ou* (a dumpling made of mixed corn and soybean flour) with dog meat. Our Chin, however, using his pedicab as a screen, and helped by our cook, succeeded with difficulty in guiding the unfortunate creature until it could dodge out to the safety of the street.

This is not the first time such an incident has happened. According to Chin, the students have already massacred and eaten four or five well-fed dogs in this way. Nor is it the last, for again this morning, but this time in the garden behind our house, we heard another frenzied barking, accompanied by yells. Then some heavy object, apparently a metal rod, clattered against our wall. After that all was still. This time the dog did not escape.

Yesterday, at Galia's insistence, she and Mrs. Sung visited some of the functionaries who ostensibly have charge of the Shansi students at Nei-wu Pu Chieh. To them they complained not only about the dog massacres but also the indiscriminate chopping of Mrs. Sung's movable timbers (for firewood) which we hear going on every night; likewise the equally indiscriminate defecations which have been making of the open area flanking the front entrance a more and more unsightly mess. The answer of one of the teachers, to whom Mrs. Sung had already complained previously, was revealing. "It wouldn't do any good for us to talk to the students," he remarked, "for they wouldn't listen to us anyway. And it doesn't do any harm not to talk to them." He then went on to convey the idea that since the teachers themselves are paid so little, and since they would receive no merit for their efforts, it would really not be worth their while to bother about such matters at all.

January 7 (Friday)

Neither Peace nor War

Ever since Chiang Kai-shek's "peace" statement of New Year's Day, the war has been in a state of suspended animation. Neither in North nor Central China does there appear to have been much military activity. Chiang's statement has been the signal for a continuing "peace offensive" from the Nationalist side. A few days ago, Nationalist planes dropped thousands of "peace bombs" on the Communists north of Nanking—leaflets urging Chinese not to kill Chinese, the need for peace, and so forth. Similar appeals, couched in highly flowery and literary language, have been issued the past few days by chambers of commerce, groups of leading Chinese citizens, and other organs in Shanghai, Peking, and elsewhere. They consist of telegrams jointly addressed to the National government and to "Mr. Mao Tse-tung and other Communist leaders." Most striking change of the times, however, is the terminology employed in the paper I now read, the *World Daily News*. In most of its dispatches the contemptuous word *fei* "bandits" has given way to the more respectful *kung* "Communists."

We ourselves continue to revel in our supply of water and electricity, though the latter is far from city-wide. A recent cold wave interrupted the water supply for twenty-four hours when our main pipe froze. This would not have happened if our students had not stolen the planks covering the pit in which the pipe and meter are situated. Another trick of theirs, discovered only with the restoration of electricity, was the complete removal of the electric bell wire which our Chin had so carefully strung between Mrs. Sung's house and our own. This wire has now been converted into aerials for the students' radios—no doubt to listen to Communist broadcasts.

"White Chinese"

This is the term certain circles are beginning to use here to describe those Chinese rich and influential enough to secure passage on the few planes flying south. It is inspired, of course, by the term "White Russian"—the major group of political exiles with which the Chinese have long been familiar. Yesterday the resumption of regular commercial plane service was promised, using the Temple of Heaven field. Over 8,000 people are said to have asked for reservations, despite the rumor that as much as US$700 is being demanded for a single ticket. Owing to local shortage of gasoline, flights will probably be limited to two a week.

As a matter of fact, Mrs. Sung, with her five children, left abruptly for the south on a noncommercial plane two days ago, thus joining the exodus that already includes the presidents of several of Peking's universities. In her place we now have a new landlord, Mr. Chen, who is the local manager of one of China's largest chemical companies. This firm has bought the entire compound—"students and all"—and, when peace returns, hopes to use it for its Peking headquarters.

A Report from Behind the Iron Curtain

Yesterday Dick showed up again on his bike from Tsinghua. Trips to the city, made at such hazard a few weeks ago, are now becoming fairly common. He told us of his return to Tsinghua after his last visit here. After being delayed a whole day by failure to have a military pass, he and his two Tsinghua companions, plus a fourth foreigner from the city, succeeded in getting past the city gate. Hardly a mile outside, however, they ran into a road block. They made a detour—and ran directly into a line of Nationalist-Communist fire. At this point two of them decided to return to the city, but the other two, Dick and Loehr, determined to push onward. The firing became worse, and finally they were obliged to abandon their bicycles and crawl the remaining several hundred yards to safety on the Communist side. Naturally they gave up their bicycles as lost; great was their surprise, therefore, when several Communist soldiers retrieved them and returned them to their owners, refusing to accept anything more than verbal thanks in return.

At present, Dick reports, Nationalist troops are hardly in evidence more than a mile outside the city walls. Beyond is a sort of no man's land, with very few people to be seen, but nevertheless controlled by the Communists simply because the Nationalists do not venture out that far.

Conditions at Tsinghua and Yenching remain quiet, says Dick. The students, enthusiastic over their "liberation," attend daily indoctrination lectures given by Communist political workers to prepare them for similar political work in the city when Peking is taken. Academic work has suffered as a result; classes, though temporarily resumed, have now again been discontinued. The Tsinghua bombing did much to destroy, among students and faculty alike, what little pro-Kuomintang sentiment remained.

January 9 (Sunday)

How It Feels To Be Rich

Never have I been rich, and never do I expect to be. Yet it is odd but true that in this beleaguered city today—short in food, in public utilities, in economic well-being, in everything, in fact, except privation, fear, and discontent—I think I understand as never before what it is to feel rich.

Perhaps, after all, this feeling is not so odd, for it depends, as I have come to realize, less upon what one has oneself than upon the ratio between what one has and what the other fellow lacks. It is the discrepancy and exclusiveness that count, not the absolute amount, and these increase in inverse ratio to the decline of a society's total living standards. Thus the difference between one and zero—between having one loaf of bread, for example, and having none at all—is infinitely greater than that between one and two or even one and three or four. From this point of view it is obvious that we, with our solid roof over our heads (unshared by soldiers or refugees, owing to our status as foreigners), our warm stove and clothing, and our simple but adequate meals, are far richer in besieged Peking than we have ever been before.

Perhaps the most tangible symbol of this feeling of wealth, as far as I am concerned, is the oil lamp beside which I now write these words (our much vaunted electricity having failed again today). The oil lamp ordinarily used in China is a primitive glass affair, hardly six inches high and without any shade to diffuse its feeble light. To read by it for any length of time puts an impossible strain on the eyes. Imagine my delight, therefore, when, the day before Christmas, I happened to pass one of the open air markets and noticed a large foreign oil lamp for sale. Its fine potbelly of gleaming white metal was capped by a broad shade of glazed white glass. I leaped from my bicycle, fortunate in the fact that a fair amount of cash was in my pocket, and, though the lamp was far from cheap, succeeded in purchasing it after some bargaining.

This addition to our household consumes alarming quantities of the kerosene we wisely bought weeks ago in a 10-gallon tin. Only after the dinner dishes have been cleared away do we huddle around it to read. At other times an ordinary Chinese lamp suffices. But as we bask in its warm glow, it produces an indescribable feeling of well-being, for we realize we are one of the very few families in Peking who can enjoy such a luxury. Only in one other household, in fact, have I seen anything like it.

This feeling of well-being, pleasurable though it is, brings with it considerable disquiet. It is unpleasant enough to run around in times like these bargaining for and buying can after can of the U.S. Army surplus foodstuffs which lie stacked in heaps of olive green on many street corners. But what is much more repugnant is to buy the foods that are of really vital concern to the Chinese: bags of flour and rice, earthenware containers of cooking oil, bottles of soy sauce and the like, knowing that only a portion of them is to be used immediately and that the greater part is to be kept under lock and key for future emergency. It is not an easy thing to do, even though some is intended as salary payment to our servants. For each bag thus hoarded means that much less to others as deserving as ourselves. Each purchase intensifies the inflationary spiral. Yet, in the absence of any over-all system of rationing, what else can we and people like us do? "Hurry! Hurry! Buy today because your money may be no longer good tomorrow." This is the motto in a city in which the race goes to him with the most dollars, and devil take the hindmost.

The moral seems sufficiently obvious: In societies in which the material goods of life are produced in sufficient abundance for all, freedom from centralized controls may well be synonymous with individual freedom. But in other, less fortunate, societies freedom from want is a primary need, and such controls are accepted, indeed welcomed, by most people as absolute essentials.

January 15 (Saturday)

The Lull Is Broken

Today marks the beginning of the second month of siege, and with it the period of inaction seems to have come to an end. On the political front, the most important development is Mao Tse-tung's statement, definitely rejecting Chiang's New Year "peace" offer and substituting eight points of his own. These call for: (1) punishment of war criminals, (2) abolition of the "false" (i.e., Kuomintang) constitution, (3) abolition of false governmental organs, (4) reorganization of all reactionary armies on democratic principles, (5) confiscation of bureaucratic capital, (6) instituting of land reform, (7) abolition of foreign treaties derogatory to China's sovereignty, (8) convocation of a national assembly of nonreactionary elements to create a democratic government.

Militarily, the lull in the North has been broken by intense fighting around Tientsin, as the result of which that city is probably already in Communist hands. Here in Peking a disturbing development has been the sporadic Communist shelling of the center of the city—aimed, it is rumored, at a munition dump in

Central Park. One shell landed barely twenty yards from the U.S. Information Service, killing a man next door. Perhaps as a consequence, commercial plane service at the Temple of Heaven airfield has been "temporarily discontinued."

One sensible step taken by the authorities is that of encouraging all refugees who wish to do so to return to their homes in the countryside. The resulting exodus is reported to involve as many as 4,000 persons daily. Early this week I paid a visit to the main east gate, where I saw a long line of persons, each with his pass, waiting to get out. Soldiers stood in force at the gate itself and at a sand-bag barricade about a hundred yards inside. As I arrived, a mad scramble was in progress to get through the gate before it closed for the night. A moment later confusion was heightened by the appearance of one of the familiar little green manure carts; the donkey, becoming excited by the crowd, rushed forward, despite the efforts of its driver, and plunged itself and its malodorous vehicle headlong into the packed ranks of pedicabs, bicycles, and pedestrians. A soldier at once began indiscriminately beating the donkey and its driver, and, by the time order had been restored, the gates a hundred yards away had been closed. A long line of disappointed people then turned back disconsolately to spend the night in the city. It was just 4:20 P.M. These night-soil carts, incidentally, each carry a triangular flag bearing the words: "Peiping Municipal Manure Cart," presumably to protect their drivers from being conscripted for labor when they go out of the city. I was heartily glad to see evidence that they are functioning.

Construction of defense works continues, especially south of the city. On Wednesday afternoon I made a trip to the extreme southern gate and on my way saw thousands upon thousands of laborers plodding southward in stolid lines with picks and shovels. The majority seemed the poorest of the poor. Many of them were either old men, some obviously in frail health, or young boys. The reason is simple: since persons with money can "hire" other workers in their place, the latter are almost invariably recruited from the poorest families. Moreover, since these families are dependent upon the able-bodied wage earners among them, they try to shelter these, if possible, and send the old or young in their place.

The main south gate itself, when I arrived, was a scene of confusion, with one long line of workers returning from the day's labor outside and another waiting inside to take its place. Turning to a small boy who was waiting in this way, I engaged him in conversation:

"How far out do you go?"

"Six *li*" ("two miles").

"Does work go on at night as well as day?"

"Yes."

"How long have you been working in this way?"

"Twenty days."

"Do you get any pay?"

"No money, only a little food."

"How old are you?"

"Twelve." (Which, according to Western reckoning, means eleven—only two years older than our Theo.) By this time a crowd had assembled, including some suspicious soldiers, and I decided to move on.

January 17 (Monday)

China Then and Now

I have just finished reading a very interesting new book, Hollington K. Tong's *China and the World Press*. Written by the former Vice-Minister of Information, a man known to countless foreign correspondents in Nanking, Hankow, and Chungking, it is an account, witty, informative, sometimes stirring, often pathetic, of the Chinese government's efforts to get its story of the war across to the outside world during the long years of 1937 to 1945. But above all it is a puzzling book; puzzling because of the unexplained gap between its earlier, heroic half—the half dealing with the battle of Shanghai in 1937, the rape of Nanking, the eleven-month stand at Hankow, and the early Chungking bombings—and the story of the depressing corruption, discord, and decay which fills its later pages. Many fragmentary accounts have been written of the external events in China between 1937 and 1945. But what *caused* these events—the psychological, economic, and political factors, some springing from the war itself, some embedded deeply in Chinese history—is a story that has not yet been told.

One key to understanding, I think, is the following vivid passage in Tong's book:

This incredible faith, which has been one of the riddles of the Chinese war to outsiders, perhaps can be best explained in terms of the father image which the Generalissimo exemplifies to the majority of our people. The Chinese feeling for a great and trusted leader is an emotion which is not easily understood by Westerners. It is a feeling which has its roots in the long Chinese custom of imputing superior wisdom to the elder. We have a great sense of security in the family and we seldom question the decisions made for the family by its head. In our political life, we have transferred much of that feeling to the head of the State or the national leader.

Generalissimo Chiang Kai-shek, in his relationship to the people of China, was behaving as a wise elder would have behaved, and we know that his decisions were made for the common good, and not for personal reasons.

The strength of this father image complex, to use Tong's very happy term, rests upon three postulations which go far back in Chinese history:

(1) The great mass of the people is ignorant and unfit to take part in government itself. As Confucius said: "The people may be made to follow a course of action but not to know the reason why."

(2) Government, therefore, must rest in the hands of a small elite whose qualifications are a mastery of the intricacies of the Chinese written language and a knowledge of the moral principles deemed necessary to give good rule. The Chinese classics were the fountainhead for these two kinds of knowledge, and the instrument for recruiting the ruling bureaucracy was, of course, the famed examination system.

(3) Spirit is superior to matter; in other words, the thesis was never questioned that morality and economics are independent of one another. To be more specific, a man who had

gained admission to the ruling class by demonstrating his knowledge of the moral principles contained in the classics was *ipso facto* deemed reliable to carry out these principles in government. The fact was disregarded that in so doing he was primarily answerable for his conduct not to the bulk of the unlettered common folk below, but to men of his own ruling class, with whom he shared a common ideology and common economic interests.

The undemocratic nature of the first of these postulates is self-evident. As for the second, one wonders about the efficacy of *any* kind of morality when it is institutionalized by being made the basis of education and, especially, the key to a man's entry into his later professional career. The third, though accepted by most philosophies and religions, puts an impossibly heavy strain on the individual unless it is checked by controls applied to him or his group by society as a whole and not merely a select portion of that society. For it is demanding too much from all but the strongest to suppose that he will remain "good" on the basis of no other control than that of inner moral conviction. Too often, if left free to act only according to his own "inner law," will he find convincing reasons why this "inner law" should coincide closely with the personal interests of himself or his group.

What is important to remember is that these three postulates still permeate the thinking of much of China's present oligarchy. A great deal of what the Kuomintang is blamed for can, I think, be attributed to the persistence of this ideology, rather than to the deliberate viciousness of which it is often accused. No modern society can be founded in China on the basis of such thinking, and the Communists are right when they attack Confucianism on this ground. The question remains whether they themselves, with their absolutist philosophy, can avoid falling into similar tendencies.

The Chinese Student

More trouble with our students. Their latest trick is to come to the rear of our house at night, smash flowerpots against our wall, and peer and jeer at us through the windows. To prevent them from further demolishing the main gate for firewood and breaking his windows to steal coal, our new landlord Mr. Chen has recently offered them a monthly sum sufficient to buy one ton of coal plus kindling. Their answer was that they would hold a meeting to consider the matter. As of today they have given no answer.*

As I observe these boys—not all of whom are destitute, because some continue to receive money from their families—I am convinced that one of the things wrong with China is the magic aura which surrounds the word "student." Stemming from the traditional separation between the educated elite and the uneducated masses, it all too often allows the former to act with an irresponsibility such as would be tolerated in no other class.

January 23 (Sunday)

Surrender!

The momentous news of the week, of course, is that the siege of Peking is now officially over. Fu Tso-yi has surrendered. At six o'clock yesterday evening he issued a thirteen-point statement, the gist of which is that his troops are to be gradually moved into the suburbs; order is to be maintained by the existing police force; administrative organs, banks, industries, schools, etc., are to continue as usual under existing personnel; aliens and alien property are to be protected, as is freedom of religion; newspapers are to continue publication; in short, life is to go on as much as possible as before. Nothing is said of Fu's future position or of when the Communists will take over.

This surrender is perhaps the result of the "peace delegation" that, on January 18, went outside the walls to talk with the Communists. This mission, composed of several prominent citizens

* The offer was later rejected on the grounds that it should include money for food and an "office" for the student organization.

headed by Ho Ssu-yüan, former city mayor, had originally been slated to leave on the seventeenth. At three o'clock that morning, however, a time bomb exploded in Ho's bedroom, followed a few minutes later by a second explosion. Ho himself, who happened to be sleeping in another room, escaped with light injuries. His wife and two children were wounded, however, and a third girl was killed. This bombing, which has been universally attributed to the die-hard CC Clique, delayed the departure of the delegation for twenty-four hours. Ho bravely accompanied it, however, when it finally went out to the Western Hills on the eighteenth.

Now, with the surrender, in the twinkling of an eye the aspect of the city has been changed from that of impending attack to a semblance of peace. Yesterday the glacis was still covered with thousands of men working like ants to extend its air strip. Today it is absolutely deserted. Unfortunately the armistice comes too late to save the many trees that have been hacked down around its border during the past week. Nor will it restore the many private houses that have been razed around the city walls— amounting, according to the newspapers, to over 16,000 *chien* (room-sections).

The futility of these and similar defense activities has been demonstrated the past few days by the way in which Communist fire has reduced the use of the emergency airfields to almost nothing. Virtually the only air activity has been that of trying to drop food into the city. Day after day, for hours at a time, the sky has been noisy with planes circling above the frozen lake of the Pei Hai and dropping bags of rice or flour upon the ice. The first attempts were far from successful. Some bags missed the lake entirely; others broke open, spilling their precious contents over the surface; at least two incautious spectators were hit and injured. After the first day, however, parachutes were used, with much better results, and it was a beautiful sight to see these planes circle the city and suddenly discharge their cargo, leaving a trail of parachutes fluttering gently down to earth.

As I write these words, our electricity remains sporadic, but today's paper promises a "great illumination" within the next two days. This, to me at least, will symbolize as keenly as anything a return to normalcy. Never, until this siege, have I been so aware of the importance of light. Never have I noted so eagerly the daily gradual increase of sunlight each afternoon following the winter solstice. To modern man, surrounded by his gadgets, such experience is needed to comprehend primitive man's joy in and adoration of light, and his fear of darkness—a joy and fear which have given to the world so much folklore and festival.

January 26 (Wednesday)

Liberation!

This is now the great slogan of the day. Everyone talks and writes happily of the "liberation" of Peking by the great "People's Army." So far as the physical appearance of the city is concerned, little has happened as yet. Fu Tso-yi's soldiers are still much in evidence, though said to be gradually moving out, and I have yet to catch my first glimpse of the Communist "Eighth Route Army." During the last two days, however, walls and telephone poles have been plastered with multigraphed posters, exhorting the population to conduct itself peacefully and work for the building of a new China. Most spectacular of all has been the arrival of the long-promised "great illumination." Tonight as I write these words, street lights are burning all over the city for the first time in six weeks.

The absence of greater change, of course, is due to the peacefulness of the turn-over and the fact that the old guard still remains in power—an old guard, however, using a vocabulary amazingly different from what it was mouthing only a few days ago. The formerly reactionary *World Daily News* is a typical example. A fair part of today's issue consists of transcripts from the Communist radio, put out, however, under the date line of the Kuomintang Central News Agency's Peking office.

Much of the new talk, of course, stems from deliberate opportunism or plain ignorance of the significance of what is taking place. Take our Shansi students, for example. During the past two or three days they have covered the walls of the compound with a rash of handwritten posters congratulating themselves and the city on its liberation. On one of these they had the audacity to write: "Protection of the people's property is our first duty." This after special workers employed by our landlord had spent the greater part of a day nailing metal sheets over a locked door which the students had broken open the night before. Another large wooden gate, leading into the rear garden, has now been completely demolished. The same students also took the opportunity to daub our gate with the slogan, "Down with American imperialism!"

Yet despite the opportunism, hypocrisy, and lack of comprehension from many sides, there is no doubt in my mind that the Communists come here with the bulk of the people on their side. As one walks the streets, the new feeling of relief and relaxation can definitely be sensed, even though it is hard to describe it in tangible terms.

January 30 (Sunday)

No Peace

Events have taken a turn for the worse since I last wrote. The Chinese New Year has come and gone. To be sure, something of a holiday atmosphere prevailed on New Year's Eve, two days ago, when we went to the market and bought a kite and a glass trumpet for Theo—traditional toys of the season—and, for ourselves, a set of door gods, a kitchen god, and "spring couplets" (strips of red paper bearing good-luck phrases). The latter we duly pasted in strategic places around the house. That night there were enough firecrackers to prevent sound sleep, though few indeed compared with former years. On New Year's Day itself it was encouraging to read of the appointment of a temporary seven-man peace committee—four Communists and three from the other side—to govern the city.

Today, however, there is neither mention of this committee nor sign of the new occupying forces. Instead we have been treated throughout the day to a series of sporadic but heavy explosions, obviously not firecrackers and some apparently within the city. One exploded this afternoon so near by that its concussion swung several of our windows open. This commotion is said to be caused by the refusal of some Kuomintang troops to accept the cease-fire order and march to their designated positions outside the city. The section of Hatamen Street fronting the glacis, which was reopened to traffic immediately following last week's "surrender," has today again been closed. Prices, which slumped at that time, have resumed their rise. Our Chin, who completed a round of belated New Year calls today, returned late this afternoon with gloomy predictions of riots and looting if the present stalemate is not soon settled.

Yesterday's *North China Daily News,* in an economic review of the year, prints some interesting statistics. One year ago, it points out, a 44-pound bag of flour could be bought for FP$1,200,000, which, at the August 19 reconversion rate, would amount to GY$0.40. Yesterday that same bag of flour cost GY$1,800. In other words, the price of flour has risen 4,500 times during the past year.

January 31 (Monday)

Occupation!

Today, less than twenty-four hours after last night's dire predictions, the "People's Liberation Army" has finally marched into Peking! At 4 P.M., while riding up Morrison Street, Galia saw the first arrivals. At their head moved a sound truck (apparently supplied by the municipality), from which blared the continuous refrain, "Welcome to the Liberation Army on its arrival in Peiping! Welcome to the People's Army on its arrival in Peiping! Congratulations to the people of Peiping on their liberation! . . ." Beside and behind it, six abreast, marched some two or three hundred Communist soldiers in full battle equipment. They moved briskly and seemed hot, as if they had been marching a long distance. All had a red-cheeked, healthy look and seemed in high spirits. As they marched up the street, the crowds lining the sidewalks, including our Chin, burst into applause. Near their head walked a rather nondescript, shabbily dressed civilian—apparently some kind of official.

Behind the soldiers marched students carrying two large portraits: one of Mao Tse-tung, the other presumably of Chu Teh, commander in chief of the People's Army. A military band came next, and finally a long line of trucks carrying more soldiers, students, and civilian employees of the telephone company, railroad administration, and other semi-official organizations. In about ten minutes the parade was over.

Yesterday's explosions, which continued this morning, are explained by the papers as having been caused either by the detonating of land mines outside the city or by exuberant soldiers inside the city who celebrated the New Year by firing their guns. We are also told that the new seven-man coalition committee will formally get under way tomorrow and that Fu Tso-yi and his headquarters have moved to the "new town" in the southwest suburbs.

February 1949

February 3 (Thursday)

The Changes Begin

Events follow each other so rapidly these days that it is hard to remember what has happened even three days ago. The People's Liberation Army is in complete control, and only occasional groups of "enemy" soldiers are still to be seen.

The entire Peking Hotel is in process of being taken over by Communist functionaries. When I went there for a haircut two days ago, a young soldier, fully equipped, walked idly up and down the room the whole time I was in the barber's chair.

The seven-man "coalition" interim committee began functioning yesterday, headed by Communist General Yeh Chien-ying, chairman and city mayor. It is subject, however, to the orders of the Peking-Tientsin Headquarters of the People's Liberation Army.

Yesterday Chin reported that he had seen long lines of carts bringing food into the city. Prices have dropped slightly, but it is obvious that few serious steps in this direction can be taken before the process of converting gold yuan into the new regime's "people's notes" has been completed. This will be done during the next twenty days at places designated by the People's Bank (into which the former Nationalist government's Central Bank has already been converted). The exchange is set at GY$10:PN$1 for all persons save laborers, students, teachers, and "poor people." These, having secured certificates indicative of their status, will be permitted to exchange up to GY$500 apiece at the favored rate of GY$3:PN$1.

All has gone smoothly so far save for one unpleasant incident: a demonstration for increased wages by several thousand municipal employees in which they wrecked the house of the former mayor, attacked and wounded the chief secretary of the municipality, pilfered a supply of ration flour, and broke into the municipal building, looting and scattering official papers. Though a hundred were arrested, they were later released after being lectured to and forced to restore what had been taken.

Today's big event has been the grand victory parade signalizing the formal take-over of the city. It unfortunately coincided with the first real dust storm of the winter. A fierce wind moaned through the scaffolding still enveloping the partially dismantled tiled archway at the south end of Morrison Street. It raised such dust from the near-by glacis that during the biggest gusts it was literally impossible to see across the field. My face was black with grime by the time I returned home.

Prominent in the parade were thousands of students and workers from schools and organizations throughout the city. Many of their colored paper banners and Mao Tse-tung portraits were torn to tatters by the wind. Among the students also marched some well-known university professors. Some groups danced to the rhythmic drum-and-gong beat of the *yang ko* or "planting song"—a simple traditional peasant dance performed in unison by large groups, which is already becoming enormously popular here as the result of the general Communist emphasis upon folk art. More familiar to me was a band of stilt walkers, cavorting merrily in colorful costumes above the heads of the crowd. Other groups, directed by "cheer leaders," chanted, as they marched, the famous "eight points" of Mao Tse-tung.

Of chief interest was, of course, the Liberation Army itself. I missed the first contingents of infantry and cavalry, as well as part of the motorized units. But in what I did see, lasting about an hour, I counted over 250 heavy motor vehicles of all kinds—tanks, armored cars, truck loads of soldiers, trucks mounted with machine guns, trucks towing heavy artillery. Behind them followed innumerable ambulances, jeeps, and other smaller vehicles. As probably the greatest demonstration of Chinese military might in history, the spectacle was enormously impressive. But what made it especially memorable to Americans was the fact that it was primarily a display of *American* military equipment, virtually all of it captured or obtained by bribe from Kuomintang forces in the short space of two and one half years.

And what about the reactions of the civilian participants and spectators? Granted that some of the former paraded only because they had been told to do so, and that many were school children too young to realize the full significance of what was happening, the fact remains that the enthusiasm of most was too obvious to have been feigned, and this notwithstanding that many had been exposed to wind and dust for some four hours before I saw them. I have no doubt that not a few on this day felt a keen sense of personal participation in an event symbolizing the beginning of a new era in Chinese history. The reaction of the spectators, on the other hand, was, like that of most Chinese crowds, less outspoken. Nevertheless they seemed in general quite favorably disposed and obviously deeply impressed by the display of power. As the stream of trucks continued, I heard several exclaim with wonder: "Still more! Still more!"

Propaganda and Press

The Communists are losing no time in beginning indoctrination. The Peking radio has already begun relaying the Yenan broadcasts, and yesterday, in one of the poorest quarters of the city, I suddenly came upon a series of Communist woodcut posters. The most effective showed a figure, obviously Chiang Kai-shek, cringing before a huge outstretched fist. At his feet lay a pile of grinning skulls; in his hand he held a sword, bearing—in English, not Chinese—the two letters, "U.S." Another poster portrayed a temple building, and beneath it the slogan, "Protect cultural monuments." Still another showed a Chinese book wrapped in flames, entitled "False Constitution." (Everything pertaining to the Kuomintang these days is invariably described as *wei* or "false.") A fourth depicted a People's Army soldier flanked by four civilians —laborer, farmer, merchant, and intellectual, symbolized by their hammer, sickle, abacus, and paper scroll. A fifth portrayed another

1   Poster prepared by students of Ch'ao-yang University. The bomb falling on Uncle Sam is labeled: "Liberation Special." The inscription reads: "Expel American imperialism from China!"

2   A Communist soldier reaches over Nanking's city wall to seize Chiang Kai-shek. The inscription reads: "Strike on to Nanking and seize Chiang Kai-shek alive!"

3   A People's Army soldier thrusts back a naval vessel carrying a Japanese admiral and being propelled by General MacArthur, which is coming to rescue the drowning Chiang Kai-shek. The inscription reads: "Oppose American imperialist support of Japan, aid to Chiang, and aggression against China!"

4 An industrial worker and a farm girl. The inscription reads: "Strike down the reactionaries and build a new China."

5 The inscription on this poster reads: "Plant the victorious banner throughout China!" (See Diary, March 4.)

6 A student (carrying a book labeled New Democracy), a worker, and a farmer. The inscription reads: "Arise, intellectuals, to unite with labor and agriculture! Construct a new China." The signpost is labeled "5/4," referring to the student demonstrations of May 4, 1919, against the signing of the Versailles Treaty by the Chinese government.

7 *Chiang Kai-shek shrinking back before an avenging fist (see* Diary, *February 3,* "*Propaganda and Press*").

8 *The mass meeting that was held in front of the T'ien An Men (front gate of the Forbidden City) in celebration of the "liberation" of Peking. The poster is a fairly accurate portrayal of the assembly that actually took place on February 12, 1949 (see* Diary, *February 13). The inscription reads: "The red flags flutter. The sounds of singing are loud and clear. Mountains and seas of people celebrate the liberation. The masses have become the rulers. The ancient palace has been transformed into a new Red Square."*

9 *Altar of Heaven, September 12, 1948, showing sleeping quarters of refugee students (see* Diary *entry of this date).*

10 *The glacis during the siege of Peking, showing laborers constructing an emergency airfield.*

11 Parading students performing the peasant yang ko *or "planting song" dance, which has become exceedingly popular in Communist China as an expression of folk art.*

12 Another yang ko *dance being performed by students who are dressed in proletarian garb.*

13   *Students, workers, and other groups participating in the great parade of February 3, 1949, celebrating the "liberation" of Peking (see* Diary *entry of that date). Poster of Mao Tse-tung in the foreground.*

14   *Close-up of poster portraits of Mao Tse-tung (right) and Chu Teh (left) over the entrance to the Forbidden City. The large characters read: "Victory of the Chinese people." The lower inscription reads: "In memory of May 1 and May 5 we must push the revolution to its final point."*

15 *Infantry approaching Hsi Chih Men (the northwest gate of the city), in victory parade of February 3, 1949. Note foundations of razed buildings outside the wall, torn down by the defenders during the siege.*

16 *First infantry detachment to enter the city, just within Hsi Chih Men.*

17 *Truckloads of soldiers.*

18 Trucks carrying troops and pulling guns toward Ch'ien Men (main south city gate).

19 Another view showing cavalry approaching Ch'ien Men.

20   *Soldiers saluting a congratulatory banner which reads: "In a hundred battles a hundred victories."*

21   *Armored cars moving toward Ch'ien Men.*

22   *Gun with Ch'ien Men in the background.*

23   *Truck float with portraits of Mao Tse-tung (right) and Chu Teh (left). The inscription reads: "Congratulations on the liberation of North China."*

24   *Band marching up Hatamen Street at the Tung Ssu Pailou (intersection of the East Four Arches).*

26 *The author, his wife and son, in Chinese costume.*

27 *Path from the front entrance leading toward the rear courtyard of the author's home.*

28 *Chinese servants in the author's household. From left to right: the amah and her two children, our boy Chin, our cook Sun, and the gatekeeper.*

soldier, his arm protectively thrown around the shoulders of a civilian. The accompanying caption read: "The People's Liberation Army is the People's Friend." This is the sort of simple but effective propaganda which now replaces the stereotyped Kuomintang slogans formerly conspicuous in all public places—slogans such as, "The liquidation of the bandits is the only way to preserve the city" or "To kill one bandit is to give life to ten people."

Most noticeable, however, are the changes in the press. The *World Daily News,* for example, now devotes considerable space to the Yenan radio, while stories from its out-of-town correspondents have been reduced and those from the Central News Agency entirely dropped. An article in its February 1 issue, "Why Is It Necessary to Put Land Reform into Practice?," argues that a situation in which seventy to eighty per cent of China's cultivated land is controlled by less than ten per cent of the total rural population not only gravely weakens China's rural economy, but impoverishes the entire nation, leaving it an easy prey to foreign imperialism.

The *North China Daily News,* former organ of the Kuomintang Ministry of Information, has already been converted into the official mouthpiece of the new regime under the name of *Jen-min Jih-pao (People's Daily)*. Here are some of the chief items appearing in its first issue yesterday:

(1) A front-page notice prohibiting all photographing of the People's Liberation Army save by accredited photographers.

(2) The text of Mao Tse-tung's eight points, accompanied by a large photo of Mao.

(3) Enthusiastic stories on the liberation of Peking and Tientsin.

(4) Attacks on Kuomintang phony peace talks.

(5) Regulations concerning the new currency and other official notices.

(6) Stalin's answers to the questions posed to him by International News.

(7) Communist gains in the recent Japanese elections.

(8) A Yenan broadcast citing the surrender of Peking as a model for what should take place elsewhere and pointing out that Fu Tso-yi, though technically a war criminal, may through this

act hope to atone his guilt. The implication is that other generals who follow his example will receive similar consideration.

(9) The text of the ultimatum delivered to Fu on January 16, the day following the fall of Tientsin, giving him until 2 P.M. of January 22 to surrender, after which the Communists threatened to storm Peking, regardless of cost. The letter promised safety to Fu's officers and men and a pardon for himself if he surrendered. This resulted in the January 18 peace delegation, following the failure of die-hards to blow up its leader, Ho Ssu-yüan, with a time bomb. On January 22, a few hours before the expiration of the ultimatum, Fu surrendered.

(10) A lengthy article, entitled "Outline of America's New Plan for Interfering in China's Internal Politics," which bolsters its thesis with extensive quotations from AP and UP dispatches, *Life, Newsweek,* the *Bulletin* of the Foreign Policy Association, *The New Republic,* and other publications. In it the author makes it clear that in his own mind, at least, there is no doubt as to who will be the controlling factor in the new China: the Communists have liberated China and they will determine its form of government; those who join that government will do so only on Communist terms. Yet at the same time he shows himself curiously anxious to remove the label of "communism" from what is now taking place. Commenting on the term "Communist government" used in an editorial of the *New York Herald-Tribune,* he says, for example: "By this is meant the Communist-led People's Government." This tendency is in line with other indications I have noticed: the army of the Communists is invariably referred to as the People's Liberation Army, the new government bank is the People's Bank, the new official paper is the *People's Daily,* and so on. The Communists are obviously anxious to foster the belief that they are the instruments of the Chinese popular will but not the sole constituents of that will.

February 13 (Sunday)

Two Weeks of the People's Government

Tomorrow it will be two weeks since Galia saw the first detachments of the Liberation Army march triumphantly up Morrison Street. What are the credits and debits of the new regime during this short period?

In physical rehabilitation much has been done. The curfew is ended, water and electricity operate continuously, the mess around the glacis has been somewhat cleared up, the electric wires replaced, and the surrounding streets reopened to traffic. Though many parks remain closed, the Pei Hai has been restored to its former tranquil appearance. Much progress has been made in communications. Streetcars run again; buses go to Tsinghua; train service to Tientsin, Mukden, and elsewhere has been restored. A British ship from Hong Kong is reported to have docked at Tientsin, and the Communists have announced that, war or no war, they are willing to barter coal for flour with Kuomintang China and to exchange letters. No planes have arrived since before Chinese New Year, however, save for that bringing a Nanking citizens' peace delegation here a week ago. Our last American mail was received on January 28, so that despite radio and telegraph, we feel cut off from the outside world.

Economically there has been little change. Prices have dropped but slightly, despite the influx of food into the city, and the hordes of silver-dollar changers remain as conspicuous on the streets as before. The conversion of gold yuan into people's notes proceeds smoothly. That the favored 3:1 exchange rate for poor people on sums up to GY$500 can give only trifling economic relief, however, is shown by the fact that this amount now buys less than six pounds of flour at current prices. One curious result of the dual exchange rate is the extraordinary lease on life it has given the gold yuan in the last days of that ill-fated currency's existence. A day or so ago I even heard a street vendor shouting his readiness to give people's notes for gold yuan. The explanation is simple: Some poor people are apparently unable to scrape together even the GY$500 which they are entitled to exchange at the favored rate. Hence they are supplied with the necessary amount by speculators, who exact a cut for themselves in return.

In organizational and indoctrination work the Communists have been particularly active. Almost all sectors of the working population, among them groups as diverse as pedicabbers and librarians, are organizing themselves into unions—or rather, being organized, for the initial steps are being taken by Communist political workers. Our Chin, who joined the pedicab union a day or so ago, was told that it would strive to improve the working conditions of its members, give them financial assistance in time of need, etc. No definite dues were demanded, but he made a voluntary donation of GY$50.

Aside from the new unions, innumerable other groups continue to issue congratulatory statements on what has been happening. Probably close to half of the *People's Daily* is devoted to such statements and to accounts of the mass meetings and parades that have been taking place almost every day this week.

Biggest of all was yesterday's super mass meeting in the big square before the T'ien-an Men (the imposing front gate to the Forbidden City), followed by a parade lasting many hours. Over 200,000 persons are said to have listened to the speeches delivered from the top of the gate, which was draped with red flags and surmounted by gigantic portraits of Mao Tse-tung and Chu Teh. Though the crush was too great to let me get near the gate itself, the cavorting paraders I saw later on seemed to be thoroughly enjoying themselves. One of the most arresting displays, according to the papers (I did not see it myself), was that prepared by students from the Mukden Medical College. It consisted of a huge turtle labeled Chiang Kai-shek. (According to Chinese folklore, the turtle is supposed to reproduce itself unnaturally, and so there is no greater insult to a Chinese than to be called a turtle or turtle's egg.) On him rode a "big-nosed" foreigner in formal attire and stovepipe hat, obviously Uncle Sam.

The papers are so full of these local doings that they give only a hazy idea of what is happening in the outside world. This is particularly true of the *People's Daily*. Aside from local news and items from the Yenan radio and Tass, most of its space is devoted to general articles of a doctrinaire nature; to a "People's Page" filled with "proletarian" essays, poems, and stories; and to occasional photos and cartoons. The result, for the outsider, is pretty dull reading.

In foreign affairs, the propaganda of the new regime follows the familiar Russian line. It bitterly attacks the British in Malaya, the Dutch in Indonesia, and the French in Indo-China, but reserves its heaviest guns for the evils of American "imperialism" abroad and American capitalism at home. Despite such propaganda, I have seen no trace of discrimination against individual private foreigners other than that, for travel outside the city, they must have special passes—apparently not readily obtainable. On the official level, however, the situation is different. On the grounds that no diplomatic relations exist between themselves and the rest of the world, the Communists resolutely deny that the foreign consulates have any legal existence. In Tientsin they have confiscated the stocks of E.C.A. flour, thus bringing the activities of this organization in North China to an end.

The biggest hornet's nest, however, was stirred up by the AP and UP dispatches telling how the People's Army was received in Peking. The UP correspondent, it is alleged here, described the local attitude as one of "wait-and-see," hardly different from that accorded Peking's six other "conquerors" of the past forty years. AP is claimed to have stated even more explicitly that the populace greeted the Communists "in the same way in which, when Japan occupied Peiping, it welcomed the Japanese; when the Americans returned, it welcomed the Americans; when the Kuomintang returned, it welcomed the Kuomintang; and even as several hundred years ago it welcomed the Mongols."

These dispatches have elicited widespread demands for the expulsion of the offending parties, and, if really quoted accurately, can hardly be denied to be not only injudicious but unfair. Who can say with assurance, for example, just how Peking reacted to the Mongols almost seven centuries ago?

Another incident heaping coals on the fire is the AP "fox story" allegedly cabled from Peking on February 7. As quoted in the *People's Daily,* it describes a group of Peking students who, happening to meet a well-to-do Chinese lady clothed in expensive furs, commanded her to crawl on the street like a fox. Though induced to desist by older people, they are alleged to have shouted as they departed: "Today we have a new China, in which no one whatever is allowed to wear fox!"

According to what I have been told, this story was written wholly on the basis of second- or even third-hand evidence. But even supposing it was accurate, was it really fair for a responsible news correspondent to single it out as representative of what is happening in Peking these days? Galia, for example, was pleasantly surprised a day or so ago when, also wearing a fur coat, she happened to drop a bundle and had it politely picked up for her by one of a group of students who were performing a dance in the street for the enjoyment of passers-by.

What, then, is the real attitude of Peking's residents toward their new "conquerors"? My own subjective opinion, for what it may be worth, is that the reaction is enthusiastic on the part of many, favorable or at least acquiescent on the part of most, and definitely antagonistic on the part of a relatively small minority. (It must be remembered that many of those most violently opposed already fled southward before the Communists arrived.) Among a group of liberal and leftist professors whom I saw this last week, the attitude was, as might be expected, uniformly favorable. But so it is among older and less manifestly liberal men, such as old Professor Chang or Galia's teacher Mr. Ma.

On a less sophisticated level, opinion is perhaps represented by the views of our servants. Our cook Sun, a cynic, is obviously skeptical. He speaks rather sneeringly of the endless meetings and parades and decries attacks made on men like Chiang, Truman, or MacArthur. "After all," he says, "Chinese shouldn't make fun of Chinese," while as for America, it is a friendly country.

Our young idealist Chin, on the other hand, is openly enthusiastic. With gusto he relates two stories. The first is that of a very poor friend of his who had run out of coal. The day after Chinese New Year (when all shops were closed) he went to his usual coal dealer to buy a few pounds of coal balls. He was angrily refused, and on repeating his plea, was threatened with a beating by some of Fu Tso-yi's soldiers who were quartered in the coal yard. A week or so later, after the liberation, he returned. This time the coal dealer greeted him with smiles and vehemently and somewhat apprehensively denied that he had ever refused him coal in the past. Moreover the Communist soldiers, who by now had replaced those of General Fu, addressed him, despite his poverty, as "old sir."

Chin's other story is that of a man on our street who recently bought 200 pounds of firewood from a street vendor. After watching its delivery, he refused to pay for more than 150 pounds, claiming that it really amounted to no more than that since its weight had been increased by soaking in water. "Why, in that case," asked the vendor, "did you first accept the wood without question?" "You can do what you like," replied the man angrily, "but I won't pay more." At this the vendor appealed to the police, who quickly compelled the man to pay the full amount. "In the old days," Chin concluded triumphantly, "these same police would probably have arrested the vendor as a troublemaker."

It is my belief that the Chins outnumber the Suns at the moment, and that the Communists can count on their continued support if—and this is an important if—they can ultimately succeed in stabilizing the economic situation.

February 28 (Monday)

Landlord and Servant in the New China

Our new landlord, Mr. Chen, is a gentle, soft-spoken man of about forty, quite a contrast to our former, extrovert landlady, Mrs. Sung, and very unlike the stereotype of the "exploiting" landlord. He is very busy these days and hence rarely comes to his office here at the extreme rear of the big garden, which he has left in charge of two young fellows who are so fearful of our student refugees that they rarely venture out of doors. This morning, however, when Galia went to pay our house rent, she found Mr. Chen present and stopped to chat a few minutes. Inevitably the talk passed to the problem of the students, quite a number of whom, Mr. Chen asserts, are not really students at all but special agents sent by Yen Hsi-shan (Kuomintang defender of besieged Taiyuan) to spy on his fellow general, Fu Tso-yi!

Mr. Chen has been working hard, he told Galia, to persuade the new authorities to take some definite action. He has called on them several times and explained the plans of his chemical company to make the compound its national headquarters as soon as it can be vacated and repaired. The Communists, eager to foster industry, are genuinely anxious, he believes, to see this happen, and so he is hopeful that something will soon be done.

"But," said Mr. Chen, "it certainly isn't easy to get to know these people. When you enter their office, you are never sure to whom you are talking. Is it an important man or just a little clerk? There's no way of telling, because all are dressed exactly alike in the same gray cotton uniform. After you've explained your case to someone, you ask his name and he replies: 'Never mind about that. When you come again, just go to this same table and you'll be taken care of.' But when I do go back, I find somebody else sitting there and have to explain my business all over again."

Recently, however, Mr. Chen succeeded in making a personal contact—a Communist whom he discovered to be a Japanese, and to whom he was able to talk in Japanese, he himself having been educated in Japan. The man was so pleased to have a chance to speak his own language that he became quite friendly and has been very helpful. Thus Mr. Chen feels that he is now on the way toward getting results.

Another matter which has given our landlord endless worry is the case of Mrs. Sung's *amah*. This woman had served Mrs. Sung for many years but is now old and not good for much work. Furthermore, she has a son to support her. Hence when Mrs. Sung fled south, she wanted to dismiss the *amah* but, instead of acting herself, left this unpleasant task to Mr. Chen. He accordingly paid her off on rather generous terms and forgot about the matter. Presently, however, the old *amah*, at her son's instigation, confronted Mr. Chen with a demand for part of the newly purchased property, which she claimed was "owing" her. Her idea seemed to be that as an old servant she was entitled to part of the money which had been paid to the Sungs. When Mr. Chen refused, she appealed to the police, who made Mr. Chen appear before them one night to face the irate woman. This little old-fashioned servant, who had always been so meek in Mrs. Sung's employ, now began a terrific rumpus. She hit her head on the floor and wailed and shrieked in a frenzy until Mr. Chen, with the police as witness, finally paid her a very considerable sum. All this had happened before Fu Tso-yi's surrender. For some weeks all was quiet, and Mr. Chen thought the case closed.

When the Communists came, however, the *amah* and her son apparently thought that now would be their real chance to make more money. Hence they brought their case before the newly established People's Court. Poor Mr. Chen was by now very downhearted. After hearing both sides, however, the judge reprimanded the *amah,* and then, in a compromise that is typically Chinese, told Mr. Chen to pay her a very trifling amount as a token settlement. This, he warned her, must be absolutely the last of the matter. Mr. Chen is very relieved over this happy conclusion to a case in which he feels he has been quite unjustly implicated.

March 1949

March 4 (Friday)

The First Month

It is now thirty-two days since the People's Army marched into
Peking. Following the spate of meetings, parades, and congratulatory messages of the first two weeks, changes of a more concrete
nature are beginning to make themselves felt. The honeymoon
seems over.

Physically, conditions continue to return to normal. The enormous piles of unsightly refuse which had accumulated in the
streets during the siege are gradually being carted away. The
reopening of the Palace Museum, and probably of many other
parks and museums, is promised within a week. Already the city
wall is open as a promenade to those who wish to use it. From
its top the evidences of destruction wrought by Peking's former
defenders are clearly apparent: on the wall itself, in the tunnels
and piles of brick and earth remaining from hundreds of dug-
outs and gun emplacements; beyond the wall, in the gray waste
of razed buildings which circle the city in a belt several hundred
yards wide. Of these, only heaps of rubble now remain, from
which boys are gradually carrying away the bricks on their backs.
At one or two places a start has been made at rebuilding, but for
the most part the scene is one of bleak desolation.

On the production front the papers are filled these days, quite
à la Russe, with enthusiastic accounts of how the workers are re-
habilitating industry to a point equal to, or even higher than,
its presiege level. Improving communications are making it pos-

sible for thousands of refugees to return to their homes, helped by free transportation and grain allotments from the government. It was inspiring to revisit the Temple of Confucius a few days ago and compare its present stately calm with the former scene of refugee squalor, misery, and confusion. Almost the last evidences of that unhappy time are the piles of refuse now being carted away in preparation for its formal reopening a few days hence. Voids remain, however, where doors, windows, and furniture used to be—all burned as firewood during the siege.

As for the economic picture, incomplete figures show that during the period of monetary reconversion ending February 23, over 817,000 workers, students, teachers, and "poor people", or not far below half of the city's population, made use of the favorable 3:1 exchange rate. Developments since that date include a census-taking of the city's poor and the distribution of 150,000 catties (Chinese pounds) of millet to an unspecified number; also a registration of the unemployed, especially those possessing technical skills.

Of more lasting importance is the activation of a new monolithic governmental organ, the North China Trading Corporation. About a week ago this organization began to sell grains, coal, and certain kinds of cloth at prices slightly below those on the open market. For this purpose it uses shops of its own as well as privately owned subsidiaries scattered throughout the city. The latter are permitted to continue selling their own commodities at unfixed prices, the theory being that in the course of time these will be forced by competition to approximate the government levels. At present it is far too early to judge of the success of this device. Prices, after continuing to rise since I last wrote, have dropped slightly during the past three or four days, but not enough to be significant. Chief defect in the system so far, according to a Chinese friend, is the inferiority in quality of government commodities to those on the open market, as well as the fact that they are sometimes mixed with the latter by certain unscrupulous private dealers and then sold at the higher open-market rates.

Coincident with these steps, the authorities have banned further transactions in the Chinese silver dollar, which must be turned in to the People's Bank for people's notes. So far, however, the ban has been only lightly applied. The hawkers who formerly blocked traffic with their numbers at certain street corners and dinned the air with their clinking, now walk singly along the streets, muttering: "Buy one! Buy one!" to passers-by.

Salaries of all workers in public institutions, including professors in the government universities, are now computed in terms of catties of millet. The immediate aim is to restore them to their late 1948 levels, which, though better than those of the siege, are still far from adequate. A professor, for example, now receives the equivalent of about twenty silver dollars monthly, compared with a prewar (pre-1937) salary of 400 silver dollars. For laborers the discrepancy is considerably less.

Shortages of imported goods are making themselves felt, particularly in gasoline, causing fewer cars than before to be seen on the streets.

In the political sphere, the last week of February saw the transfer of the North China People's Government, headed by Tung Pi-wu, from Shihchiachuang to Peking.

Far more publicized has been the arrival here of several hundred persons representing over twenty anti-Kuomintang political groups. Included are the Kuomintang Revolutionary Committee and the Democratic League, as well as overseas Chinese representatives and unaffiliated figures. These, no doubt, will become the non-Communist nucleus for the "coalition" government eventually to be created for all China. Another event has been the arrival, cordial reception, and departure after ten days, of an "unofficial" five-man peace delegation from the South.

A final item is the announcement, a couple of days ago, that the "reorganization"—in other words, indoctrination—of Fu Tso-yi's surrendered troops is now completed. Those who wish will be allowed to join the Liberation Army; others will be given three months' terminal pay and free transportation to their homes. Certainly a generous treatment and speedy metamorphosis! Fu himself apparently remains in the western suburbs, but is never mentioned.

In the educational sphere, the past weeks have seen the reopening of lower and middle schools. In that to which our *amah* sends her children, each pupil was asked to supply one table and chair —any kind would do—to replace those destroyed by Fu's soldiers during their siege-time occupation. There was nothing compulsory in the request, however, and our *amah* begged out of it on grounds of financial disability. Kuomintang textbooks, though eventually to be revised or replaced, remain in use for the time being. Peita and other government universities have at last been "taken over" by the People's Government in the sense that one or more members of that regime have been formally attached to each institution. No curricular or other changes, however, are contemplated at the present time.

Just how short the Communists are in trained personnel is shown by their efforts to recruit 10,000 men and women graduates of middle schools or higher institutions to serve in the "southern expedition." Their problem is that of finding persons who possess the requisite technical ability combined with enthusiasm for the cause and willingness to undergo great personal hardship. Many students have the latter qualities in abundance; only a few possess the former. Their eager response to the recruiting campaign is exemplified in the case of Tsinghua, which reopened classes yesterday with an attendance of only 1,804 out of its former enrollment of 2,482. Most of the 678 absent students have apparently decided to forego further studies in order to work for the revolutionary cause in the south.

With an eye to the future, the Communists are also establishing three "universities"—really gigantic indoctrination and training institutes—to be known respectively as North China University, the North China People's Revolutionary University, and North China Military Administration University. All three are now preparing to hold entrance examinations.

The notice of the Military University appearing in the *People's Daily* is no doubt typical. It announces that training in military administration is to be given to 6,000 students. A preliminary half-year term will, in the case of selected groups, be followed by a further curriculum lasting from one to one and a

half years. Subjects will include Marxism, ideology of Mao Tse-
tung, sociology, fundamental problems in the Chinese revolution,
contemporary political policy, fundamental knowledge about the
People's Liberation Army, and military science and technology.
Anyone can apply who is of good physique and habits, has graduated from a lower middle school (tenth grade by American
standards), and is between the ages of eighteen and twenty-eight.

It is in the realm of what may be called indoctrination, or, less
charitably, thought control, that we reach the most questionable
aspect of the new program. The authorities are trying, with considerable success, to see that only their point of view reaches the
people. Slogans and posters carrying their message now adorn all
public places. Many, printed in bright colors, are very effective,
for example the one depicting a galloping cavalryman holding
aloft a red banner, beneath which appears the caption: "Plant the
victorious banner throughout China!"; or that of an army officer
pointing to the way ahead, with huge tanks looming in the background.

A reading room and adjoining sales room for New Democracy
literature have been opened at a strategic location on Morrison
Street, where they attract such crowds that one can enter only with
difficulty. What I was able to examine on one brief visit proved
unimpressive: piles of tiny pamphlets containing crude black-
and-white pictures arranged in comic-strip fashion to illustrate
the evils of landlordism, the benefits of peasant cooperation with
the People's Army, and similar themes.*

Movies are now said to be subject to censorship. In the words
of the March 2 *Peiping Digest*: † "Decadent U. S. films are to be
ousted by healthy Russian films. Fifty Russian movies are already
in circulation in North China and thirteen are to be shown in
Peiping."

Newspapers have suffered a high mortality, at least seven having been closed in Peking, including that to which I had sub-

---

* This situation changed radically in later months, which saw an ever-increasing
flood of new publications pour from the presses, often very attractively printed.
Attendance remained high not only in this, but in other bookstores opened to meet
the popular demand.

† A small bi-weekly sheet of English translations from the local press, started after
the siege by a group of Peita students interested in journalism.

scribed, the *World Daily News.* This leaves the city with only
two dailies, the official *People's Daily,* and a tabloid, the *Hsin-
min Pao (New Citizen),* which is the only paper surviving from
the old regime under its own name. Others will probably be
started before long, judging from what occurred in Tientsin,
where the official *Tientsin Daily* has already been joined, or is
about to be joined, by three revamped papers. Among these, the
most important is the *Chin-pu Jih-pao* or *Progressive Daily,* a rein-
carnation of the famous *Ta Kung Pao.*

I have begun to subscribe to it again and notice that, like every
other paper, it faithfully follows the Communist line, using the
New China News Agency as its only source of information about
the outside world. Within liberated China itself, however, it
maintains something of its former wide coverage by the use of
news letters from local correspondents. These give it a piquancy
and individuality lacking in the more standardized official organs.

How many dailies are published in Communist China today?
According to the editorial reply to a letter to the editor in the
March 2 *People's Daily,* the total is 63, distributed as follows:
Manchuria (including part of Inner Mongolia), 22; North China,
16; Northwest, 6; Central Plains, 7; East China, 12. Only four
cities have more than one paper: Harbin, 2; Mukden, 4; Shihchiachuang, 3; Chengchow, 2. These figures are obviously incomplete inasmuch as they list only one paper apiece for Peking
and Tientsin.

During the past few weeks, however, I have concluded that the
integrity of the press depends on more than simply the number
of its papers, important though this may be. It does not greatly
matter, after all, if a city possesses one, two, or five papers, provided they all print essentially the same news derived from the
same source. As a matter of fact, what can be said of the press
here in China can also be made to apply, in some respects, to the
American press: too many American cities maintain only one
paper, too many papers depend for news solely on a single news
agency, too many Americans read the same feature columns syn-
dicated throughout the country. The real difference between

America and Communist China, however, can be summed up in a sentence: a speech by Mao Tse-tung has a fair chance of being at least partially reported in America; a Truman speech has no chance at all of being printed in Communist China, unless it suits the purpose of the authorities to permit it.

Most disturbing act of thought control is the February 27 order halting all further news activities of Peking's foreign correspondents. Though only seventeen persons are affected (Australian, Swiss, Swedish, and Dutch, as well as American), the order in effect means the complete cessation of news (other than over the Communist radio) from Communist China to the outside world, since Peking is the only city in North China in which foreign correspondents are stationed. The same order bans the further circulation here of the U.S. Information Service news bulletins, both Chinese and English, thus leaving the short-wave radio (for those who have one) as the only "free" organ of information from the outside world.

It is difficult to see the justification for a step which, in its sweeping inclusiveness, transcends anything attempted even in Soviet Russia. The official explanation is that of "conditions during the present state of military activity." The *Progressive Daily* goes a good bit further by beginning its February 28 editorial with the words: "Though among foreign correspondents in China good ones are certainly not wholly lacking, in the final analysis most of them are stupid and are rotten eggs." As illustration it cites the unfortunate AP and UP dispatches describing the Communist entry of Peking.

If these are the real causes for the present step, the Communists could have attained their objectives equally well either by expelling the two correspondents directly involved or by imposing general censorship. Though either step would have undoubtedly aroused criticism abroad, neither could have been as disastrous as the present move, the only practical effect of which is to close the mouths of the new regime's potential friends abroad, strengthen its enemies, and make more difficult the re-establishment of those diplomatic and commercial ties from which the Chinese Communists themselves stand to benefit.

But probably it is too much to expect the Communists to pay much attention to long-range considerations such as these in a matter in which the question of prestige with their own people is involved. Nor is it surprising that their decision should be approved by the students, always inclined to be hot-headed, or that it should be ignored by the bulk of China's toiling masses, for whom the problem of filling next day's rice bowl is far more important than the academic question of press freedom. But what about those many non-Communist intellectuals and liberals who have repeatedly in the past risked personal safety by protesting against Kuomintang violations of the press? It is disappointing that on this occasion not one has raised his voice in public criticism.

March 6 (Sunday)

Land

What is the Communist land reform program? Here is the gist of the land regulations that were approved, September 13, 1947, by the National Chinese Communist Party Assembly on Land, as contained in one of the new pamphlets now being sold on the street corners:

With the aim of realizing Sun Yat-sen's principle, "To the tiller belongs the soil," all feudalistic or semi-feudalistic land institutions are to be abolished. This means abolition of the land rights of landlords, temples, schools, and other organizations, as well as of all rural debts incurred prior to the reform. Reform will be carried out through the associations of farmers and of poor (i.e., tenant) farmers, to be created in each village (*hsiang*), district (*ch'ü*), county (*hsien*) and province (*sheng*). The village will be the focal unit for land redistribution, save in cases of special importance, which will be decided by the district or county associations.

Large forest lands, water works, mines, pasturages, waste lands, lakes, etc., will fall under government control, as will cultural and historical monuments. All other land, together with agricultural property (buildings, animals, implements, grain stocks, and the like), will be pooled for each village unit and then redistributed on the basis of quantitative and qualitative equality for all alike, irrespective of age or sex. Landlords and their families, once having surrendered their holdings to the general pool, will be reassigned amounts equal to those of everyone else. So will the families of Kuomintang soldiers and officials, and of traitors and war criminals, provided they are willing to cultivate the land themselves. Traitors and war criminals themselves, however, will not receive land. Laborers, professional workers, and others whose livelihood is dependent only in part or not at all upon land will either not share in the distribution or will receive correspondingly lesser amounts.

Once land has been redistributed, it will be regarded as the private property of its owner and may thereafter be freely bought, sold, or even rented, subject to certain regulations (prohibiting exorbitant rents and the like). Nothing is said about collectivization. Violators of the regulations will be tried in people's courts, composed of members of the farmers' associations and government-appointed individuals. The government guarantees to the people their democratic right to engage freely in criticism at the meetings of the farmers' associations and to elect or replace the committees and representatives of these associations.

Such then is the land program as it stands on paper.* To anyone acquainted with rural China, the difficulties in its way may well seem almost insuperable. There must be tens of thousands of villages in China, for each of which a farmers' association must be created. Initially, at least, this task cannot be left to the farmers themselves, but must be guided by trained political workers, preferably those intimately acquainted with local conditions. The work of awakening and activating millions of illiterate peasants to the point where they themselves can perpetuate the program is surely one of the most challenging and formidable in all history.

* For important subsequent modifications, see pp. 153-154.

What has been concretely accomplished to date? In the absence of any over-all report, one is forced to turn to whatever scattered statements happen to come to hand. Two weeks ago the papers mentioned that 90,000 *mu*,* or about 13,636 acres, of newly liberated land in northern Kiangsu province are now being surveyed for redistribution. An item in today's *Progressive Daily* describes how over 1,300 political workers have been engaged in land reform ever since October in the 1,634 villages surrounding Mukden, with redistribution already complete in some.

A story in the March 1 *Progressive Daily* gives the case history of one particular town. The place in question, Chao-kuan-ying—described as a former "bastion of feudalism"—is located in Pao-feng-hsien, southeast of Loyang, provincial capital of Honan. Its population of 2,325 individuals, belonging to 468 households, cultivates a total area of 5,860 *mu* or about 888 acres. Hence an exact land division would theoretically provide each family of slightly less than five persons with a fraction under two acres. Part of Chao-kuan-ying's population is undoubtedly engaged in occupations other than farming and so does not need land. But even if we arbitrarily grant this portion to be as much as 50 per cent—obviously far too high—each family of five would still receive an allotment of less than four acres. These figures vividly illustrate the agrarian problem that exists in China. They also reveal that even the most equitable land redistribution, as proposed by the Communists, can only partially solve this problem.

Of Chao-kuan-ying's population, 8 per cent are landlords who own 39 per cent of the land within the district (plus another 2,157 *mu* lying outside); 49 per cent are "poor farmers" who hold only 11.4 per cent of the land. At the apex of this "feudal" structure there formerly stood two families, one of which was supported by local officialdom, the other by bandits. Attempts at reform, begun with the liberation of Chao-kuan-ying in August, 1947, were nullified when the Liberation Army was subsequently driven out and the landlord association, supported by its Red Spear Society, returned to power. With the second liberation, in April, 1948, efforts were renewed. They met with continued difficulties, however, owing to the timidity and inexperience of the

* Chinese unit of area. One acre equals about 6.6 *mu*.

farmers, until in October of that year a corps of political workers began a systematic program of lectures and indoctrination. A self-defense militia corps was then established against roving bandits, and two men, one a local landowner of 800 *mu*, with a long record of exploitation, the other a notorious bandit, were apprehended and tried before a people's court. The former was fined twenty-five piculs (8,333 pounds) of wheat; the latter was executed.

Today the farmers' association of Chao-kuan-ying boasts of 349 members and is firmly established. But, as the writer of the story concludes, the real work of land reform is only just beginning.

Industry and Commerce

The *Peiping Digest* of February 25 contains a translation of "instructions issued by the Administrative Committee of the Shansi-Chahar-Hopei Frontier Area, regarding the protection of industry and commerce during the process of land reform." Some of the highlights of this document, intended primarily as a guide for dealing with small scale rural enterprise, are:

The government guarantees ownership rights, free management, and lawful business profits to all factories, workshops, and firms (public, private, and cooperative). The same guarantee applies to enterprises operated by "landlords and old-style wealthy farmers," which, if they have already been taken over by the farmers' associations, should be handed back to their original owners. Enterprises owned by "bureaucratic capital or notorious country bosses," however, are subject to confiscation and operation by the government. Every effort should be made to maintain the operation and prevent the dismemberment of all enterprises. Equipment should be confiscated from landlords only if the latter lack the manpower to operate it themselves, in which case it should be taken over by the farmers' associations. Debts between individuals engaged in industry and commerce are not to be repudiated: ["The claims to collect debts of the landowners, rich farmers, and usurers [money-lenders] in industry and commerce, when they do not fall into the category of usury, should also not be abolished." Taxation should aim at encouraging production. "Industrial and commercial capitalists" should endeavor to improve working conditions, while laborers should "actively engage in production in order to obtain reasonable profits for the capitalists." In this way "capitalists and laborers will be united in their struggle for victory in war and the reconstruction of the nation." As for the apprentice system, "except for abolishing its feudal or semi-feudal nature and making adequate improvements within economic and other necessary limitations, the treatment of apprentices should still follow the old customs."

This is a far cry from actual communism. The stipulation about non-cancellation of debts, in particular, is a notable deviation from the contrary stipulation in the 1947 land reform regulations.

"The Poor Man's Road to New Life"

This is the headline of a story in the *Progressive Daily* of two days ago, telling what has been happening the past few weeks in Ch'en-t'ang-chuang, a little town of about 2,500 persons, on the outskirts of Tientsin. A census taken immediately after liberation showed that 128 persons were in particularly straitened circumstances, owing to the siege and depredations of Kuomintang soldiery. After much persuasion, Communist political workers induced these men to organize an industrial cooperative. They were very reluctant to do so, the village having been victimized once before by a so-called "cooperative" scheme organized by a Kuomintang official. On February 7, however, the enterprise got under way with a capital of PN$14,050 subscribed by the workers themselves, another PN$12,000 contributed by the People's Bank, and tools and other equipment donated by sympathetic persons.

The cooperative began by manufacturing coal balls, which it was able to sell at less than the prevailing market price. Its next venture was to sell salt which it transported from the sea coast. By February 27 it had already made the extraordinary profit of

PN$11,200, with which it plans to expand activities by selling
fish brought from Taku and acting as local sales agent for the
government's North China Trading Corporation. In this way,
the article concludes, the poor people of this village have not only
obtained gainful employment but, perhaps even more important,
they are learning how to work for instead of against one another.

Intellectuals

Yesterday's *Peiping Digest* has an article entitled "Communist
Party Policy towards Intellectuals"—an "official statement of policy issued about two years ago." Its main thesis is that though
most professors, civil servants, scientists, engineers, and artists
come from landlord and capitalist families, they themselves are
"mental workers" toward whom "the Democratic Government
must adopt policies which will protect them and make use of
them to serve the People's Republic to the best of their capacity."
Because many suffered economic insecurity and political oppression under the Kuomintang, only a very small minority really
favor the old regime. "These people can be won over to our side.
If we can give them sound political guidance and education,
their knowledge and skill can be used." Even within the ultra-
conservative Three People's Principles Youth Corps, in fact, only
"a very small part are reactionary elements beyond redemption."

The building of a new China, the article goes on, requires
enormous numbers of educated specialists. "We can set up various kinds of training classes to give them political and technical
training, reform them gradually, then give them suitable work.
But at first we must avoid giving them key positions and be always on the alert to prevent subversive activities. . . . At the
same time we must make intellectuals out of the workers and
farmers . . . and train the most promising among them . . . so
that they can play their full part in the work of construction."

Are the Chinese Communists Really Communist?

Practically nothing of what I have been describing can be really called "communism." Government sale of grain and other key commodities is not communism. Rather it seems like a modern adaptation of that ancient "ever-normal granary" principle which, under varying names, has been sporadically practiced in China for some two thousand years. Nor is a land program communistic which not only allows private owners the right to buy, sell, and rent land but also omits all reference to collectivization. On the contrary, it, too, stems from numberless attempts in Chinese history to equalize the land, of which those by the usurper Wang Mang at the beginning of the Christian era and by the eleventh-century statesman Wang An-shih are but the most famous. Nor is an industrial and commercial policy communistic which encourages private cooperatives and leans over backward to insure "lawful business profits" to "capitalists" and "landlords and old-style wealthy farmers."

Does this mean, then, that the Chinese Communists are not true Communists? The answer is no, for two good reasons. In the first place, they accept the Marxist view of history and use such terms as "feudalism," "imperialism" and "democracy" in the same way as do other Communists. In the second place, they resemble Communists elsewhere in the propaganda techniques they employ, their almost religious faith in themselves as the sole possessors of truth, and their distrust and dislike of "imperialists."

The seeming inconsistency of their program, therefore, proves only their practical realization that immediate communism is impossible in a country as economically undeveloped as China, and their resulting willingness to accept temporary compromise in order to achieve the final socialist goal—even though "temporary" may in this case mean a span of decades. Any other interpretation, in fact, becomes almost impossible in view of actual conditions in China.

Let us take the land problem as a single example. Assume, for the sake of argument, that the land can be successfully equalized in accordance with the Communist program. Assume, too, that the pressure of population on land can be reduced by large-scale industrialization. And assume, finally, that China's huge population can during this process somehow be kept in check near its present limits.

Even granted that all three things happen, the pressure of population on land will still remain constant and inexorable, judged by Western standards. (Let us remember Chao-kuan-ying, where, if only a fifth of the existing population were to remain farmers, this would still mean less than ten acres per family.) Given this compelling fact, plus an economic system that continues to permit the private purchase, sale, and renting of land, it is hard to see how any program of land redistribution can permanently halt the gradual regrowth of the age-old rural stratification of landlord, owner, part-owner, and tenant. Nor is it easy to imagine how China's food needs can be adequately supplied as long as the land remains fragmented in small individual plots, thus preventing a mechanized agriculture without which there can be little hope of a marked increase in productivity. Some form of collectivization, therefore, seems the only way out. For this reason, if for no other, the present land reform program can hardly be more than the first, though a very essential, step toward the Communists' long-range goal.

March 17 (Thursday)

Barter Trade

Prices continue upward, as shown by the daily quotations in the papers, as well as by the recently resumed weekly cost-of-living indices compiled by Nankai University's Institute of Economic Research in Tientsin. The government does its best to slow the rise by selling large amounts of commodities to the newly formed consumer cooperatives, whose members usually are the employees of specific public and private organizations. The *Progressive Daily,* for example, reports eight such cooperatives in Peking as having already bought over a quarter of a million pounds of government sugar, together with comparable quantities of millet, corn flour, cooking oil, salt, and soy sauce. In Tientsin the government has disposed of several million pounds of millet to labor groups having a total membership of 80,000.

The new export-import trade regulations have just been published. They provide that all merchants engaged in such trade must secure operating licenses from the foreign division of the North China Trading Corporation, and that separate licenses are further required for individual transactions. Through such controls, the government aims to balance exports and imports, conserve foreign exchange, and rationalize the entire field of foreign trade in a way deemed advantageous to the total national economy. Exporters may on occasion be required to import certain specified commodities in order to export their own goods— in other words, to arrange barter deals. The North China Trading Corporation holds an option on buying such imports at prices guaranteed to give the importer a fair profit. Export and import customs duties remain fixed at their Kuomintang levels.

Meanwhile the local silver hawkers have disappeared from the streets and silver dollars are becoming increasingly difficult to buy.

A New People's Government

The formation early this month of a provisional People's Government for the Central Plains makes it appear that the Communists are in no hurry to place all occupied territory under a single government. This may not happen now before China as a whole has been taken over, which, in view of the continuing military lull, may take considerably longer than seemed possible a month or two ago.

Letters from America

During the past five days we have been happily flooded with letters from America, dating from mid-January to late February.

These, we trust, will continue coming, now that steamship contact has been resumed with Shanghai. Owing to the fact that our local stamps are not internationally recognized, we can only reply through the intermediary of friends in Shanghai.

"Jelly Belly, Tailor"

Further evidences of the new regime's strong nationalism are the regulations that all addresses on local letters must hereafter be written in Chinese, and that no non-Chinese lettering is hereafter to appear on the trademarks and packaging of products manufactured in Communist China. It has even been suggested that the latter prohibition should be applied to all shop signs as well. This, if carried out, will mean the loss of some that have for years been dear to the hearts of Peking foreigners—for example, the large placard, "Jelly Belly, Tailor," appearing over one of the shops on Morrison Street, or another labeled "Whole World & Co." * The explanation offered by the authorities is that foreign-language trademarks are earmarks of a colonial psychology resulting from China's long economic dependence on the foreigner.

Newspapers

The last two days have seen the appearance of two new newspapers in Peking: the *Chieh-fang Pao* (*Liberation News*), organ of the Peking branch of the Chinese Communist Party (in contradistinction to the *People's Daily*, which represents the North China People's Government), and the *Ta-chung Jih-pao* (*Daily Masses*), a labor organ formerly published elsewhere in liberated territory.

Regulations for the licensing of all Peking newspapers, periodicals, and news agencies were published on the eleventh. Applicant organs must state the occupation, political belief, and political affiliations of their editor and publisher, source of financial

* This suggestion, fortunately, was never carried out.

support, and present financial condition. They must pledge themselves not to violate the laws of the People's Government, not to disseminate propaganda injurious to the New Democracy or spread rumors and slander, and not to disclose national and military secrets. Violating organs are subject to temporary or permanent suspension; other (presumably more drastic) punishment will be meted out in cases entering the sphere of "criminal behavior."

I have recently asked some of the still remaining foreign correspondents what they feel is the attitude of their Chinese colleagues toward such regulations, and more particularly toward the government's ban on foreign news gathering. Their replies confirm my previous impression: Most Chinese newspapermen sincerely favor what the new government is doing and therefore accept the new regulations without hesitation. This explains the ease with which their publications have changed face since liberation, despite the fact that in many cases the staff of these publications has remained relatively intact save for a few shifts in the higher echelons. Furthermore, Chinese newspapermen have long resented the privileges enjoyed by foreign correspondents under the Kuomintang, such as freedom to write in a way which they themselves did not dare to do, or access to inside information. Hence they do not on the whole feel unhappy about the plight into which their foreign colleagues have fallen.

As for Chinese liberals, their attitude (according to these same foreign correspondents) does not materially differ from that of newspapermen. They feel, with good reason, that the Kuomintang has been corrupt and reactionary and that the United States, despite its own professed belief in democracy, has been its chief supporter. Hence they are not too sorry to see the People's Government adopt its present tactics. In other words, the United States, by its concrete policy in China, has done as much as anyone else to discredit, in the eyes of thinking Chinese, those abstract democratic principles which it would most like to see function there.

The Police State

One of the most unpleasant indications to date of a budding police state is the story, reported in the March 12 *Progressive Daily*, of how the Tientsin Bureau of Public Safety is setting up "investigation boxes" throughout the city into which anyone can drop secret denunciations of what seems to him dangerous activity. Such activity includes that of "Chiang Kai-shek's bandit adherents," "reactionaries," "traitors," persons with false identity cards, robbers, and, in general, all "destructive elements." Citizens are warned not to use this as an opportunity for making slanderous accusations or repaying private grudges, and are instructed to accompany all accusations with their own correct name and address. In return, the authorities promise anonymity to informers. Some eighteen boxes have already been set up, with others to be added. Their contents will be collected daily. So far as I know, no similar system has yet been instituted in Peking.*

Rumors

While such techniques are certainly abhorrent, it should be remembered that they are being carried out in a region in which the new regime has been barely two months in power and where many hostile elements undoubtedly remain. The arrest of notorious Kuomintang secret agents and seizure of hidden arms, ammunition, radio transmitters, and the like, have several times been reported. Under the circumstances, the absence of large-scale terroristic reprisals has been striking. Most police and other municipal employees, for example, remain unchanged from the old regime.

Even now it seems certain that rumormongers are still at work. A few days ago, for example, a letter to the editor of the *Progressive Daily* inquired whether it was true what friends had told him, namely, that all unmarried women of marriageable age living in the environs of Tientsin were to be forced into marriage

* Nor was it later instituted. In Tientsin, in fact, it was only of temporary duration, to the best of my knowledge.

by governmental decree. The editor's reply to the writer, of course, was not to believe such fabrications and to tell his friends not to do so either.

Prison Reform

During the past three days (March 14-16) the *Progressive Daily* has run an interesting series of articles on the reform program instituted in the Tientsin prisons. There, prisoners are no longer called "criminals" (*fan-jen*) but "penitents" (*hui-kuo-yüan*), corporal punishment has been abolished, "squeeze" among wardens eliminated, and care is taken that all food and other parcels sent by friends and relatives arrive intact. "The prisons have become schools." The inmates of each cell elect one of their members as their chief, and he is expected to see that all of them observe the prison rules. Livelihood committees have also been elected to look after their food, attend to their hygiene, and buy cigarettes and other supplies on a cooperative basis.

Thus, according to the *Progressive* story, every effort is made to encourage initiative and self-management and to induce the prisoners to obey the rules because of self-respect rather than intimidation. The slogan of the new prison director is: "The purpose of penal institutions is to cure persons who are ill and make them into new members of a new society."

Fixed times are now allotted for work, recreation, lessons, bathing, haircuts, etc., the story continues. Most important, however, are the daily study groups, each consisting of twelve men, devoted to "self-examination" (*fan sheng*) and "the study of life." Prisoners participating in the former are encouraged to discuss their faults frankly before their fellows, accept friendly criticism, and express repentance; in the latter they hear lectures upon the evils of the old society, the ways in which it can be reformed, and the hope this holds for their own rehabilitation.

On March 11 these small sessions culminated in a mass "self-examination" meeting, attended by over 400 prisoners, at which many stood up to make public confession, in some cases for crimes other than those for which they had been sentenced. The "confessors" included, among others, the former puppet mayor of Tientsin during Japanese occupation; a man of Soviet citizenship who had committed a notorious trunk murder in Tientsin; a dope peddler; and a robber. The robber's confession was typical:

"I am a robber. Today I have come here for self-examination. Please criticize and teach me, so that I can be completely remade. When I was born I was not a robber, but then as a youth I was led astray by bad people. . . . For the last several years I have been a pickpocket. . . . On being sent to prison, however, I found that there is food to eat and a place to live in. There is no beating or punishment. The Communists want to make us over. They do not oppress us. We must go forward with them. But we have all stepped through a cesspool. We are covered with filth. We are dirty and stink. People don't want men like ourselves. Can't we understand, then, that we must reform?"

The puppet mayor, for his part, confessed that at sixty-six he had had an affair with his wife's twenty-year-old maid. Questioning from his fellows elicited the fact that the maid had accepted his advances only under compulsion. After several further confessions and accompanying criticism, the prison superintendent expressed the hope that continued study of the nature of society, combined with sessions of self-expiation, might eventually help all to reach a state of sincere repentance and understanding, through which they could become constructive members of society. The meeting then broke up with the song: "Without the Communist Party there would be no China."

Political Revivalism

Regardless of what can be said about Communist objectives, one must admit that they bring to their cause an idealist fire that is almost religious in its earnest intensity. One of its most characteristic manifestations is that of the "self-examination" sessions just described. This technique—so reminiscent of the Oxford Movement or a revivalist meeting—differs from them in that it is more than an appeal for individual repentance. For while uttering this appeal, it asserts at the same time that every individual is essentially the product of the human environment in which he lives, and that, therefore, his own redemption is linked, in the final analysis, with the cooperative betterment of society as a whole.

This technique—a sort of political revivalism—is applied by the Communists to many groups besides prisoners. We find it, for example, being used in the Tientsin Municipal Political Training Institute, the first term of which is now being attended by over three hundred students. Its curriculum not only includes the study of such texts as *The New Democracy, On Coalition Government,* and *The Chinese Revolution and Chinese Communist Party,* but also comprises two daily meetings at which the students divide into small groups to discuss among themselves their past failings and the ways by which they may better serve society in future.

Spirit of the New China

Last Sunday, a lovely spring day, the three of us took a walk through the Pei Hai. As we passed one of the old temples that line the lake's northern shore, we noticed that two of the three large bronze incense burners before its gates had been toppled from their marble pedestals. "More of the work of Kuomintang soldiers," we commented.

A few minutes later, repassing the temple, we met eight or ten young People's Army soldiers, out for a stroll like ourselves. The next moment one of them—obviously a natural leader, though a private like the rest—noticed the overturned incense burners as we had done and ran toward them, waving to his comrades as he did so. In a matter of seconds he and three or four of the others, despite their loads of rifles and blanket rolls, were struggling to lift one of the tripods back to its pedestal. The task was terribly difficult, for the tripod was about three feet high and enormously thick and heavy, besides being so round and smooth that only two or three men could get a real grip on it. All efforts seemed doomed to failure. The burners simply could not be lifted from the ground without ropes and poles.

But then the leader had an inspiration. He called his comrades again to the task, and together they rolled the burner over the ground until it touched the foot of the pedestal. Then, pressing it with all their strength against the side of the stone, they slowly rolled it up the stone's vertical face and thus onto its upper surface. After that it was comparatively simple to pull the burner back upon its legs and slide it until they slipped once more into their original sockets, whereupon the soldier who had conceived the operation leaped happily inside the incense burner, waved his arm, and shouted in triumph. Then, jumping down again, he and his comrades ran to the other prostrate burner and within a few minutes had restored this, too, to its original position. And we three foreigners, together with a small group of Chinese children which had by now assembled, applauded and shouted: *"Hao! Hao!"* ("Good! Good!") As we did so I thought to myself: This is probably the first time in decades—perhaps in centuries—that a group of Chinese soldiers, undirected from above and with no expectation of gain or praise for themselves, have spontaneously performed an act requiring initiative, effort, ingenuity, and cooperation, simply in order to put to rights a monument belonging to the public.

April 1949

April 1 (Friday)

Cooperatives

Prices continue upward, though slowly. Even the *People's Daily* is raising its price today from PN$5 to $10 per copy. There was a time when it sold for $2. According to the Nankai University economic indices, wholesale prices in Tientsin have increased 20.3 per cent for the four weeks of February 23 to March 22, and laborers' cost of living, 16.84 per cent. Since my last entry, the North China Trading Corporation has stopped selling commodities to the general public. The official reason is that some of its fifty-five private-shop outlets were surreptitiously raising their prices and committing other irregularities, but an actual shortage of supply is probably an important factor.

The result is that the sale of government commodities is being restricted more and more to the consumer cooperatives, which are usually institutional in character, and whose membership is limited to employees of specific organizations. The rapid increase of such cooperatives, however, makes it difficult to measure the effect of the continuing inflation with accuracy.

That they do not always have easy sailing is revealed in a frank story in the March 22 *Progressive Daily* about a particular Tientsin cooperative. An official investigation revealed considerable coolness on the part of the public toward this cooperative. There were a number of reasons for this: unfortunate previous experience with Kuomintang-organized cooperatives; infiltration of unreliable personnel in the early stages of the organization; the spread of rumors that no one "with food to eat"—that is, no one

enjoying more than a bare subsistence income—would be allowed
to join; losses suffered on the first batch of corn flour, which had
been bought at higher than market prices though of second-rate
quality; and the spreading of adverse propaganda by competing
merchants.

How To Beat the Inflation

An ingenious method for protecting savings accounts against inflation, which has already been tried in Tientsin, is today being
inaugurated here by the People's Bank. This is how it operates:
The bank establishes a "unit price" which it publishes daily in
the papers. Its basis is the sum total of the average market prices
during the five preceding days of three key commodities: wheat
and corn flour (per pound) and cotton cloth (per foot). Let us
suppose that this sum, on a given day, amounts to PN$100, and
that an individual opens a savings account for that amount on
the day in question. By so doing he is, in effect, buying one
"savings unit" from the People's Bank. Now let us suppose that
three months later, wishing to withdraw his deposit, he finds
that, owing to price rises in the three basic commodities, the
value of his savings unit has gone up to $150. This means that
the bank now pays him, not his original $100, but the unit's new
value, which is $150. At the same time the interest accruing to
him is calculated proportionately.

The system is foolproof for the investor since, should deflation
cause the value of the savings unit to drop below its original level,
he is still guaranteed repayment of his original deposit in full.
The system applies, however, only to long-term accounts of three,
six, or twelve months, the interest rates on which are respectively
3.6, 6 and 9.6 per cent per annum.*

* Since my return to America, I have been informed by a Chinese economist that
this savings-unit plan is not a Communist invention, having first been suggested by
a friend of his in an article printed two or more years ago in Kuomintang China,
when, however, it was ignored. Late in 1949 the Communists applied the idea on
a nationwide scale when they announced their intention of issuing government
bonds the value of which would be adjusted every ten days according to the average
price fluctuations of four key commodities (rice, flour, cloth, charcoal) in six widely
scattered cities (Shanghai, Tientsin, Sian, Hankow, Chungking, Canton).

Business and Austerity

Increased production has become the great slogan of the day, but only of such goods as are deemed best suited to national economic needs. This means that anything smelling of bourgeois luxury is severely frowned upon and that austerity and utilitarianism have become quite the fashion. Even well-to-do Chinese—of whom there are not many left these days—make a point of dressing as shabbily as possible in order, as they themselves tell us, to avoid undue attention and make themselves look as much as possible like the *lao pai hsing* (common folk). The new mode harmonizes well with the general dilapidated and unpainted appearance of the city.

The result is that thousands of merchants formerly engaged in the "luxury" trades—often catering primarily to the foreigner—have either closed their doors or turned to other enterprises. A pewter shop, for example, now sells chemical supplies; a mirror shop sells shoes; curio shops sell watches and fountain pens; and bars of yellow laundry soap appear in the windows of shops which once sold fine porcelains. Luxury goods often go begging, even at low prices, in contrast to daily necessities, the prices of which continue upward. Formerly, for example, a yard of wool was worth a whole bale of plain white cotton cloth, but now the same bale exchanges for two or three yards of the woolen material.

One striking evidence of the new utilitarian order is what has happened to the ill fated Tung-tan glacis. From having been a polo field in the old days of the foreign legations, then Fu Tso-yi's airfield during the siege, and finally, for a short time, seemingly destined to become an assembly ground for Communist-sponsored rallies, it has now been metamorphosed into an ever-expanding shanty town of ugly mat sheds. Here hundreds of petty merchants sell everything from second-hand clothing to ancient phonographs, and almost anyone who wishes, so I am told, can stake out a claim for himself, free of rent or taxes. Many who do so are the former employees of well-established shops which, financially unable to carry on their staff, give them goods in lieu of severance pay. What has happened to the glacis is a continuation of that process whereby almost half of Peking's small business, it sometimes seems, is now conducted in the open air.

The New Democracy Youth Corps

The students continue to throw themselves enthusiastically into their new activities, though, one suspects, to the detriment of class-work. Despite much talk about curricular and textbook changes, it seems unlikely that much will be done along these lines before the fall term. One major event has been the creation of a new semi-political organization, the New Democracy Youth Corps. Membership in this organization—whose name is unpleasantly reminiscent of the Kuomintang's Three People's Principles Youth Corps—is entirely voluntary. The *Progressive Daily* has an inter-esting story describing the inauguration of the Tsinghua branch on March 20. Five hundred and twenty-six students, as well as several well-known professors, attended the meeting, which opened with the singing of the *Internationale*. Following the usual speeches, the climax came when the neophyte students recited in unison the following oath:

"I am a student of Tsinghua University, today joining the New Democracy Youth Corps. I solemnly swear to follow the organiza-tion, to follow its decisions, to follow the majority, to follow the people, to observe the organization's rules and statutes, eternally to move forward with the Communist Party, to study Mao Tse-tung's thought and cultural and scientific knowledge, and to apply every effort to self-reform so that I may be of service to laboring citizens. I guarantee that I shall exert all my strength for the revolution and shall struggle to the end for the establishment of a Chinese People's Democratic Republic."

Here, no doubt, is the organ that will prepare many future recruits for the Communist Party.

Many students are still studying for service in the southern expedition, though some have already left. The three training "universities" mentioned earlier are now in partial operation. The most important, North China University, aims at an ulti-mate enrollment of something like 10,000. Here is its Spartan cur-riculum:

Rise at 5 A.M.; 6-6:30 physical exercise; 7-9 self-study or group discussion; 9 breakfast; 10-1 P.M. reading or discussion; 1-2 rest; 2-4 classes; 4 dinner; 5-7 "organized free activity" (whatever that may mean); 7-9 study; 9:30 lights out. At least three general lecture assemblies are held weekly, each lasting three or four hours, followed by smaller group discussions. Subjects studied include the Chinese revolution, Chinese Communist party, history of social development, "philosophy of the masses," problems of coalition government, "anti-empiricism," New Democracy, and so on. Students receive free tuition, board and lodging.

Our Shansi Students

Meanwhile our compound is blissfully quiet these days, save for the crows who have made their headquarters in the great tree sheltering the front courtyard. The reason is that our Shansi students, after staying with us almost exactly four months, have at last gone elsewhere! During the past two weeks, perhaps as the result of our landlord's efforts, they have gradually dwindled away, some to be returned to the environs of their still besieged Taiyuan, some to resume classes in an unnamed spot in the Western Hills, and some—believe it or not—to study in one or another of the new Communist institutions. Their former living quarters still present a scene of chaos: windows smashed, wooden lattice work gone, deep deposits of dirt and rubbish on the floors. What they did not destroy they often stole—among other things, a bathtub, the removal of which has only now been discovered. It will take much money and many laborers to restore the place to something like its former state, and the impressions they have left will never be effaced. But today the main courtyard is clean and swept, the outer gate closed for the first time in months, and the open-air latrines beside it are lonely and unfrequented. Spring is here, the sun is warm, and the bees make a soft hum in the blossoms of our cherry tree.

Peace Plane from the South

A few minutes ago, while sitting in the sun after lunch, Galia and I heard a distant hum from the southern horizon. For perhaps a minute we were dimly conscious of it without sensing its significance. Then Galia suddenly exclaimed: "A plane!" It is curious how a sound, made familiar through constant association, retains that familiarity and thus escapes notice even when it has not been heard for many weeks. Undoubtedly this plane brings the Kuomintang delegation from Nanking that is expected here today for peace negotiations. What else, I wonder, does it bring for the people of China? . . . A great silver plane has just now passed quite low overhead, after which it circled toward the western airfield. Quite a thrill it gave us to see this tangible evidence of contact with the outside world after weeks of isolation. (Letters, however, written as late as March 13, continue to reach us from America, and so do magazines dating as far back as October and November.)

Thought Control

On March 25 the Peiping Military Control Council, to "prevent the destructive activities of counterrevolutionary elements and protect the democratic rights of the people," promulgated regulations for the control of social organizations which are very similar to those for publications issued on March 11. According to them, all societies must be registered in order to operate legally. They must submit lists of their organizers and statements as to their past and present aims, activities, political beliefs, connections with other organizations, and sources of funds. They must not violate the laws of the People's Government or engage in activities harmful to democratic principles.

In the field of art, the Cultural Control Committee has banned the performance of fifty-seven plays belonging to the traditional repertory. Included are 23 plays that are superstitious; 14, licentious; 4, derogatory to national dignity owing to the prominence given in them to acts of foreign aggression (invasions of the Huns, Mongols, etc.); 4, catering to a "slave morality"; 5, upholding feudalistic oppression; 7, "extremely boring" or lacking a definite scenario. Though I am not enough of a specialist on the Chinese drama to judge offhand whether these fifty-seven plays represent a serious loss to art, their very considerable number suggests that they do. It is a commentary on the acute moral consciousness of the Communists that among the plays, those banned for political reasons (anti-nationalistic, feudalistic, or with a slave morality) are only thirteen in number, whereas those banned on purely moral grounds (superstitious or licentious) total no less than thirty-seven.

Yesterday I was given living evidence of the continuing strength of "superstition" when I paid a visit to the P'an T'ao Kung ("Hall of Spiral Peaches"). The occasion was the birthday festival of the patron deity of this Taoist temple, the "Queen Mother of the West." The temple was jammed with worshipers burning incense or devoutly kowtowing before the images of the Queen Mother and her attendants—goddesses who send children to the childless, cure eye diseases, and perform numerous other miracles for believers. The long approach to the temple was crowded with food vendors, toy sellers, acrobats, magicians, and the other concessionaires and entertainers who are customary at such temple fairs. They did a roaring business with the crowd of festival-goers, which must have numbered in the tens of thousands. This festival, in fact, is the most striking evidence I have yet seen since my return to China of the vitality of the old beliefs. Those who attended, however, were for the most part old-fashioned folk; students and other sophisticates were conspicuous by their absence.

Love in the New China

The past couple of weeks have seen a perceptible deterioration of the *Progressive Daily*. Advertisements have been increased, news matter diminished, and in the process the often interesting newsletters from its own correspondents have been eliminated. Today, aside from local Peking and Tientsin news, it prints only what originates from the official New China News Agency. Even so it offers more diversity than the other papers, including the official *People's Daily*, especially in foreign news.

A major reason, no doubt, for the official concentration on local news is the conviction that if the people are left blissfully ignorant of what happens abroad, they will concentrate better on their tasks at home. This may be psychologically sound, but it is also obviously dangerous. Take, for example, the way in which the theme of American imperialism—symbolized at the moment by the North Atlantic Pact—is being treated here. Almost the only information available consists of the adverse statements, often Communist, and the accounts of protest meetings, that are culled from various countries. Thus the local public, while warned against the pact's sinister designs, is at the same time given the comforting illusion that few people really support it, even in America, aside from a small minority of reactionary capitalists, militarists, and government officials. The result is a reassuring but distorted picture that carefully excludes all elements of discord and uncertainty.

To return to the *Progressive Daily*, one of its most interesting sections, because most indicative of public opinion, is that of letters to the editor. These, understandably, rarely deal with politics, but touch on almost everything else: how to get rid of a bad case of halitosis; what is the meaning of the latest postal regulations; how to unsalt fields whose productivity has been lessened by brine; how the People's Bank savings units operate; the danger to health from public trash; and so forth. To all requests for information, the editor, who is a sort of doctor, agrarian expert, engineer, economist, and Dorothy Dix rolled into one, gives faithful answer.

One of the most persistent types of inquiry deals with love and marriage along lines such as these: I am a boy (or girl) twenty-two years old, deeply in love with a girl (or boy) who returns my love. But my parents are feudalistically-minded and oppose the match (often because they have previously arranged a betrothal of their own). I understand that in the new China marriage is the free choice of the couple concerned. Is this true? Do parents have any legal right to enforce a match arranged by them perhaps years ago?

To this the editor gives a stock reply: The new China wishes to destroy all class differences and social discriminations, and recognizes that marriage is a personal matter. Parents have no legal right to enforce their will. Explain this to them gently and

try to gain their approval. If this does not succeed, you are free
to do as you like.

The persistence of this theme indicates the widespread strength
of the old morality despite the efforts of men like Hu Shih to
destroy it twenty-five years ago. It gives point to the heavy Communist stress on equal rights for women, exemplified, for example,
by the great amount of publicity being given to the current session
here of the All-China Federation of Women.

Foreign Criticism

Foreign teachers at Tsinghua and Yenching now have passes allowing them to come into the city. These, however, do not permit
excursions to the Summer Palace, Jade Fountain, or other beauty
spots in the Western Hills.

Suspicion of foreigners seems to be growing, and annoying
incidents have been reported. Our British friends, the Victors, for
example, when visiting the P'an T'ao Kung yesterday, were
stopped at the temple gate by soldiers who interrogated them,
discovered that they were Tientsin residents, that their traveling
pass had expired (owing to failure of the authorities to issue a new
one in time), and straightway marched them off under armed
guard to successive police stations in different parts of the city.
It was not until five hours later that they were finally released,
with the promise, however, that the delayed pass would be issued
promptly.

Such incidents embitter many foreigners. They comment sarcastically that the Communists suffer from a "peasant mentality,"
that their new export-import regulations cannot possibly work,
that their economic position is bad and getting worse, and so forth.
Most are unable to see what goes on from any but a personal point
of view. Roberts, of Yenching, is one of the very few able to realize
that, regardless of how right the foreigners may be in certain
criticisms, the thing that really counts in China, after all, is what
happens to the Chinese, and not to a handful of outsiders.

Politics as a Religion

Developments here can be better understood, I think, if viewed in terms of a religion—a militant, dogmatic, idealistic, in some ways puritanical religion, in which the devotee, like the mystic of other religions, seeks to identify himself with the universal whole, thereby gaining spiritual release and psychological tranquillity. This no doubt sounds trite, but as I look around I cannot help being impressed by its validity. Here are some of the semi-religious elements in the New Democracy that seem significant:

(1)   The struggle between God and the Devil, good and evil. The New Democracy is always "democratic" and "progressive"; the forces of evil it opposes are always "feudalistic." Evil is primarily typified by the Kuomintang (always "bogus" or "reactionary") and the United States (always "imperialistic"). These and similar terms are applied with a blanket inclusiveness that permits no shading between black and white. Good is always good, evil always evil, and in the struggle between the two the good inevitably triumphs.

(2)   Sense of a divine mission. The Chinese Communist Party is the divine instrument of the Chinese revolution. It is notable that though official statements pay due tribute to "the people" as creators of the new China, they stress even more that they can do this successfully only "under the guidance" of the (omniscient) Communist Party or "under the leadership" of Mao Tse-tung. This concept accords well with traditional Chinese theories of government.

(3)   Dedication of the self to the cause. This is well exemplified by the oath taken by the Tsinghua students joining the New Democracy Youth Corps.

(4)   Faith rather than reason. The teachings of the New Democracy are repeatedly stated to be both "cultural" and "scientific"— scientific in the sense, apparently, that they have achieved the validity of scientifically determined laws of nature and, as such, may be expounded and commented on but are not to be seriously questioned. This, perhaps, is why "anti-empiricism," as we have seen, is one of the subjects of instruction at the North China University. Use of the term apparently means that the spirit of

scientific inquiry, and with it of individualism (now a word in disrepute), emphasized in Europe since the Renaissance, is to be discouraged.

(5) Sense of guilt. The reform of society must go hand in hand with individual reform, which must start with a readiness on the part of the individual to accept public criticism and openly confess his faults. I have earlier commented on the resemblance of the Communist technique of public confession to that of the revivalist meeting. This technique is important. Only a few days after writing that entry, a single issue of the *Progressive Daily* carried across its front page no less than three stories describing confession meetings that had been held among the workers of the Tientsin Electric Co., the porters at the Tientsin East Station, and another group, which I do not now remember. This concept of a sense of guilt is something comparatively rare in Chinese history.

(6) Puritanism. Idealism and the desire to be of public service lead to stress on personal honesty and incorruptibility. Superstition, frivolity, and looseness in sex relations are frowned upon. Chinese cheerfulness and sense of fun, however, prevent this tendency from going to the extreme of condemning pleasure simply because it is pleasure. On the contrary, the Communists like fun like anyone else, but it must be of a simple, wholesome character.

(7) Spartan simplicity. This, closely related to puritanism, leads to the willing acceptance of hardship and avoidance of luxury. It is exemplified in the curriculum of the students at the North China University. It is interesting to note in this connection that Peking's Communist mayor reportedly receives a salary less than that of the non-Communist professors in the government universities.

(8) Cult of the common man. The long-exploited *lao pai hsing* have become the heroes of the new China. Their unsophisticated arts are emphasized, so that the peasant "planting songs" hold a prominent place in the new drama. A story told by Dick is characteristic: Some weeks ago Tsinghua students produced a propaganda play to which farmers of the neighborhood were invited. On their arrival, these farmers elbowed the university people aside to get the best seats, hawked and spat loudly during the per-

formance, and generally betrayed the fact that they were unused to such surroundings. The wife of one Tsinghua professor (not a one hundred per cent supporter of the new order) afterward remarked rather bitterly to Dick, "It would have been common decency for some of the students to have told these farmers not to spit in a public auditorium. But I wouldn't have dared suggest such a thing to any students I know. If I had, they would have accused me of being counterrevolutionary."

(9) Deification of the leader. Mao Tse-tung's portrait appears far more frequently than that of anyone else, and his name and statements are always mentioned with respect. (I am sure he himself cares nothing about this.) The Communists, however, still have far to go before they achieve for him the apotheosis reached by Sun Yat-sen in Kuomintang China. (The latter, incidentally, is rarely mentioned these days. Apparently the Communists now prefer to concentrate upon their New Democracy, though a few years ago, when less secure, they played themselves up as the legitimate perpetuators of Sun and his ideas.)

(10) Exclusiveness of the "we" group. The Chinese people, "under the guidance of the Communist party," must struggle to create their own new China. Nonbelieving outsiders (foreigners) are *ipso facto* open to suspicion. This attitude, which is nothing new in Chinese history, is now being consciously reinforced through official propaganda. Judging from my daily contacts with ordinary people, its effects among them to date have been nil, though no doubt it is influencing the thinking of intellectuals to some extent.

Can a movement compounded of such elements succeed in China? Many people say no, arguing that too many are alien to Chinese temperament and tradition. They might add that several were shared by the Kuomintang in its heyday (as by many other revolutionary groups). My own opinion, however, would be otherwise. The present movement has sent its roots down into China's masses in a way the Kuomintang never was able to. Its methods are more efficient, its aims more far-reaching, its program more constructive, and its benefits more readily apparent to larger numbers of people. Moreover, it comes to power at a time when China's social and economic disintegration is much further advanced, and people therefore psychologically ready to turn to radical solutions which they would otherwise shun. History shows that in the past, during periods of stress, the Chinese have been ready to embrace ideas which, in normal times, they would have rejected as "un-Chinese."

One such period was that of the Warring States (fifth to third centuries B.C.), when the reformer Mo Tzu and his followers tried to solve the political and social crisis of their day through methods that seemed dangerously radical to their contemporaries. They organized a highly disciplined politico-philosophical group, the members of which were ready to die, if need be, at the command of their leader. They preached "universal love." They were authoritarian, dogmatic, ascetic, and puritanical, and attacked the art and rituals of the aristocratically-minded Confucians from a utilitarian and "common man" point of view.

Another such period was that of the civil wars and barbarian invasions from the third to the fifth centuries A.D., when people shunned the responsibilities of society by seeking refuge in the new Buddhist church, some chopping off fingers or even burning themselves alive in their eager fervor to gain salvation.

Both movements died, but the real reason, I think, is that neither of them ever really changed the fundamental political and economic fabric of Chinese society—Mo Tzu and his followers, because they never gained the necessary political power from the ruling class; the Buddhists, because they were never really interested in so doing. Today, however, the situation is different. The Communists possess both a dynamic ideology and the political power to make it effective. Soviet Russia proves, if proof is needed, that changes can be made in human nature, provided they coincide with changes in the human environment. Equally startling changes, I have no doubt, will take place in China, even though the obstacles are in many ways more formidable.

April 5 (Tuesday)

Confession and Criticism

The latest convert to the "confession" technique is Fu Tso-yi. On April 1 he broke his silence to issue a lengthy statement. In it he blamed himself for having exploited the people and disregarded their wishes, praised the Communists for their success in winning popular support, and closed with an appeal to all true patriots in the Kuomintang to profit by his mistakes and work for real peace on the basis of Mao's eight points. The statement was nicely timed to coincide with the arrival of the peace delegation from Nanking. Incidentally, the papers have not mentioned the delegation since that time.

More interesting is the speech made on April 2 by President Lu Chih-wei of Yenching to his students.

"Today," he said, "there is the greatest opportunity for China's intellectuals to be active. It is the time of greatest hope for China. In all past history China has never had a more noncorrupt government, or one with such concern for the people. This is our people's government, and as such we should offer it our criticisms in a spirit of complete sincerity, rather than merely sing its praises. But at the same time we should recognize the problems confronting it and so should not purposefully make difficulties for it."

All honor to the man who dares to speak with such courage and honesty.

April 18 (Monday)

We Move House

As I write these words, petals flutter down into our courtyard from the pear tree that raises itself above our neighbor's wall. What I see from my window is no longer our little garden at Fang

Chia Yuan, for on the fourteenth we moved to a new home. Perhaps it was a crazy thing to do after having stuck it out so long with our Shansi students, and with only four remaining months in China. But when we learned several weeks ago that this house was vacant, we simply couldn't resist it.

For one thing, it is far nearer than the old one to the center of the city: only a stone's throw from the Tung An market on Morrison Street, and within a few minutes' walk of the Forbidden City. But the house itself breathes the spirit of poetry and preserves, more than almost anything we have seen, the charm of old-time Peking. Unlike most houses, its entrance is from the north, not the south. From there one passes down a long garden walk running north to south, which gives access to the various courts and buildings on the right. As one walks south, one successively passes the kitchen and servants' quarters; an arbor-covered courtyard with a fine wistaria; a building containing the large guest hall and the dining room; then another courtyard, entered from the walk by a moon gate; then yet another building, containing a bedroom and bathroom. All these buildings are connected by an enclosed corridor running parallel to the garden walk on the opposite side of the compound.

Finally, at the extreme south, one reaches the most beautiful spot of all: a third larger courtyard, which is where we spend most of our time. A "rock mountain" stands in one corner, with water trickling through its stones into an artificial pool below, while adjoining it grows a small bamboo thicket. From behind the red-painted wall which bounds the garden's southern extremity rises the pear tree I have described. On the west side of the court stands a detached building containing Theo's bedroom and my study, while on the opposite side there is another building, housing a storeroom and the landlord's office (which, however, he almost never uses).

At first we felt lost in all this spaciousness; it seemed miles for us to walk when we had to get anything from another part of the house. Never would we have dreamed of occupying such a place in winter, when the cost of heating would have been impossible. For our remaining summer months, however, the house is ideal. Its rooms are lavishly furnished down to the last cup and saucer, including even an electric refrigerator—all belonging to an American *taipan,* or business "big shot," now no longer in Peking.

An impressive tiger skin which covers the floor of my study attracted much favorable comment from the movers, since the tiger is a potent protective power in Chinese folklore. It is exceedingly lifelike, too, as I discovered this morning on entering the study, when I was greatly startled by seeing the tiger suddenly crawling toward me. Its motive power turned out to be Theo, who had almost smothered himself beneath the skin while awaiting my arrival. Another object of special interest is in the bathroom— an electric reducing machine, probably the only one in Peking. It was, no doubt, formerly used by the American *taipan's* wife, reported to have been on the stocky side.

For all this magnificence we pay US $40 a month, and it is a commentary on present conditions in Peking that few foreigners and fewer Chinese now remain who can afford to pay such a sum. A year ago, before the exodus of Americans, the house was rented for $150 a month by the North China E.C.A. Director. We ourselves, in order to occupy it, have been obliged to augment our staff of cook, boy, and *amah* by taking on an old gateman-gardener who comes with the house, and for whom we have to pay an additional $12 monthly.

When Mr. Chen, our former landlord, learned of our plans, he acted in a most unlandlord-like manner. At first he suggested lowering our $30 rent, but on learning that this was not the reason for our move, he magnanimously arranged to hire movers for us through his company for less than we ourselves could have done. We are sincerely grateful for his constant thoughtfulness and wish him much luck in his chemical enterprise.

Just as the loading of our goods was in process, Galia's teacher, Mr. Ma, arrived in a state of great excitement and urged us to go at once to see the soldiers who were leaving Peking that same day on their way south to the war. He described their seemingly endless columns, all equipped with new uniforms and shoes, and the tremendous send-off they were being given by the crowd. Never before have we seen our old Chinese friend so moved and enthusiastic.

It was impossible to go at the moment, but as soon as our things had been loaded, Galia rode off in the pedicab to the new house, and sure enough, as she reached Morrison Street, met columns of soldiers still marching. The leaders carried red silk banners inscribed with slogans in gold characters—the presents of labor, student, and other groups. Apparently the spectacle was almost over, for most watchers had already gone. Each soldier had a pack of extra shoes and clothing on his back, and each wore a brand-new olive drab uniform. As Galia watched them march, she was keenly conscious of how much work and planning all this equipment represented—much of it produced at great speed during the past several months in countless little tailor shops—and what tremendous tasks and dangers lay ahead. At that moment our own activities suddenly seemed small and unimportant.

Foreign Currency

On April 7 the authorities finally proclaimed their foreign-currency regulations. All such currency must be deposited in the Bank of China within one month, after which transactions in it become illegal. Depositors of foreign currency, however, will be allowed to draw upon it in local currency at the official exchange rate then current. Persons leaving the country will be allowed to take with them as much foreign currency as they have on deposit in the bank at the time.

Coincident with this announcement, the authorities doubled the exchange value of the American dollar from US$1:PN$300 to the more realistic rate of US$1:PN$600. This sensible move, aimed at killing the black market, has so far only had the effect of forcing the black-market rate up from the lower 600's, where it had been for some time, to the 700's, and then to about 750, where it stands today. As long as inflation continues, it is difficult to see how the black market can really be stamped out.

Land Reform

Here are some of the terms that appear frequently in discussions on the land program, as defined in the April 13 issue of *Peiping Digest:*

A rich farmer is one whose "exploitation income" (income derived through hiring the labor of others) is more than 25 per cent of his total income (or 50 per cent of his net income). Such farmers are of two types: (1) "old-style"—those who regularly derive more than 25 per cent of their total income from "exploiting hired laborers in a semi-feudal mode, or from other feudal types of exploitation (such as usury and hiring out land)"; (2) "new-style"—those who do the same "in the capitalistic mode or from capitalistic types of exploitation." In other words, the "new-style" farmers' exploitation methods are supposed to leave a margin of decent living for the persons they "exploit."

A well-off medium farmer is one whose exploitation income is less than 25 per cent of his total income.

Under the program, rich farmers are allowed to own only as much land as the average medium farmer in their district; all land above this amount is subject to redistribution.

Such is the theory. As pointed out, however, in an editorial answer to a letter in the *Progressive Daily* of April 15, the land program as actually practiced does not necessarily aim at absolute equality. "It is permissible for the land retained by some of the medium farmers to be slightly more than that assigned to the generality of the poor farmers"—meaning, I suppose, that if the holdings of a medium farmer prior to land reform are only slightly above the average individual holdings, they are to be left undisturbed. Moreover, "in the case of industrial or commercial enterprises belonging to a landlord or rich farmer, these need not be divided. This is because these enterprises are beneficial to the economy of present-day society." In other words, the Communists are willing to allow certain compromises if by so doing they can maintain a high rate of production.

More Rumors

Rumormongering is still widespread, as shown by four letters in yesterday's *Progressive Daily*. The first is a variant of the rumor circulating a month ago: "It is widely reported from the outside that every unmarried male is to be given a wife. . . . What is to be done if one has an unmarried girl in one's family?" The other three all express uneasiness over the rumor that the authorities intend to tax or fine all individuals who worship Buddhist images in their homes. The editor's reply:

"The burning of incense in worship to Buddhist figures is a feudalistic, superstitious custom. In the post-liberation period, as the cultural education and awakening of the masses reaches a higher level, such surviving customs will, in the course of time, gradually disappear as the result of self-realization by the masses." However, he continues, this is purely a matter for education, and all rumors of forced suppression by the authorities are completely unfounded.

Quick Justice

Our German friend, Professor Muller, has told me an interesting story of the workings of justice in the new China. When I saw him a few nights ago, he had just returned from a three-day visit to Tientsin, where he had gone in connection with a law suit—having waited a month to obtain a travel permit. The suit had been brought by him against a well-to-do Chinese to force payment of interest and principal on a property mortgage which Muller holds in that city. On arrival, a session in the People's Court was arranged by his lawyer for the very next morning—itself a remarkable achievement.

In the courtroom, the judge solicitously asked Muller whether he knew enough Chinese to understand the proceedings without an interpreter. Muller said he did and then produced papers to show the amount owed by the defendant. The judge turned to the latter and asked a single question: "Have you paid or not?" "No," replied the defendant. "Then pay," said the judge, and, when the defendant tried to argue further, "Case closed! Keep quiet!" The whole session was over in fifteen minutes.

The method of payment is interesting. Following the session, Muller went to a Tientsin newspaper, where by consulting back files he determined the prevailing price of millet at the time that payment had been due. Comparing this with its present price, it was easy to calculate the corresponding value in today's currency. The resulting figure, when he presented it to the judge at the afternoon session, was readily accepted. At first the defendant pleaded for an eight-month period in which to pay, but on protest from Muller, this was changed to three successive monthly payments. All details were settled within half an hour. Thus in one day's time a lawsuit was disposed of which in the old days might have dragged on interminably. The case is particularly interesting because it involved a foreign plaintiff against a Chinese defendant.

April 19 (Tuesday)

Unequal Treaties

I was wrong when I recently said that readers of the *Progressive Daily* rarely write to the editor on political topics. Most of today's letter section is devoted to an editorial discussion of whether or not the Soviet Union is imperialist, and whether or not the Sino-Soviet Friendship Treaty of August, 1945 (giving the U.S.S.R. partnership in the Chinese Eastern Railroad and a military base at Port Arthur) is "unequal." This effusion is prompted by "many letters recently received from readers" on the subject, whose skepticism "is obviously the result of lengthy exposure to the deceptive propaganda of the Kuomintang" (the government which signed the treaty!). Here is an outline of the rebuttal:

The Soviet Union is the bastion of world peace. It is the first example in history of a classless society. It has always fought for the freedom of colonial peoples, and has made possible the victory over German, Italian, and Japanese fascism. Today it heads the struggle against American imperialism. With regard to China, it was the first nation to declare its readiness to renounce all unequal treaties, and it has always helped the Chinese people in their struggle for freedom, more especially by defeating Japan in Manchuria in 1945. Since imperialism is a characteristic of capitalism in its final stages, to say that the U.S.S.R. is imperialistic is "evil slander and shameless propaganda.".

As for the Sino-Soviet treaty, it obviously cannot be unequal since (1) it provided for a Russian attack on Japan in Manchuria in conjunction with the Chinese army, (2) stipulated that neither country was to sign a separate peace, and (3) was designed to prevent the future resurgence of Japanese aggression. Today it remains doubly important in view of the American rearming of Japan and the "selling-the-country" treaties that have been entered into by the Kuomintang. We should look at such matters from the point of view of what constitutes the greatest long-range benefit for the Chinese people rather than in terms of an abstract "national" benefit divorced from the actual benefit of the people.

Can such a reply, one wonders, really satisfy those readers who know the specific provision of this treaty (carefully unmentioned throughout the article)? If so, they must share the apparent conviction of the editors that a treaty is unequal only when made with a country we dislike, and becomes "equal" as soon as that country happens to share our political philosophy. Aside from this, the article is of interest as showing that some people, at least, question the Communist decision (publicly announced, I have been told) to exempt the Sino-Soviet Treaty from the scrap pile to which the other Kuomintang treaties are to be relegated.

Views of a Chinese Liberal

Today I had a talk with Fu, a young and politically-minded Peita professor formerly connected with the now defunct liberal *China Reconstruction*. "How do you like our bloodless revolution?" he began. "Much better than the French and Russian revolutions, eh?"

I agreed, but then went on to remark that its most distasteful features, from a foreign point of view, were the control and distortion of news, and absence of publicly expressed divergence of opinion. "What do you propose to write about if you get *China Reconstruction* going again?" I asked.

"Oh, probably such things as industry and economic reconstruction."

"Fine, but what about politics?"

"We shall treat this differently from before." Then he went on, "At first I was as impatient about these things as you are. But now I have come to see them in a different light. . . ."

He went on to say that everyone expected the peace agreement to be signed within a day. (On April 15 the Nanking peace delegation was presented with a proposed peace treaty—terms as yet undisclosed—and an ultimatum to sign it by the twentieth. I myself am dubious of its signing, or, if so, how effective it will be.) Then there would speedily be peace in China. A consultative conference would be held in July by the latest, at which a coalition government would be established. The emergency military restrictions would be relaxed and a new intellectual climate emerge. At the moment, however, restrictions were necessary because a state of war still existed and reactionary elements remained active.

"And what about foreign policy? What about the treatment of foreign correspondents?" I asked.

"I am sorry for my personal friends," he replied.

I interjected that the issue was much broader than one of personal friends.

"But this again," he continued, "is part of the military emergency. Once China has been unified, a new government set up, and diplomatic relations established with the foreign powers, all will change. The United States has helped and is continuing to help the Kuomintang. Therefore it is natural it should be regarded with suspicion and dislike. Even so, foreigners have been given protection and freedom."

"Not quite freedom," I interrupted. "I should like to go to Tsinghua, but cannot do so."

"Moreover," Fu went on, "communist anti-foreignism is the result of the humiliation and oppression suffered by China for the past century. The Communists are out to show their people that they are masters of their own house and that no foreigner can lord it here any more. Such domestic psychological considerations count more for them at the moment than the question of future foreign relations. Besides, the Communists are practical people. They talk big, but when the time comes for concrete negotiations, they will modify their tone. The situation is like that of their demand for war criminals: at first they make sweeping demands, but in the final bargaining they will pardon most people who repent and come over to their side."

"What about foreign trade?" I asked. "Do the Communists think China can be economically rehabilitated without foreign, particularly American, aid? And do they think foreign businessmen will be willing to continue operations here when they are told that trade must be done on a barter basis—when, for example, they are told that in order to export a load of pig bristles they must import a load of Westinghouse machinery?"

"Until now," he replied, "the Communists have made their own way, in spite of American aid to the other side. They feel that for a while, at least, they can continue to get along by themselves. At the moment, therefore, they are not particularly interested in foreign trade or help. But when the time comes, they will be ready to offer more favorable conditions, and then the Americans and others will be eager enough to do business, even on Communist terms, simply because their livelihood depends on it. Even now, in fact, there are foreign businessmen who are eager to come here and develop trade."

I tried to tell my friend that things are not as simple as he supposes. How soon peace returns to China still remains problematical. Patterns of thought control are extremely difficult to throw off once they have been established. In order to have future diplomatic recognition, it is important that the story of what is happening in Communist China be made known to the outside world *now* and not later, and from this side of China rather than via Kuomintang China. The present Communist policy of indiscriminate vituperation and falsification strengthens those elements most antagonistic to them in America, where opinion regarding China is very divided. When the time comes for trade and diplomatic relations, the Communists will find a settlement far harder than they now suppose in their present flush of success, and so forth.

I don't know what impression these arguments made on Fu. His own point of view is, I believe, representative of a great many non-Communist Chinese liberals these days, who, being in general enthusiastic about the new regime, try to find rationalizations for those particular aspects of it which do not coincide with their former liberal beliefs.

April 22 (Friday)

War

As I suspected would be the case, Nanking has rejected the Communist peace terms. Yesterday afternoon the news spread rapidly via an extra issued by the *People's Daily,* and the faces of those reading it were grave. Most had apparently hoped for better things. When, a week ago, long lines of soldiers left the city for the "southern expedition," many people believed it would be unnecessary militarily speaking. Today, as I write these lines, a long, undulating wail rises from the Japanese-installed air raid siren on Coal Hill. It is only a practice signal, but it brings home the fact that the war has started again in the south. Mao and Chu have ordered an all-out offensive against Chiang's remaining "bandit forces," and a crossing of the Yangtze is already said to be in progress on a wide front.

Nanking's rejection of the peace terms hardly comes as a surprise. The terms, first published in the papers today, follow Mao's eight points fairly closely. The preamble, written in pretty strong language, indicts the Kuomintang for its crimes. Then follow demands for: surrender of war criminals—with lenience promised to those who concretely show their repentance; revocation of the constitution and all Kuomintang laws; reorganization of the Kuomintang armies; handing over of bureaucratic capital and Kuomintang governmental organizations; and reformation of the feudalistic land system. Nanking's rejection shows that, contrary to all indications, it had hoped to the last that Mao's eight points were mere bargaining terms, to be whittled down through negotiation.

A Communist Compromise

Since the beginning of the week it has been possible to send letters directly abroad without the help of some friendly intermediary in Shanghai. This pleasant development has been made possible by a Communist compromise: the Communist stamps, bearing Mao Tse-tung's portrait, have been replaced by the old internationally recognized Sun Yat-sen stamps of Kuomintang days. These are overprinted, however, with characters reading "People's Postage." We devoutly hope the mails will continue despite the fighting.

Views of an American

A few days ago I reported the views of a Chinese liberal. Last night I heard those of a prominent Peking American, who must remain anonymous. His specific topic was Manchuria, which he knows well, but in the course of his talk he touched on many general problems. His pessimism, while characteristic of many Americans these days, has a more factual basis than most.

Manchuria, he says, long the great hope of China, is today industrially and commercially dead. Prices are low, but there is no money with which to buy. Industrial deterioration during the war, Soviet lootings and removals in 1945, mismanagement by Kuomintang carpet-baggers, and fierce civil war, in the course of which the Communists repeatedly applied scorched-earth tactics on an unnecessary scale (blowing up all spans of railroad bridges, for example, when a single one would have done the trick)—all these factors have reduced Manchuria's industrial production to perhaps only ten per cent of what it was as recently as 1945. In fact, it may be no higher than before the Japanese came in 1931 —possibly no higher than as long ago as 1919.

To restore this industry will require billions of American dollars, plus skilled personnel which not only the Communists but even the Nationalists lack. One of the greatest losses in Manchuria, aside from physical destruction, was the postwar repatriation of all the Japanese technicians who had been there. Where are the

Communists going to get the money and personnel to achieve their economic rehabilitation? Not from Russia, judging from her own needs and past policy toward satellites, and certainly not from America under present conditions.

But in China proper the situation is equally gloomy. The Communists inherit a bankrupt economy and worthless currency. Food crops threaten to be bad this year owing to drought. Demands made on the farmers are heavy. Business is dead. There is growing discontent. Nevertheless the Communists are now advancing into a food deficiency area (Shanghai, Nanking, etc.), kept from starving during the past year only by a source (E.C.A.) that will shortly be no more. They would have been better advised to have waited a year or two in North China to consolidate their power. The prospect today looks bleak. How will it be a year from now?

I respect my friend's opinion, much of which may well be factually justified. Yet there are certain factors, especially psychological, which I believe he, like many Americans, tends to overlook. In the first place, I suspect the Communists realize as keenly as anyone the dangers that face them in the south. Yet a revolution is not something that can be called off and on at will. Once started, there are inherent psychological forces that impel it forward, unless counterbalanced by still greater external forces. Who knows what might happen if the Communists now delayed their advance? Fear of increased American aid, if they paused too long, is probably as compelling a factor as any.

In the second place, I notice that Americans, even those long resident abroad, often tend to evaluate situations too much in terms of American standards. For them a railroad is not a railroad unless it permits trains to run at fifty or sixty miles an hour. But the Communists will probably be satisfied if through makeshift arrangements they can restore their train service to meet half that speed.

In the third place, Manchuria's industrial development was designed by Japanese to complement a complex Japanese economy at home. Such a high industrialization, while useful, is not essential for China's present needs. Why, for example, have steel mills geared to produce five million tons of steel yearly if the country's factories are capable of absorbing only half that amount?

In the fourth place, Russia's attitude toward her new Communist neighbor is still uncertain. Her policy toward such areas as Sinkiang and Outer Mongolia, at a time when these were within the orbit of an archaic and often disunited country, was one thing; the policy she will now adopt toward a new, dynamic, and friendly country may be quite another thing.

Finally, and most important, though most commonly overlooked by "realistic" observers, is the question of spirit. It is impossible to suppose that the Communists could have achieved their already extraordinary success without very considerable active popular support, or at least acquiescence. Predictions of growing discontent sound too much like the similar predictions periodically made about Russia. Spirit alone cannot accomplish miracles, but it sometimes achieves results which almost seem like such, especially in countries like China where the material substitutes for spirit have traditionally been in short supply. I have noticed the speed with which the Communists, despite their reputed shortage of technicians, have restored the railroads in newly occupied territories. I also remember the dire warnings made when the lights went on again in Peking, much brighter than before, shortly after the Communists entered the city. "The generators are on their last legs," said the pessimists. "The Communists are forcing them for political effect. But wait and see. One of these days the machinery will break down completely, and that will be the end of it." So far this has not happened.* Nor can I easily forget the spectacle of the soldiers replacing the fallen incense burners in the Pei Hai. All this is not to deny that the cost in human life and suffering may be staggering judged in terms of an economically more advanced society.

*When we left Peking late in August, it still had not happened.

April 24 (Sunday)

End of a Dynasty

Nanking was entered this morning! The Yangtze has been crossed on a several-hundred-mile front, and resistance is said to have virtually ceased from Hankow on down the river. Meanwhile, far to the north, the Communists have broken through the walls of long-besieged Taiyuan, where street fighting is in progress. One after another the big cities of the south fall to the ground like rotten apples. The Chiang-Soong dynasty has reached its end, even though its rulers may find temporary haven in Formosa.

It is now 9 P.M. and I have just returned from watching a series of impromptu victory parades on the strets—flaring torches, gongs, drums, a brass band, marching soldiers, cavorting students, songs, cheers, shouts of "Take Chiang Kai-shek alive!" and "On to Formosa!" Usually the streets are almost deserted by this early hour, but tonight the parading groups speedily attracted thousands of spectators, many of whom ran alongside and shouted and cheered as loudly as the marchers. In the Tung An market I saw a solitary shop girl prancing up and down behind her stall in the *yang ko* dance. All this is the most impressive example of spontaneous joy and enthusiasm I have yet seen in China. Even the victory parade after the taking of Peking, though far more grandiose, evoked nothing like it.

According to the radio, the troops defending Nanking pulled out well before the entry of the occupiers, leaving the city a prey to widespread looting. The big shots flew by plane for Shanghai, Canton, and other places of refuge. Some planes, it is reported, were piled high with household belongings, sometimes even including pianos.

Of special interest to foreigners is the shooting affray on the Yangtze between British warships and Communist shore batteries, in which at least one ship, H.M.S. *Amethyst,* ran aground. Though already several days old, the affair is reported in the

local press today for the first time. The Communists accuse the
British of having fired first and say they will hold them strictly
accountable. Fitzhugh, a self-announced English Conservative,
told me quite frankly that even if the Communist version is not
wholly correct, he believes the British were at fault. For, he says,
since it is obvious that a war is in progress, they should have informed not only the Nationalists, but the Communists as well, of
their intention to sail upriver.

April 29 (Friday)

The White-haired Girl

Yesterday I attended a performance of the most famous of the
new plays, *The White-haired Girl*, beautifully produced and ex-
pertly acted by the Artist Workers Group of the (Communist)
North China University. This semi-operatic drama is an elaborate production, written by four persons and requiring a cast of
twenty and an orchestra of twelve. Seeing it was an exciting and
memorable experience, despite its length of four hours and the
fact that, as all tickets were unreserved, I had to come more than
an hour early to insure getting a seat.

The plot, laid in a small farming village near the mountains
of northwestern Hopei between 1935 and 1939, is said to be
based on actual fact. Its theme is the struggle of the farmers
against landlord oppression, and their final liberation. Happy
One, the seventeen-year-old daughter of a widowed farmer, is sold
by her father, under compulsion, into the service of the landlord
as payment for debt. The father then commits suicide. In the
landlord's family, Happy One, after constant abuse, is raped and
made pregnant by the landlord. Seven months later her master,
having decided to marry someone else, plans to sell her into a
brothel. Her attempted suicide is prevented by another servant,
who helps her to escape. From that day onward her one aim is to
gain revenge for herself and her father. She finds refuge in a

mountain cave, where she gives birth to her child and maintains
a precarious existence during the next several years by making
nightly forays to steal the offerings from a lonely mountain temple. Diet deficiency, coupled with the fact that she never sees the
light of day, causes her hair to turn white, so that to the people
of the locality who occasionally glimpse her she becomes known
as the "white-haired immortal fairy." Then comes the Sino-
Japanese War and the landlord turns into a Japanese puppet official. But the Eighth Route Army guerrillas arrive at the village,
and with them Happy One's farmer lover. The guerrillas organize the farmers, and the lover rescues Happy One and her
child from the mountain cave. The last scene is the public trial of
the landlord by the enraged farmers—an enactment of what has
actually happened innumerable times in rural China during the
past few years. Happy One appears at the trial to give her testimony, and, as the curtain falls, the trussed-up landlord and his
emissary are dragged away to their execution.

Technically, the play is a highly successful blending of new
and traditional elements. The realistic settings of the farmer's
hovel, the landlord's mansion, the mountain temple, the cave,
and the threshing enclosure where the trial takes place, are new
and aroused great enthusiasm from the audience. So are the stage
effects of snow, wind, thunder, lightning, and sunrise. The shift-
ing of scenes is rapid and skillful, with action continuing in front
of the curtain during changes of sets, so that the entire four
hours of the play are broken by only one intermission. Traditional, however, is the concept of a fourth invisible front wall
separating the audience from the interiors shown on the stage.
The actors, as they come and go, constantly open and close the
unseen doors which lead through this wall and step high to avoid
the unseen threshholds.

The music, which is charming and often poignant, is neither
Western nor does it include any of the falsetto singing of the
traditional Chinese opera. Much of it is based on Chinese folk
music. As in Chinese opera, certain motifs are associated with
certain characters. The orchestra is a combination of Western
string instruments (violin, cello, and contrabass) with the native
erh hu (Chinese type of violin), flute, drum, gong, and wooden

clapper. In some themes the Western instruments predominate; in others, the Chinese. The result is remarkably successful and constitutes a new musical genre. Most reminiscent of the old-time drama is the use of drum, gong, and clapper to punctuate and accentuate the movements of the actors. This technique is highly effective when, for example, the percussion instruments burst into a crescendo of fury during a pursuit or a scene of violence. As a result, this play, despite the realism of its plot, resembles—as does the old-time drama—a stylized ballet. Even when the actors are not singing, they frequently move about the stage with the rhythmic steps and gestures seen on the traditional stage.

Ideologically speaking, there is nothing subtle about this drama. Mood is suggested by certain obvious stage tricks. The bleakness of the farmer's home, for example, is heightened by the raging snow storm which we see without; the joy and hope of Happy One as she is rescued from the cave by her lover, by the crowing of a cock and flooding of the cave entrance with rosy light—symbol of the dawning of China's New Day. The characters remain types rather than fully rounded individuals. Happy One's old, bent father is the symbol of the passive despair of China's peasants under millennia of oppression. The sly landlord is a monster of heartless cruelty, meanness, and corruption. Happy One herself symbolizes the will to live and gain revenge. The Eighth Route guerrillas typify the purposeful, organized, idealistic activity which can bring to the old China new life and hope.

This is not to say that the actors do not do their work well. They act magnificently, but according to the directions of the script. As a matter of fact, the stylization is less jarring than one might suppose, because the opera-ballet technique of the play permits certain conventionalities and exaggerations that would be out of place in a more realistic portrayal. Even so, as I watched the sobbing heroine being dragged away from her father's corpse to serve the landlord, I could not help wondering: Is this artistically true to life? Granted that such scenes do happen in China and that there are thousands of landlords whose underlying motives, in the final analysis, are as heartless as this one's, would it be typical of many to act with such complete disregard for at least the external appearances of decency? These thoughts prevented me from full satisfaction at the triumph of good over evil in the final trial scene. On the contrary, its mob violence unpleasantly suggested the Communes of the French revolution, and this despite the fact that the scene has been toned down for urban audiences: in its original version it showed the farmers mobbing and killing the landlord; in the revised play, the curtain falls as he is being led to execution.*

It is obvious, however, that no such considerations disturbed the minds of the audience (among whom I was probably the only foreigner). Emotionally, they were completely one with the play and, during tense moments, roared their disapproval of the landlord, shouted advice to the heroine, and cheered the arrival of the Eighth Route Army. "Let her get him!" shouted my neighbor—a mild-looking youth two seats away, who before the play had been reading a pamphlet entitled *The Chinese Revolution and Chinese Communist Party*—during one exciting episode in which the heroine is restrained by her comrade from attacking the landlord.

The behavior of the spectators, in fact, was in some ways almost as interesting as the play itself. They filled every seat and overflowed into the aisles. During the hour or so of waiting before the play began, some groups passed the time by singing the new revolutionary songs at the top of their voices. True, the audience was predominantly youthful and contained many students and soldiers; yet there were many older people. The man to my right, for example, was an oldish worker—apparently illiterate, judging from the fact that he barely glanced at the program I gave him. A good part of the row in front of me was occupied by a respectable old gentleman, his wife, and their several grown-up daughters, complete with teapot and melon seeds. The theater is a good-sized one (seating perhaps 2,000), and the play has been running for over a month—an exceptionally long time for Peking. Though slated to close tomorrow, it could easily run for

---

* Since returning to America and reading the many case histories of landlord conduct narrated in Jack Belden's *China Shakes the World* (Harper, New York, 1949), I am less certain than I was that this criticism is justified.

an additional month, judging from the capacity houses. The whole experience of seeing it, in fact, gave overwhelming proof of the strength of the new ideas in revolutionary China. Let any man beware who glibly assumes that these ideas are the monopoly of but a few visionary fanatics beneath whom lies a sea of "growing discontent."

May 1949

May 10 (Tuesday)

Air Raid

Shanghai remains untaken, while the Communists are swinging around it to the south to occupy Hangchow. Likewise they have left Hankow alone while pushing southward toward Nanchang. Apparently they hope by these tactics to avoid the destruction of industry in these important centers. With the occupation of Taiyuan and two other northern cities, all of North China is in Communist hands with the important exception of Tsingtao, where American personnel has long been stationed. Judging by the silence of the papers, the incident involving the firing on British ships in the Yangtze seems to have frittered away to nothing.

Far though we are from the front, we got our taste of war on May 4, when at seven-thirty in the morning the wail of sirens signaled an impending air raid. As I climbed the roof of the house to get a better view, a strange silence descended upon the city: the sirens died away, the voices of children from the nearby primary school ceased as they marched into the building, and all traffic stopped. Then, far to the south, I heard a faint hum but could catch no sight of planes. It was two hours before the all-clear sounded. At the same time light and water, which had been turned off, were restored. From the brief notice in next day's papers we learned that six Kuomintang planes had bombed the southern airfield, killing seven or eight people, wounding some forty more, and doing unspecified damage.

The next day, at about the same time, the raid was repeated.

No results were revealed. Apparently the chief purpose of these militarily useless tactics was to disrupt the celebration of the thirtieth anniversary of the famous May 4 incident of 1919— when Peking students, demonstrating against the terms of the Versailles Treaty, were fired upon by gendarmes and many killed. At any rate, the parade scheduled for this day was cancelled.

Land, Cooperatives, and Taxes

Prices, especially of grain, have been jumping. The many weeks without rain, coupled with intense, drying winds which have made this spring the windiest and dustiest in my memory, have created serious fear of drought. The authorities do their best to allay anxiety. Newspaper stories describe the digging of wells and development of irrigation in the countryside. Others stress the fact that huge quantities of grain, especially millet, are now being brought here from Manchuria by the North China Trading Corporation. Yet there just doesn't seem to be enough to keep prices down.

Tomorrow is the last day for turning in foreign currency to the Bank of China. After that, its use becomes illegal. In view of the weakness of the local currency, however, most people doubt that the black market can be stamped out. People's notes are pouring from the presses in large numbers these days, judging from the many new bills that are making their appearance.

On the constructive side, the May 8 *Progressive Daily* prints a long report on the growth of Tientsin cooperatives. In April alone consumer cooperatives increased from 35 to 224, and their membership from 68,307 to 356,022. (This in a city whose population is under two million.) During the same month these cooperatives sold 3,495,185 catties of coarse grain (millet, corn, corn flour), and 2,237,872 catties of wheat, at prices 25 per cent below those on the open market. The resulting saving to members amounted to PN$42,977,649. By comparison, the record of producer cooperatives is poor; only seven were established during the month, with a membership of 350. The report admits that their growth has been hampered by poor organization and certain misconceptions—one of them being that they should be exempt from taxes. Meanwhile, here in Peking there are now 71 cooperatives, with a membership of 96,000.

Considering the jaundiced view many businessmen have of these and similar activities, it was refreshing yesterday to hear the opinions of Mr. Ho, a Chinese businessman who, because of his background, might be expected to object as violently as any. The new taxes, he stated quite freely, are in his belief fair and not unduly onerous. By way of contrast he pointed to what used to happen in the old days. During the last three months of the Kuomintang, for example, the Tung Hsing Lou, one of Peking's oldest and most famous restaurants, with a staff of about seventy, paid a tax amounting to only GY$7.30 (less than US$2.00 at the original exchange rate of the gold yuan). For the same period a small adjoining radio shop, employing only three men and lacking official connections, had to pay a tax more than ten times that amount.

In the field of export trade, the May 6 *Progressive Daily* proudly prints Tientsin's customs figures for April. They show uniform increases for wool, dried eggs, soybeans, and other items over the corresponding figures for April of last year. The two most important exports, however, suffered sizable drops: pig bristles, 1,483 boxes, as compared to 2,856 of the year before; hides, 92,664, as compared to 230,803. No import figures are given, but here the drop must be even more marked. One evidence of a growing gasoline shortage is the equipping of all Tsinghua and Yenching buses during the past week or so with wood burners—a throwback to wartime China.

The *Progressive Daily* in its April 25 issue carries a story on land reform in the suburbs of Tientsin. Two instances of what is happening are striking. One is that of 1,273 *mu* of land (about 193 acres) owned by three families. These customarily leased it out to a secondary landlord, who subleased it to a group of tertiary landlords, who in turn subleased it to its actual peasant cultivators. This land has now been confiscated *in toto,* though the story fails to explain how it is to be redistributed. The other instance is that of a wealthy farmer-landlord who, though owning only

13.5 *mu* of land himself, rented yet another 750.5 *mu*. Of this amount, he himself, helped by hired labor, customarily cultivated 48 *mu;* the remainder he subleased to others. Under the new program he has been allowed to retain his own 13.5 *mu* as well as that portion of the rented land which he himself cultivates. All the remaining subleased land has been taken over for redistribution.

Schools and Intellectuals

The salaries of university faculty members have recently been fixed at the following rates (all payable in cash, but calculated in terms of catties of millet in order to safeguard against price fluctuations): presidents, 1300-1500 catties per month; professors and associate professors, 800-1300 catties; lecturers, 400-800 catties. These figures amount roughly to a one-third increase over the salaries of the latter part of 1948. They mean, in the case of a university president, that he may conceivably earn a maximum of about US$75 monthly, though in actual practice I imagine the amount comes to considerably less. In terms of purchasing power, of course, it represents considerably more here than it would in America.

The Tsinghua historian, Wu Han, in a recent speech before the National Youth Congress, offers statistics on the social backgrounds of children now going to school in Hopei province. In central Hopei, 93.2 per cent of the lower-school students come from poor and middle-class farming families. At the normal school in Hsing-t'ai (a town on the Peking-Hankow Railroad line), the percentage of such children is 83. In the middle schools of P'u-yü 89 per cent come from middle-class farming families. Among the 2,469 middle-school students in Shihchiachuang, 62 per cent are the children of poor farmers or hired agricultural workers; 6.3 per cent are those of urban laborers.

I happened to see Miss Hill (an American Fulbright student) recently and asked her if she still retained contact with her group of Peita students. Most of them, she told me, have joined the southern expedition. She still sees one boy, however, who apparently has not been completely won over to the new order. From him she learned of what is being told to university students who want to know why the Russians removed industrial installations from Manchuria in 1945. The official line, it seems, is that this was done to "protect" these installations from imperialist aggression until such time as they might be handed back to a friendly Chinese government.

I also asked her whether she retained contacts with liberal professors at Peita. One, she replied, she saw fairly recently. His views, as she reports them, coincide remarkably closely with those I heard from Professor Fu some weeks ago. As she was leaving the house of her friend, she asked him to visit her on a certain date. At first he pleaded another engagement, then, after an embarrassed pause, added, "I'm afraid I won't be able to visit you in the future. But I'll always be glad to see you here."

The Foreigner in China

There have been some unpleasant incidents here lately. An American military officer, for example, was cut on the face when the window of his car was hit by a stone. Two or three other stonings have also been reported. The police, however, seem to be genuinely anxious that such incidents should not recur.

I myself have never witnessed anything of the kind. All my contacts with Chinese, in fact, have remained uniformly friendly except for those with our former Shansi student refugees. I particularly remember the two Shihta (Normal University) students who were my neighbors at the theater the night I attended *The White-haired Girl.* I think they were pleased that a foreigner would come to see this famous revolutionary play. At any rate they offered me cigarettes, explained various fine points of the play as it went along, and, during its less tense moments, kept up a running fire of comment and question, such as, "Isn't it terrible how great is the poverty of the Chinese farmer!" "Have you had a chance to see the life of farmers in China?" "Is there oppression such as this also in America?" "We want to be friends with the American people! Can't we write letters to someone in

America?" "What do you think of our government? We would like your criticism."

They were so sincere and at the same time so naïve that it was hard to explain why friendship between the two peoples is now difficult. But it would be well for Americans to remember these two students and the many others like them. To those foreigners who approach the Chinese student sympathetically and without snobbery, he will almost always respond with warmth. The trouble is that too many foreigners are either unwilling or unable to approach him in that way.

On the official level, there has been a relaxation in the granting of travel permits. Several foreigners have recently been allowed to travel to Tientsin, and I myself, in a single morning, succeeded in securing a permit for the whole family to visit Tsinghua, Yenching, and the Summer Palace any time during the present month. What lies beyond the Summer Palace in the Western Hills, however, remains forbidden territory.

Group Effort

One of the things which the Communists are trying to teach the student class is the dignity of manual labor. Galia saw an example this morning while riding along the large east-west avenue which flanks the Tung-tan glacis near its northeast corner. When Fu Tso-yi built his emergency airstrip during the siege, great quantities of earth were removed from the glacis itself and piled in unsightly mounds north of the avenue. Until now, occupied with more important work, the authorities have allowed it to remain where it was. This morning, however, Galia saw large numbers of young people—many apparently in their early teens and all wearing the usual official gray uniform—vigorously attacking these mounds with picks and shovels. They were members of the National Young Congress which for the past several days has been in session here.

It was a pleasure, Galia commented, to see the eagerness with which they went about their task, singing group songs as they worked. The enterprise was well organized. Empty trucks that had brought the crowd to the spot were now waiting to take the earth away. On a table in the center stood a large blackboard, decorated with a bright cloth inscribed with names and slogans. Its purpose was apparently to keep score for the several teams working in competition. So numerous were the workers and so rapidly did they dig that even as Galia passed she noticed the mounds perceptibly diminishing. It would be a very few days, she thought, before the last traces of the siege at this spot would be completely obliterated.

May 20 (Friday)

Food, Prices and Business

Despite moderate rains on May 11 and 16, and our first thunderstorm of the season last night, unpleasant rumors continue that crops are drying up, people eating leaves in the countryside, and famine is impending. It is said that the rains have come too late to save the winter wheat.

Many people obviously feel concerned about the future. In reply to letters asking why, since liberation, price rises continue, today's *Progressive Daily* prints an official statement from the Department of Industry and Commerce.

Following the liberation of Peking and Tientsin, it points out, these two largest industrial centers of the North have become saturated with the money of persons from the countryside anxious to buy goods of all kinds. The effects of this inflationary concentration of currency have been further aggravated by the fact that China's largest industrial center, Shanghai, still remains unliberated. Drought has been another factor. Still a third has been the Manchurian regime's embargo upon grain shipments into China proper, imposed in order to stabilize prices in Manchuria, and only recently removed. (This is the first official implication I have seen that food may also be in short supply in Manchuria.) The fourth factor is the recent liberation of long-besieged Taiyuan and other cities, which has resulted in a flood of orders from these cities for commodities of all kinds. But, the official statement concludes cautiously, with the removal of the Manchurian embargo, arrival of rain, crack-down on commercial speculation, and imminent liberation of Shanghai, prices in Tientsin and Peking "will in future tend to become settled."

Such explanations, honest and reasonable though they seem, fail to allay the criticism of foreigners, many of whom take rather bitter pleasure in pointing out the numerous "mistakes" of the new regime. Some time ago, for example, the authorities instituted an income tax—a withholding tax at the source—which, though going as high as 15 per cent for those in the upper income brackets, would not seem unduly onerous considering China's present needs. Being quite unprecedented in China, however, it naturally aroused the resentment of many of its "victims." Recently this tax was repealed, probably because it could not be carried out effectively in an economy as amorphous and decentralized as that of China. This repeal, nevertheless, is regarded by one Englishman with whom I have been talking as a profound mistake. Why? Because it lessens public confidence in the permanence of any future measures undertaken by the government.

Thus, the government is blamed when it takes measures to modernize China's economic and political structure. Then, when it discovers by trial and error that it is moving too fast, it is blamed for canceling these measures. This seems hardly fair. When the Communists came into the big cities, they frankly admitted they were new to many problems and would necessarily make mistakes, which, however, they hoped to correct. Why not give them the chance to do so?

Their biggest mistake so far, according to the same Englishman, is the foreign-currency conversion. In Tientsin, according to final figures, a total of US$214,608 was acquired in this way; in Peking, US$88,870. These sums, he says, while insufficient to kill the black market, are enough to create many enemies.

Complaints are loudest among Tientsin's export-importers. "Sets business back two thousand years," is a favorite comment on the export-import barter regulations, according to a recent visitor to that city. Businessmen remark bitterly that the Communists are babes in the wood when it comes to foreign trade. Though forced to use the middleman who has the necessary know-how, they are unwilling to pay him adequately for that knowledge.

Recently, for example, the North China Trading Corporation collected a large quantity of hog bristles from the countryside which it handed over to Tientsin traders for export. It failed to realize, however, that in order to sell these abroad, they must be graded according to certain specifications. The result was that the traders were forced to do the grading themselves. When they had finished, however, the government was unwilling to pay them for this extra work.

Or again, the Jen Li Rug Company, the largest concern of its kind in North China, was told that in order to export rugs it must contract for the import of a certain amount of paper. After much trouble the company succeeded in making the necessary arrangements abroad, only to be told that by this time the government no longer needed paper, but wanted copper wire. While such stories are no doubt true, I suspect that in this as in other fields the authorities may change some of their rulings when experience proves that doctrinaire assumptions do not always lead to successful practice.

The Communist levy of taxes on general business is an interesting process. Instead of telling each individual concern what it should pay, they determine the total amount they think ought to be raised by the business community as a whole and then set quotas for each particular trading and industrial group. These quotas are subject to discussion between the authorities and the leaders of the business groups concerned. After that it is left to the members within each group to work out among themselves how much each firm must pay in fulfilling that group's quota. This they do in guild or association meetings, thus bringing into the business world the same pattern of group discussion which has become so generally prominent under the new regime.

This technique is efficient in that it saves the authorities much administrative work by allowing them to deal with major groups instead of scattered individuals. It is "democratic" in the sense that it leaves it up to the members of each group to discuss in-

dividual payments. And it agrees with Chinese tradition by util-
izing the long-accepted principle of group responsibility.

From the foreign point of view, however, it suffers from one
major defect. The foreign businessman has traditionally (and
usually rightly) been regarded by his Chinese business rivals as
economically better off than themselves. But at the same time he
occupies a minority position. The temptation is strong, therefore,
for the Chinese companies to gang up against the foreigners in
the group meetings and, by outvoting them, oblige them to pay
a disproportionate share of the total.

Reform and Reconstruction

Here are four items on the constructive side:

The entire railroad from Tientsin to Pukow has been restored,
save for the large Huai River bridge. Considering the shortage
of materials and trained personnel, the widespread destruction,
and the continuing war, this seems quite a remarkable achievement.

"Non-interest loans worth nearly four million kilograms of
millet have been extended by the People's Government to owners of houses burnt or destroyed by the Kuomintang army in
Tientsin before liberation," according to today's *Daily News
Release.** No doubt similar steps will later be taken here for
those miserable people whose homes outside the city wall were
razed during the siege. It is scarcely surprising that reconstruction activities of this kind should cost money and help inflation.

Last night our Chin attended a district meeting of his recently
formed pedicab union. Some two hundred were present. They
were asked to contribute what they could toward repair of the
rooms which are to be their permanent headquarters and in
which a night school will eventually be organized. They were
also told that until further notice the rental of pedicabs is to be
frozen at $30 per day, and that privately employed pedicabbers

* A small English-language publication launched in Peking on May 1 by the official
New China News Agency. It replaced the *Peiping Digest* previously put out by a
group of Peita students.

should report to their union if they are inadequately paid. On their own part, they should not charge unreasonable fares. In the face of rising prices, Peking's pedicabbers are having a hard time of it these days. The political organizer explained that at present these conditions can't be helped, but that later, after all China has been unified, more positive measures will be instituted, such as insurance, medical care, loans, etc.*

Official attention is beginning to be paid to the beggar problem. According to the May 14 *Daily News Release,* the 913 who have been registered in Peking are being classified and dealt with as follows: (1) Those capable of work have already been sent to the People's Institute for Trade Training to learn a productive occupation. (2) Those who came to Peking as refugees are being returned to their homes. (3) Those who took to begging because of illness will be granted loans to set them on their feet again. (4) Those who are still sick or disabled will be provided for in relief homes and gradually absorbed into productive occupations. (5) The professional beggars, who form the most difficult category, have been put into groups in which they follow a fixed daily routine and are constantly indoctrinated with the idea that "those who do not work do not eat."

This seems a more constructive approach to the problem than that of the Japanese, who, according to report, periodically used to round up Peking's beggars from the streets and load them into trucks for trips into the country from which they never returned. During the last week or two I have failed to see the groups of beggars who used to beat their wooden clappers in front of the shops on Morrison Street until given a handout. The old man who spent his days on Gold Fish Hutung beating his head to the ground and wailing, *"Lao Yeh! T'ai-t'ai!"* ("Old sir! Mistress!") to all passersby seems also to have disappeared.

* Far-reaching plans were announced at another union meeting held some two months later, at which Chin and his fellow pedicabbers were informed that the municipality intends eventually to develop more efficient means of communication, as the result of which it will be possible to abolish pedicabs entirely, or almost entirely. When this time comes, existing pedicabbers will be given the chance to learn other, more useful, trades at trade schools and the like. Meanwhile, since the present number of pedicabs is already greater than warranted by demand, no further licences will be granted to new applicants below the age of thirty-five.

The Southern Campaign

The military advance continues on a wide front in the south, where Hankow has been taken and Shanghai completely surrounded. Conditions in Shanghai must be fantastic. Reports speak of US$10 or more being paid for a single pound of meat, of prices doubling and redoubling in the course of a day, and of GY$500,000 notes being printed, but refused by merchants, who do all business by barter. There are the usual stories of Kuomintang arrests, extortion, and destruction. How the Communists will be able to rehabilitate this chaos is hard to imagine. In places like Nanking, however, they seem to have acted with speed and efficiency. In a matter of days they had public utilities and government offices going again, the worthless gold yuan notes were being turned in for new currency, the Communist radio and official newspaper were operating full blast, and huge crowds were seeing performances of *The White-haired Girl* and buying Communist literature in thousands of copies.

All this is being done simultaneously in dozens of newly taken towns that have already fallen behind the front as the army continues its push southward. How the military advance is maintained is portrayed in an account of Lin Piao's army in the May 18 *Daily News Release:*

Many of the men in this army have marched all the way from Harbin and Mukden. Nearly all have marched from Peiping to the Yangtze—800 miles in the heat and blinding dust. But they did the march in an average 40 days, and in one army, less than one man in each 140 dropped out because of ill health or bad feet and there was not one deserter. Ahead of the troops, great granaries, food stores and mobile hospitals were set up, from which the army could draw its supplies without disturbing the economic life of the countryside through which it passed. This entailed months of preparation.

Along the whole route of the march, a giant complex organization was functioning smoothly, arranging facilities for provisioning, sleeping, drinking and cooking. In front of each column, a few hours ahead, advance parties went to prepare for the night's rest, food, animal fodder, entertainment and education. Signposts at every few miles explained the next part of the journey—warned of bad sections or encouraged the men to maintain their efforts. . . . On the march, they are able to wash their feet every night and bathe their eyes with boric acid solution. . . . The march of the people's army to the south will go down in history as a triumph of mass support, political consciousness, minute efficiency and unbounded self-sacrifice.

Two Art Exhibits

A few days ago I attended a large exhibition of "proletarian" paintings in Central Park. Its several hundred pictures, almost all produced since the liberation, met with obvious interest and approval from the good-sized crowd, consisting mainly of plain folk. Most of them had probably never seen so many paintings before.

In subject matter the exhibit marked a conscious break with the past. Favorite themes were scenes of peasants laboring in the fields and of workers in the factories, of the People's Army fraternizing with civilians, and of the happiness and prosperity of the future China.

Some pictures were blatantly propagandistic—for instance, a photographically realistic scene showing Mao Tse-tung leading his men on horseback beneath a billowing red banner. Others, however, were ingenious and arresting. For example, there was a portrait of one of Peking's innumerable night-soil carriers, complete with barrel and scoop, and beside it the inscription, "Wherever you go, a stench always follows, but you are performing a necessary service for the people." A landscape, with the traditional background of distant mountains bathed in mist, showed, in the foreground, a row of factory chimneys belching smoke into the sky. A file of wild ducks silhouetted in flight was entitled: "Organized Life."

In technique, however, most of the pictures were garish, stiff, crude, and poor in workmanship. I hardly saw a one I would really care to own.

Afterward I wandered, quite by chance, into another art show, an "Exhibition of Famous Painters," also in Central Park, though in a less conspicuous building. How different the atmosphere here! The technique—in some cases, at least—was delicate and graceful, and the subjects were the traditional ones of landscapes, birds, flowers, and calligraphy. Many of the best pictures were the work of Peking's most famous artist, Ch'i Pai-shih, who now proudly prefixes his signature with the words, "In his eighty-ninth year." Yet even in these technically outstanding paintings the net effect was stilted, artifical, and dead. Though something of the old form lingered, the spirit was gone. How far removed this was from that exhibition of great early paintings I saw at Tsinghua last October!

In art, as in many other fields, China has reached the end of the old road without entering the new. The past has spoken so long that its words no longer convey meaning, but the future has not yet learned how to talk. In China, as elsewhere, revolution is not the time for great cultural creation, save possibly in literature. That creation must await the later age of "emotion recollected in tranquillity."

The Old Scholar in the New Society

The *Progressive Daily* of May 17 carries a long and beautifully written "open letter" from Ch'en Yüan, president of Fu Jen University, to Hu Shih, former president of Peita. Professor Ch'en, a well-known historian, now in his seventies, who is steeped in Confucian tradition and ignorant of any Western language, elected to remain in Peking when the Communists came. Dr. Hu, westernized scholar, famed as a former leader of progressive thought, suddenly left at that time, as we all know, first to South China and then to America.

"Why," Ch'en writes, in essence, to his friend, "did you choose to run away? You said there would be no freedom here and cited Kravchenko's *I Chose Freedom* as illustration. But it is not as you say. Now, for the first time in my life, I have seen what freedom really is. I have been free to read many things I had never heard of before: such books as Mao Tse-tung's *Chinese Revolution and Chinese Communist Party*, his *New Democracy* and *On Coalition Government*, and Edgar Snow's *Red Star over China* [in Chinese translation]. You have long lived abroad. Is it possible that you never read Snow's book? You own forty editions of the *Water*

Classic Commentary [an ancient geographical work on which Dr. Hu has long been doing research]. Why is it you never owned a single book by Mao Tse-tung? In reading these works, a new world has opened before me. I realize for the first time that our whole study of history has been subjective, unscientific. Man's mind is determined by his society. We must study that society in order to understand the individual, and can reform the individual only through reforming the society. All culture follows politics and at the same time leads politics. The realization of this fact is the freedom that the new government has brought to me."

Here is an eloquent and, I believe, sincere expression of the feeling of widened mental horizons and spiritual exhilaration that Marxism has recently brought to not a few traditional Chinese scholars. These men, having been nurtured for a lifetime on the old Confucian concept of a static, individual, and idealistic morality, are now suddenly confronted with the new and dynamic concept that an interplay exists between the thinking of the individual and his social environment. This concept, so ignored in traditional Chinese philosophy, yet so seemingly simple, logical, and coherent, comes to these old-time scholars with the blinding impact of a sort of "instantaneous enlightenment," to quote a Buddhist expression. These men, we must remember, have never known the Western tradition of empirical inquiry and scientific analysis. Their own Confucian, humanistic tradition was very different from the Renaissance and post-Renaissance humanism in the West. Unthinkingly they accepted this tradition, and with it a form of society that, they later discovered, had somehow gone wrong. Now Marxism tells them in simple terms *why* it went wrong and at the same time promises a short cut to its betterment. The result, for its converts, is a new feeling of mental freedom. This, I think, explains in part the readiness with which so many Chinese intellectuals accept a "freedom" in certain ways so strikingly unlike its classical counterpart in the West.

June 1949

June 1 (Wednesday)

Shanghai

The big news since last writing is, of course, the taking of Shanghai on May 27. This event brings immeasurably nearer the day when all China will be ruled by a single nonmilitary government. It also draws the Communists inescapably into the complicated web of modern commerce and industry and the problems of foreign affairs. For us personally it arouses the selfish hope that our two-month interruption of mail contacts with the outside world will soon come to an end.

The difficulties and hopes brought by Shanghai's capture are clearly recognized in yesterday's New China News Agency editorial:

The liberation of Shanghai has caused the whole Chinese people and all progressive humanity to rejoice. . . . The enemies of Chinese revolution have threatened the Chinese people by saying: "You dare not occupy Shanghai because you have no way of administering the city. You have no other way but to surrender to us." These shameless braggarts drew on all kinds of fabrications in order to comfort themselves and each other. But now their last card is played. . . . Now, for the first time, industrial workers, laboring people, intellectuals and the patriotic national capitalist class have joined hands freely. . . .

On the road of advance we shall, of necessity, meet all sorts of obstacles—both expected and unexpected—which result from the war, from the long years of destruction wrought by the enemy, from the continued sabotage by the enemy through subversive means, and from our own lack of mature experience. We should never adopt a disdainful attitude to these difficulties. If we disdain them we shall tend not to adopt seriously the proper methods of overcoming them and we shall certainly commit grave errors. . . .

The Chinese people have long made plain their standpoint regarding international affairs. On the last occasion it was in [the following] statement made by General Li Tao, spokesman of the General Headquarters of the Chinese People's Liberation Army on April 30:

"The Chinese People's Revolutionary Military Committee and the People's Government are willing to protect all foreign nationals in China who engage in normal vocations . . . [They] . . . are willing to consider the establishment of diplomatic relations with foreign countries. These relations should be established on the basis of equality, mutual benefit, and mutual respect for each other's independence and integrity of territorial sovereignty, and, above all, foreign countries must not aid the Kuomintang reactionaries. . . . The People's Government will not accept any action of an intimidating nature from any foreign government. If foreign governments are willing to consider the establishment of diplomatic relations with us, they must sever their relations with remnant Kuomintang forces and withdraw their armed forces from China."

This statement is both fair and rational. . . . But certain foreign governments, not only in the past but also today, have stood, and stand now, with the reactionary Kuomintang clique against the Chinese people. It is not surprising, then, that the people recognize that the attitude adopted by these governments toward the Chinese people has been of an unfriendly nature. . . .

Relaxation

The reiteration of this statement on foreign policy coincides with other indications—some perhaps only imaginary—suggestive of a more tolerant official attitude. One is the ease with which almost any foreigner can now get a pass to go out of the city. Another is the less stringent customs examinations of departing foreigners recently reported. A third is the recent lifting of the ban on curio exports. And a fourth is the fact that anyone—Chinese as well as foreigner—can now exchange foreign currency freely at the Bank of China with no questions asked, and at a rate slightly above that of the black market (US$1:PN$1,040)—this despite the fact that

since early May all foreign-currency transactions have been officially illegal. Even the daily newspaper blasts against Western
imperialism seem a little less shrill these days, though this may
be only imagination.*

There is one peculiar thing—all the liberation slogans are being
obliterated from the walls of hundreds of buildings throughout
the city.

Culture

A few days ago, not having the necessary pass herself, Galia sent
our boy Chin to see what has happened to the British cemetery
outside the southwest corner of the city, where a relative of hers
is buried. Chin's report was distressing. The stone cross above
the grave has been broken and removed, and so has the marble
name slab; the little sheltering pine has been cut down. Almost
all the other graves are in a similar condition. The doors and
windows of the chapel have been torn away; the surrounding
wall has been completely demolished, leaving the cemetery open
to any kind of looting or vandalism.†

All this, it is worth pointing out, was not done by Communists.
It was the work of Kuomintang soldiers who, quartered there during the siege, burned the trees and wooden fixtures, sold the
tombstones, and encouraged outsiders to loot what was left. Yet
when we mentioned this at a dinner party a couple of nights ago,
it was shrugged off with the remark that a similar fate had likewise befallen the Russian cemetery—also outside the city—and that
such acts are inevitable in time of war.

When the Communists took over Peking, one of their eight
slogans concerned the protection of historical monuments and the
encouragement of culture. Too many foreigners here forget this
fact and forget the past. They are oblivious, for example, of the
fact that more simple folk than ever before now swarm into

* This observation proved premature. The following months saw a crescendo of
propaganda attacks, which perhaps reached their climax on August 19 with a New
China News Agency editorial entitled "Bye-bye Leighton Stuart!"
† This description was later confirmed by Galia when she visited the cemetery herself.

the parks and Forbidden City owing to the low admission prices, and that these places are everywhere placarded with new signs bearing such statements as "This park is the property of the Chinese people. Respect it!" Or that much publicity was recently given to the National Library's acquisition of a unique twelfth-century edition of the Buddhist canon in 4,000 volumes—a work which Eighth Route Army guerrillas, at the cost of several lives, saved from Japanese seizure during the war by concealing it in an abandoned coal pit.

A week ago we spent several hours at the Temple of Heaven. What a joy to see this magnificent structure restored to its original condition, and what a contrast to the human filth and degradation we saw there when it was occupied by the student refugees. Now all signs of dirt and destruction have been removed and new exhibits opened, including one of a fine set of musical instruments formerly used in the imperial sacrifices.

One enclosure, however—already quite dilapidated when I last saw it, more than ten years ago—still remains unrenovated. It is that of the building where the emperor used to pass the night prior to offering sacrifice to Heaven. On this visit we found part of it being used as a stable, and, lying on a manure pile in the middle of the enclosure, a magnificent large bronze bell of the Yung-lo period. According to a custodian who was obviously unaware of its age, this bell had been removed from its tower by the Japanese, probably with the expectation of shipping it to Japan. The wooden frame from which it had hung was later burned by Kuomintang soldiers.

Above the entrance to the building itself we saw, smudged but still legible, what must surely be almost the last Kuomintang inscription surviving in Peking—large characters of Kuomintang blue quoting one of Sun Yat-sen's most famous sayings: "The revolution is not yet completed!" How bitterly Chiang Kai-shek and his companions, for whom this slogan was long a favorite, must realize its truth today!

Signs of the Times

The elimination of business enterprises not regarded as socially or economically beneficial goes steadily forward. Gold and silver shops, for example, will probably soon become things of the past. Though permitted to sell out their existing stocks of finished merchandise, they have been ordered to surrender all unworked precious metals to the government bank in exchange for people's notes. A similar fate has already overtaken the pawn shops. Of the forty-six that flourished in Tientsin prior to liberation, all save nine, according to the May 28 *Progressive Daily*, have closed their doors or turned to other business; these nine are themselves now in process of dissolution.

Tientsin's incense manufacturers, regarded by the authorities as encouragers of superstition, are likewise turning to new trades, though not under direct compulsion. Out of thirty, only four or five still exist, according to the same paper. The largest of all, which during the "flourishing days of superstition" under the Japanese employed seven or eight hundred workers and produced one boxcar load of incense every three days, has now decided to manufacture matches. It has asked for a government loan to assist its reconversion.

The *Progressive Daily*, in its May 30 issue, urges its readers to consider the advantages of cremation funerals. Traditional Chinese funerals, it points out, are enormously wasteful in money, coffin wood, and land. Tientsin's municipal crematory, on the other hand, is available to everyone at a nominal cost for fuel and labor. If this movement really gains headway, it will mark one of the sharpest breaks with tradition since the philosopher Mo Tzu vainly fulminated against the Confucianists for encouraging lavish funerals.

Self-criticism

Some very frank criticism appears in an official report on consumer cooperatives published in the May 28 *Progressive Daily*. Though some cooperatives, it admits, operate efficiently and honestly, these are "very few" in number and "the majority still have shortcomings." Some are actually corrupt, "the managers of the majority are solely interested in personal benefit," and a few violate the whole spirit of the movement by trying to compete instead of cooperate with one another. This report exemplifies the Chinese Communist technique of self-criticism.

Imperialism and "Emperor-countryism"

Taking advantage of newly acquired traveling passes, we recently spent a delightful day at the Summer Palace. It was the first time in more than six months that we had gone outside the city walls. On the bus we fell into conversation with a Tientsin merchant and his wife, a well-dressed couple in their early forties, apparently comfortably off, exceedingly friendly, and woefully ignorant of what goes on in the world.

"Are you Soviet Russians?" was the first question, a common one these days, though the number of Soviet Russians here remains infinitesimal compared with other foreign groups. On being told our actual nationality, the conversation as usual shifted to a comparison of America with China.

"America is a very *comfortable* country, isn't it?" asked the couple. "In America there are many skilled technicians, but China has very few, because the Chinese are so stupid."

"Not stupid," I replied, "only lacking in experience and opportunity, but their handicrafts show how clever they can be with their hands."

Then came the inevitable questions on American politics. "America has an emperor, hasn't it?" was the bombshell dropped by the merchant's wife.

Though I hastened to disillusion her, she seemed puzzled and unconvinced. Now how could this good woman have fallen into such an error? To anyone acquainted with the intricacies of the Chinese language the answer is simple.

In the first place, "But the American ruler lives in a *Pai Kung*, doesn't he?" she asked. Now *Pai Kung*, the Chinese rendition of "White House," literally means "White Palace." Our bus was standing at the time outside the entrance to the Forbidden City, and to this woman the words *Pai Kung* no doubt suggested something not unlike that vast array of palace buildings. I had to explain to her that the American *Pai Kung* is only a fraction of the size of the Forbidden City, that it has no wall but only an open fence, and that, unlike the Forbidden City of imperial days, its unoccupied portion is daily open to the public. In Moscow, I went on, there does exist a place called the Kremlin which is more like the old Forbidden City, being a walled enclosure not accessible to the public. But in America this is not so.

The major cause of confusion, however, became clear a moment later when I heard her muttering to herself, "But there is so much talk in the papers these days about the *Mei-kuo ti-kuo chu-yi*." *Mei-kuo*, literally "American country," is the Chinese term for America or American. *Ti-kuo chu-yi* signifies "imperialism," but literally it means "emperor-countryism." Because *Mei-kuo ti-kuo chu-yi* is a clumsy way of saying "American imperialism," and because the term appears so constantly in the papers, it is commonly abbreviated to *Mei ti,* which literally means "American emperor." No wonder, then, that this unsophisticated lady—and probably thousands like her—draws the conclusion that America is ruled by an emperor. The incident illustrates, as vividly as any I know, the dangers of high-powered propaganda when it operates upon an unsophisticated population.

Our conversation was interrupted a moment later by a loud whirring behind the bus. We turned to see clouds of smoke billowing from a boilerlike tank attached to the rear of our vehicle like the hump of a hunchback. Such tanks are now the common badge of the many trucks and buses which have been rigged with wood-burning devices, to save gasoline. The ticket taker was furiously cranking a rotary bellows to help along the combustion of wood inside. Several minutes of this activity generated sufficient gas pressure. The driver stepped on the starter, the engine burst into song, and we chugged slowly off.

June 3 (Friday)

Modern Literature

What have been some of the major characteristics of Chinese literature since the beginnings of the literary renaissance movement some thirty years ago? Last night I heard an interesting talk by Miss Hill on this subject.

In the first place, as she points out, Russian literature, both pre- and postrevolutionary, has—commonly via Japanese translation—had a greater influence on modern Chinese literature than that of any other country. Compared with it, American literary influence has been negligible. This statement agrees with what I was told last fall by a group of Chinese intellectuals.

Her second point was that modern Chinese literature can be understood only in terms of politics. Its major changes are generally dated by political events, notably the May 4 and May 30 movements of 1919 and 1925 respectively. The major controversy in Chinese literature of recent decades has been between art for art's sake, on the one hand, and, on the other, the theory that literature is an expression of society. According to this theory, all literature produced in a traditional, i.e., nonrevolutionary, society is reactionary unless it is consciously directed toward arousing class consciousness, sharpening the class struggle, and furthering the objectives of the proletarian revolution. Already as early as the thirties this Marxist viewpoint gained dominance among most major writers. This fact helps explain the ease with which intellectuals have now gone over to the Communist camp. In other words, Marxism has long been influential in Chinese intellectual circles—more so than most Americans realize.

Despite this orientation toward the left, however, the effectiveness of the literary movement has often been weakened by inter-clique bickerings springing from personal rivalry rather than basic theoretical differences. Literary figures have tended to shift from one clique to another in a way which, to the outsider, smacks a good deal of opportunism. An outstanding example is the way in which the Creative Society (headed by Kuo Mo-jo, now the leading literary figure in Communist China), in the middle twenties suddenly abandoned the theory of art for art's sake and adopted the Marxist one.

Another weakness of many leftist writers is that they seem to have written in something of an intellectual vacuum. Thus, while writing prolifically on literary theory, they have often failed to exemplify their theories through concrete literary accomplishment. While debating on how to write for the masses, they themselves have often written in a far from easy style which could reach and influence only a small group of fellow intellectuals. While the "practical" Communists were establishing successive regimes in Kiangsi, Yenan, and elsewhere, many of these writers were seeking refuge from Kuomintang persecution in the foreign concessions of Shanghai and other treaty ports, where they could maintain only indirect contact with communism as a political movement.

The general tenor of Miss Hill's remarks confirms criticism I have repeatedly heard since coming to Peking, namely that the Chinese intellectuals are a "wavering class" which has failed to make really effective contact with the masses, and that their concrete contribution to the Chinese revolution, especially in late years, has been less than their vociferousness would indicate.

June 10 (Friday)

Beggars and Black Marketeers

Tsingtao, last Kuomintang outpost in North China, has at last been taken over (June 2). . . . Still no letters from the outside world. . . . In Shanghai a few days ago according to the papers here, "more than 200 corpses of workers, students, professors, and other citizens" were recovered from a mass grave into which they had been cast shortly before the taking of Shanghai. They had been executed on orders of the Kuomintang police commissioner.

Many bodies were so badly mutilated that identification was impossible. Also in Shanghai, the conversion of the gold yuan into people's notes has been completed. In the last few days before the fall of the city the Kuomintang was printing gold yuan notes in denominations of one and five million dollars and preparing to issue others of ten million. Here the highest denomination in people's notes I have seen is one hundred dollars.

In North China, for the first time since early April, the price spiral has leveled off, at least temporarily. The official exchange value of the American dollar, after remaining for some time at 1:1040, has been raised to 1:1100 and then 1:1200, which is well above the black market. The latter, as a result, has virtually disappeared, the more so as penalties for currency violators are severe. Today's paper reports the conviction of a Morrison Street jewelry-shop proprietor for having engaged in black-market currency operations "fifty-five times." He was sentenced to two years in prison and confiscation of his "stock in trade," consisting of 15 ounces of gold, 115 Chinese silver dollars, and US$180.

The quarterly installment of the municipal tenant's house tax on the house we rent has just been announced. It comes to PN$1,770 or about US$1.50—a pittance for this two-courtyard mansion, and far from enough to support the allegation of some that the new regime is taxing the people to death.

A few days ago over three hundred former beggars paraded the streets of Tientsin, dancing the *yang ko* "to celebrate their own reform and the liberation of Tsingtao." They had partially completed an indoctrination program being given by the Tientsin municipality. According to the papers, the sight profoundly impressed large crowds of spectators. Here in Peking eight hundred beggars are participating in a similar program. A few days ago, nonetheless, an old crone approached me for alms in the Tung An market. On telling her that begging is now frowned upon by the authorities, she abruptly disappeared.

The other day I saw, for the first time, four white people (two men, two women—all young) wearing the ubiquitous gray-blue uniforms of functionaries of the People's Government. They were out for an evening stroll near the American Consulate, but I was too far away to hear what language they were speaking.

Wonder of wonders! Certain governmental representatives recently asked the U.S. Information Service for the loan of two U.S.I.S. posters, one about Labor Day, the other about Byrd's Antarctic explorations. The American flag appeared prominently in the second one. Not only this, but the request was followed by an expression of interest in certain U.S.I.S. educational movies.

The Capitalist in New China

"If I were a 'Citizen Capitalist' " is the title of a persuasive article by Ch'ien Tuan-sheng, Peita political science professor, in the June 5 *Progressive Daily*. By "citizen capitalist" he means one who has not been connected with the Kuomintang bureaucracy, especially with China's "four ruling families." The hero of the article is a hypothetical capitalist who, in present-day China, at least, seems almost too good to be true. He is a man who has stayed clear of politics, avoided dishonest speculation, been kind to his workers, never defaulted to his stockholders, paid all his taxes, supported philanthropic enterprises, and endowed chairs of economics in two universities. What, asks the article, is the future of such a man in the new China? As answer it quotes several reassuring statements by Mao Tse-tung and others. But even these, it admits, may not fully convince our capitalist, owing to his ignorance of the Communist program and to his long exposure to British and American propaganda. The remainder of the article therefore tries to settle his doubts on seven specific points:

(1) Since the Communist party is committed to the support of the proletariat, will this not interfere with capitalist expansion? The answer is that the Communist party is in actual fact committed to the "mutual benefit of labor and capital alike." This has already been demonstrated in such earlier-liberated cities as Mukden and Tientsin. There is no question that the People's Government is dedicated to the improvement of labor conditions. But at the same time it is unalterably opposed to all unreasonable labor demands which interfere with maximum industrial production.

(2) Deficiency of raw materials. This problem, often present

in the past, will disappear once the country has been unified and normal communications restored.

(3)   Raising of capital. This too has often been difficult in the past, owing to the control of the nation's banks by a small number of selfish bureaucrats. But now, with the breaking of their control, it will become far easier to arrange for loans on productive enterprise.

(4)   Selling of manufactured commodities. This will be facilitated by the restoration of communications and improvement of rural economy, resulting in a much larger domestic market.

(5)   Adequate profits. The People's Government, being vitally interested in industrialization, is committed to the principle of adequate profits for all private investors in productive enterprise.

(6)   Enlargement of enterprise. The People's Government places no restrictions on the enlargement of private enterprise as long as it conforms to the laws of the country, is not oppressive, and "does not gain a position in which it controls the people's livelihood."

(7)   The most vital question of all: What will happen to the capitalist when China passes from New Democracy to full-fledged socialism? The answer is that it is naturally impossible for any capitalist, living in a capitalist society and subject to the ideology of that society, to view with equanimity the future disappearance of his class. In the China of the New Democracy, however, the situation is different, for the simple reason that the psychological forces at work are different. "Suppose," the author has his hypothetical capitalist say, "I really come to recognize that I form one of those classes which, under the New Democracy, exercises political power; that I have previously contributed to the building of the new China; and that I, like those of any other class, have become warmly interested in the still newer institution of socialism. This being so, when the nation evolves from New Democracy to socialism, I too shall evolve from being a citizen capitalist to being a manager in the new socialistic industrial enterprise. I shall continue to have a function to perform and thereby shall continue to enjoy the respect of my fellow citizens."

The final moral drawn by our now converted capitalist is that "my future road and that of the new China are equally bright."

Marriage, New and Old

The *Daily News Release* of June 1 carries a story headlined "Old Marriage Customs Dying Out Fast." The "horrible feudal practices" of arranged marriage and sale of girls, it says, such as flourished under the old government, are now rapidly disappearing in the liberated areas. An example is what has happened in a certain village about a hundred miles southwest of Peking. Out of 267 couples living in that village in 1938, the marriages of 95 per cent had been arranged by the parents. But of the 157 marriages that occurred subsequently, between 1938 (when the village was liberated) and 1948, only 22 per cent were arranged. All the others were by free choice of the couples concerned, and no case whatever was reported of buying or selling.

All very true, no doubt, and yet the process of change begins slowly. Take, for example, the case of our boy Chin.

Chin is poor, honest, unsophisticated, uneducated beyond a few years of primary school, and a filial son to his widowed mother. Aside from quite an unusual intelligence, he is not unlike thousands of others in Peking. Because he is young and strong, he recently decided he would like to marry. Did he have some particular girl in mind? Not at all. The conditions of life for him and most other young men of his class permit little opportunity for meeting eligible young girls. (No doubt this situation will change with the growth of labor unions and similar Communist-fostered organizations.) So he appealed to a male friend to act as matchmaker.

This friend knew of a girl who he thought would do—the daughter of a petty street vendor. The first we learned of the proceedings was when Chin asked for time off one day to meet the girl's father. Would he also see the girl, we asked? Oh no, he replied, the first step would be a restaurant dinner given by the father for the purpose of sizing up the prospective son-in-law.

The dinner having passed off successfully, the next step was to arrange for the prospective couple to have an actual glimpse of each other—a striking concession to modernity. The medium was a "chance" encounter on the bank of the Shih Ch'a Hai (Lake of Ten Temples)—a popular place of promenade in summer.

There, at a certain hour one morning, Chin, with his mother, appeared for a stroll, while from the other direction came the girl and her father. As she and Chin passed each other, they were able to have a look at one another. Here is Chin's report of the results to Galia:

Galia: "Well, is the girl good-looking?"

Chin: "Not too good but also not bad. However"—making expressive curves in the air with his hands—"her body is good."

Galia: "And did you talk to her?"

Bashful Chin: "Oh no. As soon as I had one look at her, I ran away."

Galia: "And what about the girl? What did she think?"

Chin: "She told her father: '*K'o-yi*, will do.'"

Galia: "Is she intelligent? Can she read characters? To get ahead in the new China, you ought to have a wife as clever as yourself."

Chin's reply was indefinite—he thought the girl could read "a little." But the meeting was obviously successful, for the wedding was now planned to take place about a month hence on a day deemed mutually propitious according to the couple's horoscopes.

In preparation, Chin requested and received a one-month advance in wages, part of which, he explained (and here appears a Western touch), was to be spent on an engagement ring. After the exchange of rings, he continued, it would be permissible for him and the girl to see and talk to each other.

But at this point an unexpected hitch developed. The girl's mother—and it is remarkable how often the *lao t'ai-t'ai* ("old lady") of the family is the stumbling block to progress in China—insisted that *her* daughter must have a proper wedding. This meant a covered sedan chair with several bearers, an escort of musicians, and all the other trappings, such as she herself had enjoyed when she was married. Today, however, all this would cost the equivalent of about 30 American dollars—an inordinate sum for people in their circumstances. Moreover, as immediately pointed out by objectors in both families, it would not be in keeping with the present trend toward simplicity and austerity; it might, indeed, evoke unfavorable comment.

Chin himself, supported by his mother and the matchmaker,

flatly refused to make this concession to tradition. The girl's father took a similar position and is reported to have pounded the table violently in an unpleasant family scene. But all in vain. The mother remained adamant and (as so often in China) won the day. The result is that the match has been called off. The girl's family has lost much face and Chin and his family none, but neither has he gained a wife. Now he has hopefully appealed to his friend to find another girl. The latter has suggested one reportedly skilled with the needle, but as yet no action has been taken. Thus, in this case at least, the old has triumphed over the new.*

June 12 (Sunday)

The New China and the Soviet Union

Although there is still no evidence here of material collaboration between the People's Government and the Soviet Union—aside from a few Russian technicians, probably recruited mostly from Harbin rather than the U.S.S.R. itself—official propaganda continues to stress the community of interests between the two governments. T'ien Chün, prominent Manchurian writer, best known abroad for his novel, *Village in August*, has recently been officially reprimanded for suggesting in a Harbin newspaper that "there may be various colors to imperialism." His implication was that there may be a red imperialism as well as a white one. This is the first indication I have seen of possible dissatisfaction among Manchurian intellectuals over the provisions of the 1945 Sino-Soviet Friendship Treaty.

Foreign Minister Chou En-lai has likewise warned in a recent speech that "people will be disappointed if they think there will ever be a Tito in China." On the other hand, he and others in

* Some months after returning to America I was delighted to receive a Chinese letter from Chin, in which he happily announced his marriage. It had also been arranged by his matchmaker friend, but was a "modern" one nonetheless, for the bride came in an automobile instead of the traditional but now expensive sedan chair. Like the other girl, however, Chin's wife "reads only a few characters."

the Communist hierarchy have repeatedly stressed their determination to protect China's national integrity and independence.

The Devil's Tunes

Last Sunday, while cycling up Morrison Street, I passed thirty or forty people attending an open-air service in front of the Salvation Army building, among them four or five wearing the gray-blue Communist uniform. As I stopped to listen, the crowd burst into song. The words, posted in large characters on the wall, were those of a hymn. The tune itself, however, I recognized as one of the hits from the popular play, *The White-Haired Girl!* So apparently the Salvation Army has not forgotten the advice of General Booth, who is reported to have said: "There is no reason why the devil should have all the good tunes!"

A Chinese professor whom I saw yesterday (not an ardent supporter of the new regime) seems well enough satisfied with the new university salary scale, which at present exchange rates gives a full professor something like US$60 per month—two or three times what he often received during the past few years. Factory and other workers also do somewhat better than before, on the whole. Office clerks and administrators, on the other hand, have suffered. A university treasurer, for example, now receives less than a professor, whereas formerly his salary would have been about the same.

This same source confirmed the existence of what I have already heard rumored—a weekly newspaper restricted to the inner circle of the Communist party and closely associated non-Communists. At Yenching University it is received by four or five individuals. Labeled "secret," it consists of news dispatches taken from non-Communist sources (AP, UP, Reuter's, the Kuomintang Central News Agency, etc.). In its pages, therefore, such terms as "Communist bandits" still appear; only the headlines reflect editorial opinion.

June 26 (Sunday)

"Coalition Government"

The big news of the week is the announcement on the twentieth that a Political Consultative Conference is soon to be convened in order to institute a Democratic Coalition Government for China. Its 510 delegates will be drawn from 45 "representative units," to include: 14 political parties (142 delegates), most important of which will be the Communist party, the Kuomintang Revolutionary Committee, and the Democratic League (16 delegates each); 9 nonpolitical regional groups (102 delegates), to be drawn from all parts of China; 6 army units (60 delegates), all of which, of course, are Communist; 16 people's organizations and groupings (206 delegates). This last group will comprise labor, peasant, women, youth, and student divisions, industrial and commercial circles, literary, scientific, educational, social science, and journalist groups, minority nationalities, "democratic overseas Chinese," and "democratic religious circles."

The P.C.C will be notable for its inclusion, besides the Communist party itself, of all other political parties which have broken away from the Kuomintang (many of which, however, might more properly be called cliques rather than parties). Other than this, it will follow the Soviet pattern fairly closely. As in Russia, it will be a composite of regional, military, occupational, and racial groups. Since all "reactionary elements" are to be excluded, it will obviously not be a truly representative body, judged by Western democratic standards. Even though the Communists will be outweighed in point of actual numbers, there is no doubt they will remain the final arbiters of policy.

Yet it would be extreme to conclude that the P.C.C. will be nothing more than window dressing. Within certain basic limitations, I believe, the Communists are genuinely willing to receive suggestions and make occasional concessions, the more so because of their self-admitted inexperience in various fields. I have heard it said, for example, that the Democratic National Construction

Association—a group that aspires to represent industrial and commercial interests in the new China—has already pointedly criticized parts of the present economic program, and that its remarks have at least received respectful Communist hearing. As in any Communist-dominated coalition, however, such internal differences may be expected to be kept under cover, and all decisions, once reached, will be presented to the world as unanimous facts.

New Publications

With the appearance on the 17th of a new newspaper, the *Kuang-ming Jih-pao* (*Glorious Daily*), organ of the Democratic League, Peking's dailies have been increased to five. Aside from a few special newsletters from Hong Kong, the paper seems to differ little from its rivals.*

According to a summary in the June 15 *Progressive Daily* of the results of the third registration period for Peking's newspapers and periodicals, the registrations of 10 were approved, bringing to 40 the number of periodicals now published here. The registration of six has been refused and that of two others indefinitely postponed.

Despite paper shortage and resulting high prices, the bookstores continue to be crowded with people eager to buy the publications pouring from the presses these days. The variety of these is wide. There are treatises on Marxism, communism, and the New Democracy; scholarly reappraisals of Chinese history, sociology, thought, and literature from a Marxist point of view; works of pure literature; translations of Soviet books. The number of Russian imports is growing. A bulky treatise on Marx-Leninism, for example, excellently printed in Chinese and selling at a price less than that of comparable books published here, bears a Moscow imprint. English-language Soviet magazines include a political periodical, *New Times*, an illustrated magazine, *Soviet Woman*,

---

* Peking's dailies jumped to six on July 16 with the inauguration of the *Daily Worker*, representative of labor interests. August 1 saw the appearance of the *North China Liberation Army*, organ of the North China Military Headquarters, but on the same date the semi-official *Liberation News* merged with the ultra-official *People's Daily*.

and a de luxe heavy-paper publication similar in format to, though thinner than, *Fortune Magazine,* in which good colored photos portray life in the U.S.S.R. in idyllic terms. I try to buy what I can of the more important local publications, and regret the lack of time which prevents me from reading them.

Law

At the moment we are living in a legal vacuum, for though all Kuomintang laws have been officially abrogated, nothing has as yet been formulated to take their place. Justice, therefore, is of the rough-and-ready sort. A group of experts, however, is now in process of drawing up a new code. One of these men, to whom I talked a week ago, was reluctant to say much more than that the code would not lean exclusively on Soviet law and that he was at that very moment beginning work on the section dealing with alien rights.

More informative is a story in the June 18 issue of the *Progressive Daily* reporting a series of meetings of high officials on the subject.

The guiding principle of the new code will be to "express the Chinese revolutionary thought of Mao Tse-tung." In concrete terms this means:

(1) It "must recognize that the Chinese revolution and Chinese nation are in their nature based upon the New Democracy," that is to say that "the forces opposed to the revolution are those of feudalism and bureaucratic capitalism," and that the aim of the revolution is to create "a nation based on the joint democratic dictatorship of the proletariat and the peasant, and dedicated to the development of a classless society."

(2) As such, the code must be framed so as to facilitate the carrying out of four major points in Mao's political program. These are, "joint concern for society and the individual, mutual benefit for labor and capital, mutual assistance between city and countryside, mutual intercourse between China and foreign countries."

(3) The code must give recognition to the fact that "the China

of the New Democracy is a preparatory and transitional stage for a socialistic China."

(4) In order better to carry out these aims, the framers of the code should study the legal and political experience of the Chinese Communist party during the past twenty odd years.

The general conclusion is that Marxism, Leninism and the thought of Mao Tse-tung should be carefully studied for the purpose of the code; that the legal theory current in the U.S.S.R. and other "democratic" countries should be used as basic reference material; but that this should be supplemented by study of the codes of the capitalistic countries of Europe and America.

Prices, Cooperatives, and Austerity

Prices continue their slight but encouraging decline: wholesale prices by 1.27 per cent and laborers' cost of living by 4.31 per cent for the period of June 1-21.

Yesterday's *Progressive Daily* gives a further report on the development of Tientsin's cooperatives. In May they sold a total of 13,456,076 pounds of grains, together with other daily necessities worth PN$83,005,208. The resulting total savings to members amounted to PN$97,632,281. Sales of coarse and fine grains during April averaged ten and fifteen pounds respectively per member (not much when it is considered that most members probably have families to feed). These achievements were countered by continuing weaknesses. Owing to faulty inspection, for example, some cooperatives "purchased not a little grain that was spoiled or of secondary quality, and which they were therefore unable to sell."

The past two weeks have seen a major press campaign urging reduced consumption and general austerity, and describing numerous cases in which public organizations are reducing their consumption of electricity, water, etc. Much publicity has also been given to the decision of needy university students, following a series of public discussions, to accept smaller living allowances from the government, often at considerable personal sacrifice. On June 18 Peking's post-office employees likewise voted a salary reduction for themselves totaling 300,000 pounds of millet a month. By fostering public acts of this kind, the authorities are trying to ward off the difficult economic times ahead.

The Public Mood

I have just returned, this lovely summer evening, from a walk past the moat south of the Forbidden City, through Central Park, and thence home by way of the south gate to the palaces. Throughout this walk I was struck again by something I have noticed several times recently—the changed mood of the people from that prevailing when we arrived in Peking ten months ago. As I started on my way this evening, I was greeted by the usual vociferous cries of *"Ting hao! Ting hao!"* ("Very good! Very good!") from the swarm of dirty little children at play in our *hutung*. A little later I was startled by sounds directly behind me and turned just in time to see a bicyclist crashing to the ground. He had miscalculated my movements and had fallen from his bicycle rather than run into me. A good-natured grin was on his face as he picked himself up, and loud guffaws rose from several people who had witnessed the mishap. Farther on I paused to join a group of amused bystanders watching the antics of four or five young people who, rather self-consciously, were practicing the steps of a *yang ko* dance.

Next I came upon a group of soldiers making horseplay with each other and singing a snatch of song ending with the words: "Down with Chiang Kai-shek!" On noticing that they were being watched, they burst into good-humored laughter, as if pleased to have aroused the attention of a foreigner.

Finally I reached Central Park and found it filled with people. Among them were none of the fashionably gowned, exquisitely slender, sophisticated beauties who used to be so conspicuous here twelve years ago. On the contrary, these were simple folk, dressed in the most nondescript clothing, and out for a stroll on this beautiful Sunday evening which they were obviously enjoying.

In short, all these people encountered on my walk have lost that grim tension so noticeable during the first six months of our stay here. In their readiness to smile, to sing (the new songs are enormously popular), and to talk freely to one another, they have regained that carefree ease and friendliness that I remember so well from the old days and have missed so greatly since our return. Economically, perhaps, most of them are little or no better off than they were before. But they do seem free at last from the old fears and buoyed up by hope for the future. May they not be disappointed this time!

Walking home by way of the imposing outer gate to the palace, I saw a vendor beside one of its huge stone lions selling *ping-kun-er* or "ice-sticks," as the Chinese call popsicles. On the side of his little hand-cart were painted two large characters, *Hsieh Li*, "United Effort." United Effort! If the Communists can succeed in giving this one precious gift to China, they will have achieved much indeed.

June 30 (Thursday)

Unpleasant Intrusion

This morning, while working in my study, I was suddenly conscious of a dark shadow outside. Looking up, I saw four young fellows in official uniform standing silently in the courtyard. Waiting behind—instead of leading them in, as would have been customary—were two of our servants, who looked troubled and apologetic at having been unable to announce the unexpected visitors. Galia quickly joined me, having been warned in a few hurried words from Chin that the visit in some way concerned the housing situation.

One of the visitors spoke English and the conversation was conducted both in English and Chinese. Their manner was blunt, and, as we immediately learned, their purpose was to see if part of our house could be occupied as an office for a local bureau of the municipality. They wanted to know how many people lived in the house, how many rooms it had, and were full of scorn when they learned there were only three of us in this large establishment. We tried to explain the nature of my work and the need for concentration and quiet if I were to complete it within the time remaining to us in Peking. This had some effect, especially when the English-speaking official (apparently a former local student) learned that I was translating a history of Chinese philosophy written by a Peking professor.

But only after considerable discussion, concluded by Galia's suggestion that they investigate a vacant house a few doors away, did they grudgingly agree to go and leave us in peace. We had been quite alarmed at the prospect of our remaining weeks in Peking being spoiled by the intrusion of a noisy office, and were happy to learn later in the day that they have apparently arranged to take the other house. The visitors were all of student age, but their attitudes differed. While the English-speaking man was understanding and reasonably pleasant, the others had a more threatening air, especially one whose burning eyes seemed to express his hatred for all people like ourselves who are both "foreign imperialists" and "rich exploiters."

July 1949

July 4 (Monday)

Birthday of the Communist Party

July 1 was the twenty-eighth anniversary of the founding of the Chinese Communist party. According to figures published in the *Progressive Daily* on that day, the party now has a membership of "over three million"; in 1945 the figure was 1,210,000. (In 1938 it is said to have been only about 200,000.)

A congratulatory message received by the party on this day ends with the words, "We fully believe that the Chinese people will unite forever under the leadership of your party, that a people's democratic and industrialized China will of necessity be built up successfully, and that your party will live forever with the Chinese people." This message is signed by the leaders of the Kuomintang Revolutionary Committee, the Democratic League, and seven other political groups—all of them founded, and, until recently, operated, in complete independence of the Communist party. All are now slated to participate in the forthcoming Political Consultative Conference. Their latest message suggests the degree of unanimity that may be expected at that conference.

"On the People's Democratic Dictatorship"

Mao's lengthy statement bearing this title, issued on the occasion of the Communist anniversary, is one of his major policy pronouncements to date. The following are some of its highlights (captions mine):

Communist Utopia

When a man reaches old age, he dies; it is the same with the [Communist] party. When classes are eliminated, all the instruments of class struggle, political parties, and the state apparatus will as a result lose their functions, . . . gradually wither away, . . . and travel toward the higher plane of the society of mankind. We are quite different from the political party of the bourgeoisie. They are afraid to talk of abolishing classes, state authority, and party. But we openly declare that we struggle hard precisely for the creation of conditions to accelerate the elimination of these things.

And Communist Reality

"Don't you want to eliminate state authority?" Yes, but not at present. We cannot eliminate the state authority now. Why? Because imperialism still exists, the domestic reactionaries still exist, and classes in the country still exist. Our present task is to strengthen the people's state apparatus, which refers mainly to the people's army, people's police, and people's court.

International Relations

Only one imperialist country in the world, the United States of America, suffered no loss [as the result of the war]. However, the domestic crisis of America is very grave. She wants to enslave the entire world and she aided Chiang Kai-shek with arms to slaughter several millions of Chinese. . . .

"We want to do business." Entirely correct. Business has to be done. We only oppose domestic and foreign reactionaries who hamper us from doing business. . . .

"Victory is also possible without international aid"—this is an erroneous thought. In the era when imperialism exists, it is impossible for the true people's revolution of any country to win its own victory without assistance in various forms from international revolutionary forces. . . .

"We need the aid of the British and American governments." This is also childish thought at present. At the present time, rulers in Britain and the United States are still imperialists. . . . Supposing that these countries are willing in future to lend us money on the condition of mutual benefits, what is the reason for it? It is because the capitalists of these countries want to make money, the bankers want to gain interest to relieve their own crises. . . . Internationally, we belong to the anti-imperialist front headed by the U.S.S.R., and we can look only for genuine friendly aid from that front.

Communism and Sun Yat-sen

A common conclusion has been reached, namely, "The firm belief that to attain victory we must awaken the masses of the people and unite ourselves in a common struggle with those peoples of the world who treat us on the basis of equality." Sun Yat-sen has a different world outlook from us, and started out from a different class standpoint, . . . but on the problem of how to struggle against imperialism . . . he arrived at a conclusion which was in basic agreement with ours.

No Middle Road Possible

"You lean to one side." Precisely so. The forty years' experience of Sun Yat-sen and twenty-eight years' experience of the Communist party have made us firmly believe that in order to win and consolidate victory we must lean to one side. . . . Without exception, the Chinese people either lean to the side of imperialism or of socialism. To sit on the fence is impossible; a third road does not exist. . . . Not only in China but also in the world, without exception, one either leans to the side of imperialism or of socialism.

Democratic Dictatorship

"You are dictatorial." Yes, dear gentlemen, you are right, and we are really that way. The experiences of several decades amassed by the Chinese people tell us to carry out the people's democratic dictatorship. That is, the right of reactionaries to voice their opinion must be taken away and only the people are to be allowed to have the right of voicing their opinion.

Who are the "people"? At the present stage in China, they are the working class, the peasant class, the petty bourgeoisie and national bourgeoisie. Under the leadership of the working class and the Communist party, these classes unite together to form their own state and elect their own government to enact dictatorship over the lackeys of imperialism—the landlord class, the bureaucratic-capitalistic class, and the Kuomintang reactionaries and their henchmen. . . . The democratic system is to be carried out within the ranks of the people, giving them freedom of speech, assembly, and association. The right to vote is only given to the people and not to the reactionaries. These two aspects, namely democracy among the people and dictatorship over the reactionaries, combine to form the people's democratic dictatorship. . . .

The methods we use in this field are democratic, that is, methods of persuasion and not coercion. . . . After their political regime is overthrown, members of the reactionary classes . . . will also be given land and work and a means of living to re-educate themselves through work, provided they do not rebel, disrupt, or sabotage. If they are unwilling to work, the people's state will compel them to work.

Peasants

The grave problem is that of educating peasants. The peasants' economy is scattered. According to the experience of the Soviet Union, it requires a very long time and careful work to attain the socialization of agriculture. Without the socialization of agriculture, there will be no complete and consolidated socialism. And to carry out the socialization of agriculture, a powerful industry with state-owned enterprises as the main component must be developed.

Workers

The people's democratic dictatorship needs the leadership of the working class, because only the working class is most farsighted, just, and unselfish. . . . In the era of imperialism, no other class in any country can lead any genuine revolution to victory. This is clearly proved by the fact that the Chinese national bourgeois class led the revolution many times and failed.

National Bourgeoisie

The national bourgeois class is of great importance at the present stage. . . . Only when China's industries are developed and China no longer depends on foreign countries economically, can there be real independence. . . . China must utilize all urban and rural capitalist factors which are beneficial and not detrimental to the national economy and people's livelihood and unite with the national bourgeoisie in common struggle. Our present policy is to restrict capitalism but not eliminate it. The national bourgeois class, however, cannot be the leader in the revolutionary united front and also cannot occupy the main position in the state.

Basis of Communist Success

A party with discipline, armed with the theories of Marx, Engels, Lenin, and Stalin, employing the method of self-criticism, and linked closely with the masses; an army led by such a party; a united front of various revolutionary strata and groups led by such a party—these mark us off from our predecessors. . . . Our experience may be summarized and boiled down to a single point—the people's democratic dictatorship based on the alliance of workers and peasants and led by the working class (through the Communist party). This dictatorship must unite . . . with international revolutionary forces.

Future Difficulties

We must overcome difficulties and master what we do not know. We must learn economic work from all who know the ropes (no matter who they are). . . . We must not pretend that we know when we do not know. Do not put on bureaucratic airs. . . . The Communist party of the U.S.S.R. is our best teacher.

This statement may be attacked on the basis of its ideas. But one thing must be said for it, it is a clear, cogent, dynamic presentation of the Communist point of view. It lets us know exactly how we and they stand. And it is selfless. Compare it with Chiang Kai-shek's moralistic generalities and his mystic identification of himself with "China's Destiny." In that comparison a measure of the difference between the two men emerges.

"Democratic Dictatorship" in Action

One of the most hated features of the old regime was that whereby Peking was administered through a series of regional units known as *pao* and *chia*. It was through the local heads of these units that the populace was spied upon, conscripted for military training or public works, and taxed in many ways, often illegally. When the Communists entered Peking, they abolished this system and replaced it with one consisting of twenty larger *ch'ü* (districts), each with its local bureaus of education, culture, labor, mediation, and the like, staffed by thirty-five to forty persons. It was planned that the heads of these bureaus would eventually be elected by the people living in their *ch'ü*; until now, however, they have been appointed by the municipal government. Each *ch'ü* was in turn subdivided into several lesser *chieh* (street) governments.

A few days ago this system was in turn abolished. It will be succeeded by a simpler system of smaller administrative units based upon the local police-station precincts throughout the city. Each precinct will be staffed by a single municipally-appointed chief, aided by a few assistants, all of whom will be responsible to the Bureau of Public Safety, i.e., the police bureau. The official reason for the change is that the *ch'ü* system was too cumbrous and complex, and no doubt it is true that the new system will effect a considerable saving in badly needed personnel. At the same time, however, it seems a step toward greater police control over the people. A further unexpressed reason may be that even in such a comparatively sophisticated city as Peking, the population has not yet reached the degree of political maturity needed for the effective political participation apparently envisaged in the original *ch'ü* system.

Confirmation of this was provided by the mass meeting of our own *ch'ü*, held June 29, at which it officially abolished itself. Because every family in the *ch'ü* had been urged in advance to send at least one member to the meeting, the good-sized movie theater in which it was held was well filled by the time proceedings got under way. Because, however, the meeting was held on a week day and in the morning—as the theater would be in use that afternoon—those present were mostly women (many old and probably illiterate), as well as innumerable children of all ages. I seemed to be the only foreigner there.

At 10 A.M., half an hour later than scheduled, the program began with a moment of silent bowing before a large portrait of Mao Tse-tung mounted on the stage—very reminiscent of the obeisance to Sun Yat-sen performed on such occasions in Kuomintang days. Five or six persons, some in the gray uniform of civil functionaries, others in khaki police uniform, and one in civilian dress, sat on the stage; additional civilian leaders, distinguished by paper badges in their buttonholes, occupied the first row. The chairman (in gray uniform), a tall, forceful young man with powerful voice, began matters by explaining the reasons for the proposed change. He emphasized the excellence of the police who were to handle the new setup and received loud applause when he remarked that "the police are now the people's police."

The subsequent speakers, however, unfortunately lacked his lung power, so that their soft voices became gradually drowned in a rising babel of squalling babies, mischievous children, and chattering women. Even from my second-row seat I could only occasionally hear what was said. Twice the chairman strode forward and called loudly for order. Each time his withdrawal was followed by a renewal of noise. Finally he advanced a third time, determinedly halted the current speaker in the middle of a sentence, and shouted above the din, "If there is no further discussion, it is the decision of this meeting that the *ch'ü* system be abolished!" The formal vote, if it had ever been contemplated, was dispensed with.

This closed the business part of the proceedings. Thereafter groups of school children performed, very charmingly, a series of *yang ko* dances and songs, including the popular number, "Without the Communist Party There Would Be No China." The change in the behavior of the audience at this point was truly remarkable. Such a hush fell upon the theater that even the words of a boy-and-girl duet could be heard with comparative ease. Half an hour later the crowd dispersed, apparently well satisfied with the morning's proceedings.

Mass Justice

Five days ago the proprietor of a Peking shoe store was sentenced to three and a half years imprisonment on charges of having repeatedly beaten and otherwise maltreated an apprentice. He was further ordered to pay the apprentice ten bags of flour as compensation for "mental and physical suffering."

What gives this case interest is that it was handled as a mass trial, attended by almost a thousand shop proprietors, employees, and apprentices from the defendant's district. The district head of the Municipal General Labor Association acted as prosecutor, testimony was taken from the plaintiff's fellow apprentices, and apprentices from other shops contributed their remarks. According to newspaper accounts, the affair reached its climax when "the general assembly, with one voice, shouted such slogans as, 'Promote the spirit of respect for masters and love for apprentices!' and 'Down with feudalistic oppression!' " Sentence was then pronounced by a member of the Municipal People's Court. The whole technique, reminiscent of the innumerable mass trials of landlords conducted during the past few years by the farmers' associations in the countryside, may seem, to some, a direct borrowing from Soviet Russia. It accords well, nevertheless, with the traditional Chinese abhorrence of formal court procedure and preference for informal settlement arranged within the sphere of one's own occupational or social group.

The Dance as an Instrument of Ideology

A small item in the June 28 *Progressive Daily* points out that the growing popularity of the *yang ko* dances has led to the appearance of certain undesirable characteristics. To check these, the Peiping Municipal General Labor Association has laid down four rules for its many *yang ko* performers:

(1) Male performers are forbidden to dress as women.
(2) Feudalistic and superstitious tendencies, such as the portrayal of Buddhist and Taoist priests, demons, etc., are henceforth banned.

(3) No vulgarity is to be permitted—for example, the portrayal of Chiang Kai-shek as a black turtle.

(4) Cosmetics are to be used with restraint.

These prohibitions—which, if strictly applied, will deprive the *yang ko* dances of not a little color—are reminiscent, despite their Communist origin, of the traditional and somewhat puritanical Confucian insistence upon moral propriety.

July 16 (Saturday)

Through Train from Shanghai

Latest step in the restoration of communications is the inauguration of through trains from Shanghai, made possible by the repair of the large Huai River bridge. A traveler arriving on the initial train, on July 5, reported the trip of slightly more than forty-five hours as comfortable and uneventful. It is strange to think that it is the first through train from Shanghai since shortly after the outbreak of the Sino-Japanese War in 1937.

Business and Taxes

How the North China authorities try to stimulate industry, and what types of industry they give top priority, is revealed in an order by the Tientsin municipality on July 5 proclaiming that various industries and trades are to be granted remission of taxes for the first half of 1949 according to the following schedule:

(1) Forty per cent remission: machine tool industries.

(2) Thirty per cent: mining industries; producers of communications and electrical equipment, smelting equipment, chemicals.

(3) Twenty per cent: producers of chemical fertilizers, agricultural tools, cultural, educational, medical, and health supplies; exporting and shipping concerns; manufacturers of export goods.

(4) Fifteen per cent: producers of printing equipment, substitutes for imported products (kerosene, gasoline, batteries, glass, hemp bags, etc.), building materials, tires.

(5) Ten per cent: producers of non-machine-communications implements (wooden carts, boats, etc.), repair tools, everyday necessities (cotton cloth, pottery, needles, nails, matches, etc.); makers of handicraft products; hospitals; transport concerns.

How to Increase Production

In a letter to Mao Tse-tung, the 10,000 workers of a Dairen glass factory proudly proclaim the completion of their factory's 1949 production quota in six months' time. "The letter," reports the July 10 *Daily News Release,* "said that the livelihood of workers and staff members had been greatly improved owing to the application of the principles of 'more labor, more pay,' 'progressive bonus' and 'piece-rate wages.' " In other words, the same speed-up methods are praised which, if reported from America, would be denounced as examples of sweated labor. The difference, according to the official line, is that in America such practices serve only to profit the private capitalist; here they benefit the nation as a whole, and thereby the workers themselves.

July 30 (Saturday)

The Joys of Travel

The gap in this record is due to no lack of news but to sheer pressure of other work. At the moment we are preparing for our departure from China—not a particularly easy thing to arrange these days. One of the difficulties is the Kuomintang-imposed naval blockade, which throws uncertainty into the thin trickle of passenger steamers between Tientsin and Hong Kong—now the only means of exit from Communist China. This in turn makes

it difficult to coordinate our prospective arrival in Hong Kong
with the plane flight from there to San Francisco (purchased last
fall during the mass exodus of foreigners).

The fact that my letter to Pan American's Hong Kong office,
sent over a month ago, remains unanswered, makes things even
more uncertain. This morning I learned the possible reason
when I tried to send another letter to Hong Kong, only to have
it refused at the post office on the ground that I had failed to
write the complete address in Chinese. How, unless one knows
them already, is one to write the Chinese ideographs for such
names as Miller, Dupont Corporation, or Marina House? What
I did was to scribble characters having some phonetic resemblance, and the letter was then promptly accepted. But who
knows, perhaps my first letter, because it lacked these symbols, is
still lying around in the post office here.*

Floods, Typhoons, and Prices

It is now 4 P.M., and since 6:30 this morning the rain has been
descending in an unending roar. Shortly before lunch we were
startled by a dull rumble rising above the sound of the rain.
Looking out, we saw that a sizable section of the water-logged
garden wall had collapsed, burying a lovely little bush beneath
its bricks.

This is the climax to an unprecedented rainy season which
began about mid-June on the heels of an equally unprecedented
spring drought and has continued with few interruptions ever
since. At Tientsin the river has risen well above the danger
point, and in the South the Yangtze floods are rumored to be the
worst since 1931. Our papers report ten million persons homeless
in the Kuomintang area, with 127,000 dead in Kwangtung and
Hunan alone. Though little is said about conditions in Communist China, it is obvious that natural disasters are no respec-
ters of political boundaries.

* This suspicion proved unwarranted, for on arriving in Hong Kong on September
5 we found that my first letter, mailed June 25, had preceded us by about two
weeks.

As if this were not enough, a few days ago a typhoon struck Shanghai and, coinciding with high tides and flood waters, inundated almost the entire city. Thousands were made homeless and on Nanking Road, Shanghai's Broadway, the water reached thigh level in front of the Wing On department store.

What all this means economically is shown by the catastrophic rise in prices since early July. During the four weeks of June 29 to July 27 wholesale prices went up by 84.20 per cent, and laborers' cost of living by 103.87 per cent. The outlook for the winter is grim, and rumors already circulate that the peasants, forced to supply the cities with large quantities of food, are in a state as bad or worse than that under the Kuomintang. These rumors, however, come from people admittedly hostile to the new regime. For us foreigners, confined almost entirely to the city, it is as hard to check up on their truth as it is to determine the real state of industrial production from the glowing accounts appearing in the papers.

Interrogation of Foreigners

The past month has been bad for the foreigner. Aside from stepped-up anti-imperialist propaganda, several unpleasant incidents have been reported from Shanghai, notably the case of the temporary arrest of "former" American Vice-Consul Olive. In Tientsin the Chase National Bank has closed its doors rather than open its books, like other banks, to government inspection. In all the Communist cities in which the U. S. Information Service functioned, its offices have been closed on the grounds that no diplomatic relations exist between the United States and the regime here. Its British and Soviet counterparts, however—the British Council and VOKS—have been spared, ostensibly because they do not fall under the jurisdiction of their respective foreign offices.

Here in Peking the entire foreign community has been undergoing re-registration at the Bureau of Public Safety. The procedure is long and onerous. It involves several visits, the writing of quadruplicate answers in Chinese to a fairly detailed questionnaire (rejected if answers are incomplete or wrong), and submission of six photos. The climax is a personal interview, lasting anywhere from fifteen minutes to an hour, at which all answers are carefully recorded.

On the day of our interview, we found the Bureau's small waiting room crowded with foreigners of numerous nationalities, with others pacing somewhat nervously up and down the courtyard outside. After waiting about half an hour, we heard our name called, only to learn to our surprise that we were to be interviewed separately. I was summoned first and asked to sit at a table occupied by four interviewers. Several I recognized as hold-overs from the Kuomintang regime, but in a corner behind me, taking no part in the proceedings, sat a fifth man who, I suppose, must have been a Communist.

In my case the proceedings were conducted entirely in Chinese, but in Galia's an interpreter was supplied. The main questions concerned my educational background, purpose of residence in China, friends, especially Chinese, and whether I had any political affiliations. Nothing was said about my source of income or other financial matters, but these topics were stressed when Galia's turn came to be interviewed. The questioning throughout was polite and unexceptional, and, after about twenty minutes each, we were through.

Some other foreigners, however, have been asked amusing or impertinent questions: "Do you have many boy friends?" "Do you have a Chinese mistress?" "What kind of books do you read?" "Do you smoke?" "Do you like to dance?" The prize one was that asked of a Rotarian: "What is this Rotary Club anyway? Some kind of a dancing organization?"

Trade and Imperialism

Imperialism or no imperialism, one fact remains of some importance—America continues to be the best trader with Communist China. Tientsin customs figures for June show exports at PN$4,-139,660,618—more than double those of May. Imports, however, were only PN$1,168,270,889—13 per cent off from May. The

United States held first place in both categories by an easy margin, 42.36 per cent of the exports and 38 per cent of the imports. Dried eggs were first in exports, comprising 16.73 per cent of the total; newsprint was the most important import, comprising 22.56 per cent.

Early this month the provisional trade regulations for East China (meaning primarily Shanghai) were published. They provide that exporters suffering from temporary financial difficulties may seek assistance from the Bank of China, and that priority will be given to the import of machinery and of supplies needed for manufacturing export goods, as well as to exporters trying to develop new foreign markets. Exports will be inspected by the government so as to improve and standardize their quality. Those below specifications will be refused clearance. No apparent mention is made of the "link barter system" (balancing of each individual export against a corresponding import), which has proved such a bone of contention in Tientsin.

Meanwhile, here in the north, all outgoing products have, at about the same time, been exempted from export duty. Thus, in foreign trade at least, the authorities seem to be learning through experience.

Collectivization

In China proper there is no hint as yet of any effort to hurry the land program beyond its first stage of redistribution of land to private owners. Manchuria, however, provides possible clues to what may eventually happen. The July 22 *Daily News Release* tells of the existence of seventeen "publicly operated farms" in Manchuria, totaling 55,000 acres and operating 231 tractors. These farms, created only this spring through the reclamation of waste land and opening of virgin soil, are expected to harvest over 33,000 tons of crops.

How the Land Program Works

It is easy to criticize Communist mistakes in urban administration or foreign affairs—fields in which they are least experienced —while forgetting their solid achievements in rural reform about which few of us foreigners have any first-hand information. I felt fortunate the other evening, therefore, to meet a man—a young non-Chinese sociologist—who has spent many months observing how the land program works in a small village in northern Honan. Here are a few of the things he saw and learned:

This community, typical of the innumerable villages that dot the great North China plain, has a population of about 1,400. Though first occupied by the Eighth Route Army as early as 1941, no serious land reform was attempted there until around 1945, and even then very gradually. The aim of the team of political workers in charge was to educate the peasants at each step to the point where they themselves would be willing and able to proceed on their own. This was done through a Poor Peasants' Association, membership in which consisted of one elected representative from every twelve peasant families.

Several of these representatives, though illiterate, later joined the Communist party. According to my informant it was remarkable how quickly they came to understand Marxist ideas. Their terminology was amusing. The haves were called "mounds," and the have-nots "holes." "Levelling the mounds" and "filling up the holes" were the terms used to express the aim of the land program. "Struggle-fruits" was their designation for daily necessities, such as food, shelter and clothing, for which the struggle of existence must be waged; "struggle-objects" was what they called landlords, usurers, and the like against whom this struggle is directed.

Initially (1945) the program was limited to the reduction of rent and interest rates; actual land redistribution did not start till 1947. Even then, in fact, the only land legally subject to confiscation was that of landlords and "rich peasants"—those who derive one fourth or more of their total income through "exploitation," i.e., the hiring of outside labor.

Since, according to Communist statistics, only some ten per

cent of China's rural population belongs to these two classes, this means, in the words of my informant, that the land reform aims at "egalitarian distribution" rather than absolute equalization.

In this particular village, as a matter of fact, most landlords had already been "liquidated" before land redistribution was actually attempted. This had been brought about by demanding immediate payment of all back taxes of several years standing—from which their privileged position had formerly exempted them. Unable to pay in one lump, they had no alternative but to surrender their land. Such was the situation when the first of three widely spaced meetings of the Poor Peasants' Association took place. At these, each peasant was called upon to declare before the Association the amount of his land and annual income.

At this first meeting the peasants were still timid and hesitant. Because of "face" considerations, the statements of certain individuals were allowed to pass unchallenged, even in cases in which they obviously understated the value of their land. Much greater outspokenness prevailed at the second meeting, however, and the third, when it took place, served primarily as a recheck upon the results of the second. No land assignments became final until after this third meeting. In making them, account was taken not only of the amounts of land involved but also their fertility, nearness to the village, and similar considerations. The aim was to consolidate properties and eliminate uneconomical strip holdings as much as possible. Simultaneously a campaign was launched to restore to cultivation the ancestral grave mounds that have long taken from the farmer so much of his potentially arable land.

With the growth of peasant political consciousness, the traveling team of political workers was reduced from thirteen to three, and eventually withdrawn altogether. Thus the future operation of the program is to be left entirely in peasant hands, save for occasional check-up visits.

Like so much that the Communists do, this program tries, through mass meetings and public confession, to lift the individual to a high pitch of moral fervor. At the later meetings, in fact, so much enthusiasm was generated that some peasants could hardly be restrained from surrendering land which they obviously were in no economic position to give up.

So successful was the effort of making everybody into a middle-class peasant that a graduated tax, instituted during the early stages, was later abolished as no longer necessary. Present taxes, though lighter than those under the Kuomintang, yield more to the authorities, according to my informant, because of the absence of corruption. Former landlords, having been dispossessed of their original holdings, were then reassigned land according to their new status as middle-class peasants. Now they receive exactly the same treatment as everyone else. Nor are any restrictions laid upon the so-called "new rich peasants." These are the peasants who, following the land reform and abolition of high rents and usury, succeed through their own unaided efforts in forging ahead of their neighbors.

One important feature of the program is that of the mutual-aid peasant groups, the members of which work in common to cultivate each other's fields, and especially to perform such tasks as are better suited to cooperative than to individual effort. Careful count is kept of the labor contributed by each member—with the labor of a donkey or mule sometimes counting for more than that of its owner. Thus a balance is kept between what each individual contributes to his group and what he receives in return. Through this institution more than anything else the Communists seem to be laying a psychological basis for that ultimate stage of collectivization toward which, as they themselves state, the present program is only a first step.

As I listened to what this worker for the Communists had to say, I could not help being struck by his evident sincerity and spirit of self-sacrifice—qualities also apparent in another non-Chinese worker whom I have recently met. To undergo the hardships and the isolation from their countrymen, willingly accepted by these men, calls for a genuine idealism such as no one, not even the severest critic of their cause, should deny them.

Three Years of War

According to recently issued statistics for the three years of civil war from July 1, 1946, to July 1, 1949, the territory occupied during this period is slightly less than one third of China as a whole, but contains over 58 per cent of the population and 80 per cent of the railroads; more than 79 per cent of the latter have already been restored to traffic. It is further claimed that, whereas at the beginning of the war the Kuomintang armed forces enjoyed a numerical superiority of 3.58:1 over the People's Army, today that ratio has been reversed to 2.68:1 in favor of the latter.

Kuomintang manpower losses during the three years are said to total 5,691,400, of which 27 per cent represent casualties, 60 per cent prisoners, and 12 per cent soldiers who went over to the Communist side. The comparative statistics for the People's Army are particularly illuminating: 1,432,900 total losses, of which 86.09 per cent are casualties, 13 per cent missing, and *only 0.73 per cent prisoners.*

Culture in the New China: Theory

Organizational activity continues intense, apparently with the aim of eventually placing all members of the population within some particular organization. Most prominent among recent congresses has been the First All-China Conference of Writers and Artists, attended the earlier part of this month by "more than 207 literary workers, 86 artists, 250 playwrights, stage directors, actors and actresses, and cinema workers, 68 musicians, and 3 folk-dance experts, from all parts of China." Included among the many big names was Mei Lan-fang, the famous old-time actor. Kuo Mo-jo, leftist poet and archaeologist, was chairman.

The conference produced numerous statements on the function of literature and art in the new society. Among them was that of Ch'en Po-ta, assistant head of the Central Propaganda Department of the Communist Party:

Workers in literature and the arts should possess ideology and their works should be ones possessing ideology. . . . The popularization and raising of the level of literature cannot be done without ideological guidance. . . . [Writers should] learn to depict Communist party leaders after they have learned to depict the masses. Writers cannot produce good works on the mass movement if they write only about the masses and fail to depict the leading cadres and the leading role of Mao Tse-tung's ideology. . . . Mao Tse-tung's ideology is not to be worshiped, but his method and style of work should be learned. . . . [At the same time writers and artists should] eulogize the people and the proletariat. Eulogizing does not mean flattering, for the people also have shortcomings. Therefore, apart from eulogizing, there must also be criticism and self-criticism.

Another statement, by Ch'ien Ch'un-jui, secretary of the Chinese Delegation to the World Peace Congress held this spring in Paris and Prague, is unpleasantly reminiscent of the current Soviet attacks on "bourgeois cosmopolitanism":

So-called "cosmopolitanism" is a tool of American imperialism in its attempt to dominate the world. The aim of this "cosmopolitanism" is to ignore the independence and characteristics of various nations and weaken their self-confidence and self-respect. . . . We should love the people, history, and excellent arts and cultural traditions of China and create works of proletarian patriotism and proletarian internationalism.

Thus in China, as in Russia, the present wave of ultra-nationalism leads to an unresolved contradiction: in the context of China's relations with the outside world, the word "excellent" is to be used to describe her arts and cultural traditions; in the context of China's internal social development, however, these same arts and traditions must be branded as feudalistic, since, according to Marxist theory, they are the products of a feudalistic society.

Culture in the New China: Practice

Can art and literature be great and at the same time propaganda? Of course they can, but only when two conditions exist: The artist or writer must wholeheartedly believe in the message he tries to convey. At the same time he must retain sufficient artistic integrity to avoid the sacrifice of artistic reality to propagandistic formula.

What happens in a society in which all cultural workers are told to produce according to a given ideology? A few, especially in the first flush of revolutionary enthusiasm, may create great art. The works of others, however, even with the best will in the world, will probably be stereotyped and fail to realize the full potentialities of their creators. For it is idle to suppose that a man who may be an excellent imagist poet can at the same time be an equally good writer of Marxist plays, any more than a man who by temperament is an idealist philosopher can suddenly become a convincing exponent of materialism.

The Marxist answer, of course, is that no man is temperamentally this or that unless certain factors exist in society that induce him to be this or that. Remove, for example, the social factors that make for idealistic philosophy, and idealist philosophers will no longer exist. To which the non-Marxist will reply that genius (and with it, more specific mental characteristics) appears or does not appear irrespective of birth and social background. Abraham Lincoln was great, though he was born poor; Franklin Roosevelt was also great, though he was born rich. And thus the argument can continue ad infinitum.

To get back to culture in the new China: The exhibition of "proletarian" paintings held in Central Park some two months ago, interesting though it was, was essentially unsuccessful owing to the failure of technique to live up to conception. Quite otherwise was the impression produced by the large exhibition—filling seventeen good-sized rooms—that was held at the College of Fine Arts early this month. Its many forms included oils and water colors, sculpture and engravings, cartoons and posters. Some were the sophisticated work of semi-westernized artists in Shanghai and Hong Kong, some the childlike and truly "proletarian" drawings of untutored peasants, soldiers, and laborers. Many professional works were derivative, but others were powerful and original. Notable, for example, was a sculptured group labeled "Air Raid," in which a fleeing mother crouches low to the ground and stares apprehensively upward over one shoulder, while holding one child by the hand and a second to her breast. Or a black-and-white cartoon depicting a huge ship labeled "U.S.A.," a glaring eye on either side of its lofty prow, which crashes with demoniac force through a conglomeration of toppling city buildings.

Most interesting, however, were the less sophisticated works prepared by Communist propagandists for use among the peasants. There were colored lantern slides illustrating the prowess of the Liberation Army or its cooperation with the people; lithographed wall newspapers in which the news of the day was presented in the form of brightly colored pictures arranged like American comic strips; colored New Year pictures (traditionally posted in peasant homes at Chinese New Year) in which the traditional God of Wealth and the Eight Immortals are replaced by such up-to-date themes as peasants working together in the field or participating in a "bean election" (voting for village officials by casting beans into jars set beneath the names and pictures of candidates); "scissor pictures" (designs cut with scissors from red paper —a traditional art of peasant women), likewise modernized to show Liberation Army soldiers or peasants at work.

Many statistics accompanied these displays. Nineteen lantern-slide performances, for example, were given in two months to 17,700 people by the cultural corps of the Third Field Army. Four hundred kinds of New Year pictures were printed in the liberated areas during the past five years. Wall newspapers had a total circulation of 296,000 among an estimated population of three million in the Shansi-Suiyuan area.

The entire exhibition left two dominant impressions. One was the dynamic force that graphic art can have when it is harnessed with conviction and skill to certain guiding ideas. The other was the extent to which the Communists, as no other group in Chinese history, have succeeded in conveying their message to China's rural millions.

In the field of drama, on the other hand, we recently saw what can happen when artistic values are excessively sacrificed to purposes of propaganda. The play, *Song of the Red Flag*, differs from the far superior *The White-haired Girl* in that it is entirely a spoken drama—aside from one theme song. Its subject is the life of girl workers in a postliberation spinning mill. It treats their perpetual squabbles resulting from misunderstanding of the new ideology, the inability of the mill owner, himself a product of the old regime, to deal with these squabbles, and, by way of contrast, the success of the Communist-appointed manager, a hero of almost unbelievable gentleness, tact, and patience. Action centers around the struggle for the soul of one particularly unregenerate girl. Fired by the owner in a fit of temper, she bitterly resists the new way of life until he atones for his action—at the persuasion of the manager—by sending her three sacks of flour. She then suddenly realizes that "the factories are now the people's factories," and sees the light with revivalist fervor. The final act ends in triumph as she leads her comrades in a production race which wins for their factory the coveted red flag.

As an educational tract for Chinese factory workers, the play no doubt serves a useful purpose. It portrays *ad nauseam* all the problems in human relations that might conceivably arise in a factory and the ideal way of handling them. As a play, however, I found it dull, lacking in dramatic impact (save for one or two episodes), too long, too didactic, and too unrealistic.

August 1949

August 2 (Tuesday)

"Union at the Heavenly River"—Revised

Yesterday, the seventh day of the seventh lunar month, was the festival of the Cowherd and the Weaving Girl. Each year on this day a play called *Union at the Heavenly River* is customarily presented to commemorate the legend of this celestial pair.

The story is that of a young cowherd who, constantly abused by his elder brother and sister-in-law, runs away from home accompanied by his supernatural cow, spies a group of beautiful goddesses bathing in a river, steals the clothes of one of them, the celestial weaving girl, and thus compels her to be his wife. The pair live happily together and become prosperous. Meanwhile, however, the cowherd's evil brother and sister-in-law suffer sucessive misfortunes culminating in the destruction of their home by heavenly fire. Finally they are forced to come as indigents to the despised younger brother, who forgives and aids them. About this time, however, his wife discovers the garments which she had worn as a goddess, puts them on, and returns to Heaven. The cowherd pursues her, only to be balked by the barrier of the "Heavenly River" (Milky Way). Thereupon the ruler of Heaven decrees that one night in every seven the pair shall be allowed to meet. They mistake him as saying, however, that it shall be only once a year on the seventh day of the seventh month. Every year on this night, therefore, the magpies form a bridge with their wings over which the cowherd and the weaving girl (believed to be two constellations on either side of the Milky Way) may rejoin each other.

Members of the theatrical world, both here and in Tientsin, have lately been discussing ways of bringing this play into line with current ideology. Typical is a Tientsin meeting reported in the July 24 *Progressive Daily*. At this meeting it was agreed that the good points of the play are its portrayal of the rewards that come with hard work, and its implied criticism of lack of freedom in selecting a marriage partner. It was also agreed, however, that it suffers from certain defects, notably oversexiness (the bathing scene) and overemphasis on superstition (the incident of the heavenly fire). Several ways to overcome these faults were suggested. Least radical would be the addition of a prologue and epilogue in which the play's weaknesses would be pointed out in speeches to the audience. More radical would be deletion of the heavenly fire and portrayal of the impoverishment of the brother and sister-in-law as the direct result of their own idleness and bad conduct. Most radical of all would be to strip the play of all supernatural elements and place it into a wholly mundane setting. Each theatrical group was left free to work out its own solution.

As the result of this and similar meetings, all Peking and Tientsin theaters are now advertising themselves as producers of "new" versions of *Union at the Heavenly River*. Yesterday afternoon we went to see one for ourselves, fully prepared for sharp surprises. We were pleased, however, to find most of the story played as in former years, the only major change being the deletion of a short final scene in which the ruler of Heaven decrees the future time of rendezvous for the couple. This deletion was accepted without comment by the audience.

Last night, however, our boy Chin attended another performance of the same company. On that occasion the audience was apparently made of sterner stuff, for as the curtain fell without the final scene, many people set up a clamor of "Not finished! Not finished!" Not only this, but they refused to leave the theater even after a member of the company stepped forth to explain that the cut was made in order to combat superstition. His appearance, in fact, was greeted by added protest, emphasized by a shower of melon seeds from the front rows. It was almost ten minutes before the audience finally filed sullenly out. This, to my knowledge, is the first instance of popular protest against changing the old into the new. Obviously it was induced by the inept way in which the company had arranged its new version.*

August 14 (Sunday)

Uncertain Exit

We are now scheduled to leave Peking on the twenty-third and Tientsin on the twenty-sixth, blockade permitting. This blockade has become more than a joking matter. The grapevine reports that several ships have been prevented by Kuomintang naval vessels from entering Tientsin the last four or five days, that some have been searched, and that two, of Chinese registry, were even sunk. Not a word of this, of course, in the local press.

Food and Grumbling

Price rises continue, though at a considerably slower tempo. The rainy season, thank God, seems to be tapering off. Floods continue, however. Today's *Progressive Daily* reports that in our Hopei province alone more than ten million *mu* (about 1,666,666 acres) have been inundated, affecting 3,288 communities with a total population of about 300,000. Train service between Mukden and Tientsin has been cut for a number of days. All government employees in Hopei have consequently been ordered to eat one ounce less of grain per day per person, while the general populace is exhorted to cooperate in a one-bowl-of-grain-per-meal-only movement.

In the South the economic situation is obviously even more difficult. A Chinese friend wrote from Shanghai on August 6: "Already owing to a number of reasons, rice here is something like

* On August 8 a two-month indoctrination course for theatrical workers was introduced in Peking. Attended by 450 persons, it consisted of three weekly morning sessions of lectures and group discussions in which emphasis was laid on how to bring revolutionary content into the old plays.

US$30 a picul [about 133 lbs.] instead of the US$5 before liberation. Generally speaking, conditions are more difficult with us
than they were before. As our university faces the coming year with
smaller enrollment and lower tuition (with the faculty and staff
remaining the same), and therefore a smaller budget, our pay is
likely to be further reduced."

Though here in the North, teachers' salaries are protected
against inflation by being calculated in terms of millet, I have
twice heard complaints recently that even this device is not entirely successful. The reason is the time lag of two or three days
between the periodic calculation of salaries and their actual payment, during which sharp price rises may occur. Today's *Progressive Daily* announces a partial remedy for this situation. If, during
this interim period, the price of millet rises by more than 20 per
cent, this increase will be compensated for when the next salary
payment is made.

Here in Peking, or so it seems to me—and this, of course, is a
highly subjective impression—there is a slackening of enthusiasm
compared with a month or so ago. Complaints are frequent about
the difficulty of making ends meet, and rumors persist, seemingly
more widespread than before, of suffering in the countryside.

What percentage of the population remains definitely antagonistic to the new regime? Of course there is no way of knowing.
All I can say is that lately I seem to have heard more overt criticism
than formerly. Recently I was invited to an elaborate dinner party
attended by seven or eight oldish Chinese scholars. As course followed course in rich profusion, the conversation consisted of an
almost uninterrupted series of grumblings and criticisms. Sarcastic
remarks were passed about some of the "democratic personages"
whose statements now figure so prominently in the press. The
word "opportunist" occurred more than once. The new leftist
scholarship was criticized in no uncertain terms—one man's style
is poor, another's scholarship inadequate, and so on.

From this particular group of older scholars such sentiments
are not too surprising. But what about the younger intellectuals,
among whom the Communists find their most enthusiastic support? A few days ago I met two young Chinese artists, one of whom
could speak, haltingly, a few words of English. I asked how he had

learned them. "By listening to the radio," he replied. "I have a short-wave radio, over which I hear BBC, Voice of America, New Delhi, and many other stations." Then, after a pause, "How long I shall be able to do this, I don't know. As time passes, conditions will become tighter. But at the moment we still have freedom of ear." To which his friend, who was conspicuously wearing a Mao Tse-tung button, added, "You see this button? It cost me only $100. It says nothing important. Simply 'Mao Tse-tung, Chairman of the Chinese Communist Party.' So I bought it, thinking it would be helpful when I go in and out of the city."

Such are the sentiments of a few scattered intellectuals. But what about the common people? Here is the way a Chinese we know well, an intelligent man who is himself sympathetic to the regime, sums up what he believes to be the feelings of many:

"Food is the important thing. Maybe conditions will be fine a year from now, but the *lao pai hsing* don't care about that. What they have to think about is how to fill their stomachs today, tomorrow, and the day after. It doesn't matter that food shortages may be caused by drought, flood, the blockade, or other things for which the Communists are not responsible. A government is good if the people have enough to eat; it is bad if they don't have enough. That's how the *lao pai hsing* feel, not what I think myself. Everybody hated the Japanese because they didn't give us enough to eat. My mother and wife used to go to the grain shop at midnight and sleep in line until next morning, and even then they might be able to buy only a couple of pounds of bad millet between them. So everyone was happy when the Kuomintang came back, and for a while American flour helped a little. But then things got worse, so everyone was happy when the Kuomintang was kicked out and the Communists came in. But now things are getting bad again. What's going to happen next? That's what a lot of people are asking."

My friend went on to describe the weekly meetings in his local police district of those families whose chief wage earners have entered the government here or joined the southern expedition. These meetings, held under the auspices of the district administrator of military dependents' affairs (a woman veteran of the Liberation Army), are attended by some twelve families, including that of my friend. Chief item on the agenda is the difficulty several of these families have in supporting themselves now that their chief wage earners have gone southward. When this movement started, some months ago, the authorities pledged themselves to give economic aid to all dependents who might fall in need. Now, however, the government is itself so hard pressed that it finds it difficult to carry out this promise.

At one meeting, for example, an old lady of seventy, now left alone in Peking with a three-year-old grandson, rose and with tears in her eyes read a letter she had recently received from her son in Hankow. "Have you," he wrote, "been receiving the grain promised by the government when I went away?" The answer, the old lady pointed out, was "no." At this juncture my friend rose with her and declared that the government should not have made pledges which it has since been unable to fulfill. To this the chairwoman protested vigorously. The People's Government, she pointed out, is a government for the people. How then could it possibly have accepted able-bodied men for the army without promising security for their dependents? Its present difficulties, she continued, were the temporary result of drought, flood, and other unforeseen factors. Later, however, she admitted that the government is now no longer making such commitments when asking for recruits. (In this connection it should be understood that there is no such thing as a draft under the People's Govern ment; all recruiting is entirely voluntary.)

What is being done concretely to cope with this situation? Several things, my friend told me. He and others in his district, for example, have been given tickets allowing them to buy grain in the cooperatives. Factory jobs have been promised to unemployed members of some families. In the case of my friend himself, his younger daughter has been promised free tuition in a private middle school. But the case of the seventy-year-old lady remains unsolved.

Further questioning elicited from him the information that few Peking cooperatives (whose membership now exceeds 185,000, according to latest published figures) still sell directly to the general public. Membership is largely limited to the employees of specific factories or other organizations, or to persons like my friend who for special reasons are given membership tickets. Furthermore, prices are sometimes only slightly lower than those on the open market.

What about the factories, I then asked? How do they find places for these newly employed dependents of military personnel? His reply was that some jobs have opened up as the result of factory workers themselves volunteering for the southern expedition, some have been created through expanding production, and in certain cases persons with reactionary tendencies may have been dropped from their positions.

I then asked whether the private middle school to which my friend's daughter has been promised free admission had any choice in the matter. His reply was that it did not. Such schools, as their contribution toward alleviating the situation, have been asked by the authorities to accept a certain quota of deserving students tuition-free. (It should be remembered in this connection that Peking's public middle schools are insufficient to meet the educational demand.)

Such are the comments of an intelligent though irritable and sometimes excitable Chinese, whose opinions I have nevertheless always found provocative.

Manchuria and the Soviet Union

In the midst of this depressing situation, much fanfare has been given to the one-year trade agreement between Manchuria and the Soviet Union, the signing of which was announced from Moscow on July 30. Under it Russia is to supply Manchuria with industrial installations, motor vehicles, petroleum, cloth, paper, medical drugs, and instruments, in return for soybeans, vegetable oils, corn, rice, and the like. The quantities involved are unspecified.

How do people in Peking, Shanghai, and elsewhere feel about the export, at this time, of Chinese *grain* in return for "industrial installations" quite possibly in part the same as those the Russians originally removed from Manchuria in 1945? The newspapers, of course, give the impression that the reaction is one of unqualified enthusiasm. Statements by workers, industrialists, intellectuals, all hail the pact as another demonstration of Soviet friendship and a crushing reply by the Chinese people to the "imperialist blockade."

This pact, signed in the absence of formal diplomatic relations, suggests a cooperation between Russia and Manchuria seemingly greater than that between Russia and China proper. So, perhaps, does the announcement made in Mukden on August 7 that "Russian will be the first foreign language in all high schools and universities." Here in China proper, though an expansion of Russian-language teaching is planned, English continues to hold its traditional primacy.

How To Lose Friends and Antagonize People— Communist Style

The fourth anniversaries of the Soviet declaration of war on Japan on August 8, 1945, and of the Japanese surrender on August 15, have been signals for a renewed "sell Russia" publicity campaign. Typical is the August 8 broadcast of Hu Yu-chih, "Chinese expert on foreign affairs":

"Without the troops of the Soviet Union in Manchuria, Japan might not have surrendered. Even if she did surrender, a great part of China would temporarily have become the colony of American imperialism, as South Korea and the Philippines are at present. It would not have been easy for the people of the Northeast and those throughout the country to win their swift victory today."

Today's *Progressive Daily* elaborates on the same theme in its answer to a reader who asks: "Whose force brought about the surrender of the Japanese pirates?" The editorial reply is:

The surrender of the Japanese pirates resulted from the heroic eight-year resistance of the Chinese people, and especially of the Eighth Route Army under the leadership of the Communist party. . . . At the same time it resulted from the alliance of the various allies then linked in the common struggle against Japanese fascism. . . . The final factor bringing about the Japanese surrender was the Soviet declaration of war on Japan on August 8, 1945. . . . Within a week the Soviet Red Army, in conjunction with the forces of Outer Mongolia,

. . . destroyed or captured 764,000 men of the Japanese Imperial Kuantung Army. . . . If the Soviet Union had not sent troops into Manchuria, a military decision could not have been reached so speedily, because Japan still retained a very powerful army at the time . . . with which it could have continued resistance against the allied forces. . . .

The American imperialists, however, with their running dogs, the Kuomintang reactionaries, spread propaganda to the effect that the defeat of Japanese fascism resulted solely from the use of two atomic bombs. Such talk is completely deceptive, for even though Soviet participation in the [Japanese] war came late, the fact remains that, if the Soviet people had not been ready, with their spirit of lofty self-sacrifice, to resist and destroy Hitler's great armies in the West, America would certainly have been unable to conduct her offensive against Japan in the Pacific. And if, after Germany's surrender, the Soviet Union had not participated in the war against Japan and destroyed her exceedingly powerful Kuantung Army, the war against Japan could not have been concluded with the August 15 surrender four years ago. . . .

The purpose of this deceptive talk on the part of the Americans and their running dogs is to conceal their sin of seizing and holding the fruits of victory for themselves alone, and, by exaggerating the power of the atomic bomb, to terrorize the people of the world's various peace-loving countries in order to facilitate their own dark designs for conducting new aggression as conditions permit. . . .

Such is the picture of history that the Communists and their supporters—it should be remembered that the *Progressive Daily* is not officially a Communist organ—wish to give their people. One wonders how many they hope to convince. Their most difficult psychological task, as I have been told repeatedly, is that of explaining away Russian actions in Manchuria and of reinterpreting in terms of noble altruism the 1945 Sino-Soviet Friendship Treaty (the one Kuomintang treaty which the Communists never refer to as "Kuomintang"). This topic is one that cropped up frequently during the summer indoctrination course for university students recently concluded at Tsinghua, and the official way of handling it failed to arouse great enthusiasm.

How To Lose Friends and Antagonize People— American Style

The effect here of the State Department's White Paper on China (issued August 5 but first made known in Peking on the twelfth) has been disastrous. Here are some of the passages from Mr. Acheson's introduction that have aroused particularly violent comment:

(1) "The Nationalist armies did not lose a single battle during the crucial year of 1948 through lack of arms and ammunition." The real cause of defeat was that their "government had lost popular support." These facts notwithstanding, the United States continued its "historic policy . . . of friendship and aid toward the people of China" in the form of several billion dollars' worth of military and economic aid to the Nationalist government.

Comment: What kind of "friendship" toward what "people"? Everywhere the document blames Kuomintang incompetence for what has happened in China. Why does it nowhere blame the United States itself for maintaining a policy that was morally wrong and politically disastrous?

(2) Full scale American intervention "would have been resented by the mass of the Chinese people, would have diametrically reversed our historic policy, and would have been condemned by the American people."

Comment from the New China News Agency: "Really strange! If the American government actually harbored a friendly attitude towards the Chinese people, why should extending the sphere and scope of such a friendship . . . evoke the indignation of one party . . . and denunciation by the other? . . . American imperialist elements fancy that the whole world is stupid, but the results show it is only they who are stupid."

(3) "The Communist leaders have forsworn their Chinese heritage and have publicly announced their subservience to a foreign power, Russia."

Comment: If that is so, why does Mr. Acheson himself admit that the Chinese revolution "was the product of internal Chinese forces, forces which this country tried to influence but could not"?

If the Chinese Communists, by taking their stand with Russia in the present world schism, are to be accused of having "forsworn their Chinese heritage," why should not the European signatories to the North Atlantic Pact be accused with equal justice of having forsworn their European heritage?

(4) "Ultimately the profound civilization and the democratic individualism of China will reassert themselves and she will throw off the foreign yoke. I consider that we should encourage all developments in China which now and in the future work toward this end."

Comment: This statement has been seized upon as an open threat to interfere in Chinese internal affairs—a threat which ill accords with America's reiterated policy of respect for the territorial and administrative integrity of China. In particular, the term "democratic individualism" (translated into Chinese as "democratic individualists") has aroused heated reaction, and Chinese intellectuals are falling over themselves to deny that they could possibly fit into such a category. It is a commentary on the differences between the two countries today that this term, so respected in America, has in China become one of opprobrium. The reason is that a long tradition of highly "individualistic" opportunism and self-seeking in Chinese public life has today made of the word "individualism" a synonym for selfishness.

"All the News That's Fit To Print"

In general the Communists have succeeded remarkably well, without use of force, in inducing non-Communist newspapers to toe the ideological line. This record broke down on August 2, however, when a minor Tientsin daily, the *Po-ling Jih-pao,* saved itself from closure only by printing a front-page apology for the fact that ever since liberation it had "uninterruptedly been issuing errors." As listed in a New China News Agency dispatch of August 6, these included:

(1) Falsification of statements issued by the Military Control Commission.

(2) Disturbing of public order by making fabrications concern-

ing the arrest of a certain Chang Pi-hsien (unknown to me), member of the Kuomintang Legislative Yuan.

(3) Continued use of certain terms, such as "struggle" and "reckoning accounts with," which distort present official policy (inasmuch as the Communists, since entering the big cities, no longer emphasize the class struggle).

(4) Frequent abbreviation of the dispatches of the New China News Agency.

(5) Use of terminology which is disrespectful and immoral, for example: "Being a pedicabber is good business; you can get a wife and also get rich."

(6) Printing short stories which are reactionary in their ideology. For example, ones where oppressed peasants refer to their landlords as "My Lord in Heaven! My Lord of Heaven and Earth! My dearly beloved first exemplar!"

August 18 (Thursday)

Clash of Old and New

Many are the family strains and heartaches resulting from the eagerness of the younger generation to join the new movement despite parental objection.

Last night, at a wonderful farewell dinner of Peking roast duck given us by a Chinese professor of Peita, Galia was talking to her table neighbor, the wife of another Chinese professor.

The talk turned to their children, and Galia learned that the lady's daughter, of college age, is now working with the People's Army in the South. The mother had recently received a letter and seemed pleased that the news was good.

When Galia asked how she felt about her daughter being so far away and living under such difficult physical conditions, she replied with a face which showed her conflicting emotions, "My daughter joined the Southern Expedition against my wishes and ran away from home."

What a jolt it must have been to this mother and to her youth-ful-looking husband, both of whom definitely do not belong to the modern, westernized set of Chinese intellectuals. At first, she told Galia, she had cried a great deal, but now she had gradually adjusted herself to the idea. As she told her story, there was a mix-ture of pride and embarrassment in her face—whether she was embarrassed at her daughter's behavior or at her own "backward-ness," Galia could not tell.

The group enthusiasm aroused among the young through meetings and discussions is highly contagious. Some weeks ago a Tsinghua Chinese professor told us the story of the daughter of one of his colleagues, a girl who is not very strong. Soon after the coming of the Communists, she joined one of their indoctrina-tion courses and, like all her classmates, followed a very strenuous regimen. She was required to rise at five, go for a half-hour run before breakfast (compulsory for everyone joining the Communist cadres because so much of their wartime advance has been made on foot), and continue classes and study until evening with but few interruptions. Only two meals were served daily, commonly consisting of kaoliang porridge, *wo-t'ou,* or cabbage soup.

After some weeks the girl fell ill and was compelled by her parents, supported by the family doctor, to give up her training. Thereafter she spent lonely days at home, sometimes visited in the evenings by her friends who were continuing their studies. One fine day, however, she disappeared from the house. Her parents soon learned that she had run away to rejoin her student group, which had gone south with the army. Our friend has not heard how she has since fared.

Galia's teacher, Mr. Ma, is another man whose family has had its share of upheavals. Though versed in traditional Chinese learning, he has a remarkably open attitude toward new ideas. Like most scholars with a Confucian background, he does not take much stock in religion, which he regards as *mi hsin* (superstition). He was glad when the Communists came, and has since been read-ing philosophical treatises on Marxism (some of which, he admits, have been rather tough going). His wife, however, is a really old-fashioned *t'ai-t'ai,* with no education and no mind for anything outside her family.

They have an attractive fourteen-year-old daughter who, like the others in her school, has been drawn into many new activities —discussion groups, political lectures, mass singing, participation in victory celebrations, and the like. Among them is a drama group whose purpose is to train recruits for acting teams sent south to propagate the new ideas in dramatic form. Ma's daughter was very anxious to join this group, for which she seemed to possess particular talent. Her mother, however, flatly forbade her even to think of such a thing. Her daughter a singing girl, an actress? Never! What could be more degrading! So despite her father's willingness, the girl was forced to renounce her wish.

Later she actually did join, though secretly. When the mother discovered a registration card showing this fact, a real family drama developed. In good traditional manner, the mother wailed and cried and declared she would take poison if the daughter continued. The daughter no less vehemently declared that she herself would do the same if not allowed to continue. Poor Ma, placed between two fires, spent many sleepless nights. As for the daughter, she fell ill and lost all interest in school or life. Finally, her elder brother, also an ardent follower of the new order, persuaded her to placate her mother by agreeing to wait a year before again discussing the matter.

Thus the clash between old and new continues in many families.

The other evening we heard our *amah*'s two children, a girl of thirteen and boy of eleven, singing the new songs they have learned in school. The tunes are catchy and the children were undoubtedly enjoying themselves. Even small children delight in singing these days. A lower primary school stands near our house, and often in the early morning we are awakened by the sounds of singing and dancing to the rhythmic, monotonous beat of the *yang ko*. It is also a common sight to see truckloads of children lustily singing as they are taken for an outing. Their exhilaration comes from doing things together (an idea little stressed in traditional Chinese child life). In the beginning they probably hardly understand what they are singing, but gradually the new ideas undoubtedly sink in.

August 22 (Monday)

Malthus and Marx

Here is a remark by Kuo Mo-jo, writer and archaeologist, who is one of the most notable "democratic personages" supporting the new order. It appeared in an August 13 broadcast commemorating the fourth anniversary of the Sino-Soviet Friendship Treaty.

"The food problem in China is not due to overpopulation but to excessive economic exploitation by foreign capitalism acting in connivance with the bad eggs in China. The Chinese people have now turned the tables on their exploiters and *in the near future* [italics mine] there will be no food problem in China even though there is an increase in population."

One of the weaknesses in Marxism is its refusal to recognize overpopulation as a possible factor affecting a nation's well-being. Many people doubt that China, whether Communist or not, can ever achieve a standard of living comparable to that of Western nations as long as her present population pressure remains un-checked. So far as I know, the Communists have never gone to the extreme of Sun Yat-sen, who once expressed fear that the Chinese would be swallowed up by the white race. On the other hand they have also, so far as I know, never put themselves on record as favoring birth control, which to many observers seems essential for any long-term solution.

Sudden Conversion

On the one hand, the Communists have officially pledged them-selves to respect religious freedom; on the other, they reserve and exercise the right to attack it verbally as a form of superstition which, they maintain, will gradually die a natural death as the result of popular education. Here in Peking they have so far acted with exemplary correctness toward the Christian missions. In certain rural areas, however, it is rumored that some missions suffer difficulties because of increased taxation and similar measures. Treatment has apparently sometimes varied from place to place.

Meanwhile what about the indigenous Chinese religions? The August 16 *Progressive Daily* carries a curious item describing the experience of twelve monks belonging to a Buddhist temple at Wusih, near Nanking:

"Since the liberation of Wusih these monks have been accused by society of being 'parasites' whose livelihood consists of abstract talk; nobody there invokes the name of Buddha any more or prostrates himself." On August 3, therefore, the head abbot, "seeing that conditions in the new society are no longer favorable for Buddhist monks, . . . proclaimed to all the monks the dissolution of the monastery and expressed the wish that they embrace the bosom of the new China and work for the New Democracy." The next day "all the monks returned to lay life, collectively bought the revolutionary literature, and began to engage in study. On the eighth they furthermore registered at the school for the training of revolutionary cadres, desiring to act for the service of the people."

Here indeed, to use a Buddhist term, is "instantaneous enlightenment" with a vengeance. Offhand it would be hard to imagine a greater contrast than that between Buddhism, with its renunciation of life, and the extremely practical New Democracy! Though obviously not typical, this incident symbolizes, I think, what will become a growing trend. It is, in fact, a continuation of a trend that was already evident before the arrival of the Communists.

Changes in the Schools

Few changes have as yet been made in the curricula of schools and universities. The major ones will come only with the fall semester. Several recent newspaper articles, however, give a hint of what some of them will be. Many new textbooks have been written during the summer and many old ones scrapped, though some Kuomintang texts have been retained with revisions. The same is true of certain Communist texts which, originally prepared for rural use, have now been revised to meet the demands of an urban population. None have as yet appeared for sale.

Changes planned for middle schools include curtailment or elimination of certain classes and a corresponding expansion of self-study and extracurricular activity. For example, chemistry and physics are to be abolished and mathematics curtailed in the case of arts students. On the other hand, history and geography will be abolished and Chinese curtailed in the case of science students. Both groups of students will take a new two-hour weekly course in "new philosophy." This will include the methodology of thinking and dialectic materialism.

The teaching of Russian will be generally increased, though in ways varying from school to school. Some schools will make it compulsory in the first year and elective in the second and third, while retaining English as before; some will require a choice of either Russian or English in the first year; some will make Russian an elective in the first-year, and English in the second and third years.

Political-science courses will be made more concrete by synthesizing abstract principles with a greater amount of material drawn from actual life.

Rising costs will force "slight" tuition increases for a number of private middle schools—in one school, 77 instead of 66 pounds of flour per semester for its lower division, and 88 instead of 70 pounds for its upper division; in another, corresponding increases in terms of pounds of millet of 210 instead of 125 and 220 instead of 185.

Regulations issued by the Peking municipality on the 18th for private primary and middle schools provide that all private schools must reregister and, in the process, must pledge themselves to act in conformity with the ideals of the New Democracy. Principals and teachers who fail to do so are subject to removal by the municipal board of education. The curricula of their schools must conform with those of the public schools. "In order to preserve students' freedom of belief," compulsory religious instruction and attendance at religious services are henceforth forbidden. (This provision does not differ materially from that already in force under the Kuomintang.) Private schools suffering from financial difficulties may appeal to the municipality for assistance. All schools will be required to submit reports to the board of education at stated intervals.

As regards universities, both national and private, the major general change seems to be the introduction of two new compulsory one-semester freshman courses, each three hours weekly. The first will deal with dialectic and historical materialism; the second with the New Democracy and its background in earlier revolutionary movements. They replace such subjects as the "Three People's Principles" and others compulsory under the old regime.

In addition, all arts students will be required to take a one-semester three-hour course on political economy. The arts colleges of the different universities are to be reorganized to include departments of literature, history, philosophy, politics, economics, law, and education. This means that, for example, Chinese and Western languages, formerly separate departments, are now to be merged into a single department of literature.

At the educational meetings at which these changes were discussed, it was emphasized that the present economic situation precludes any major expansion of curriculum in the near future. On the contrary, courses that seem too much like "unnecesary frills" must be either curtailed or eliminated.

Spare Our "Plowing Friends"

A touching letter in the August 18 *Progressive Daily* comments bitterly on a news item carried by that paper a few days earlier, in which it was stated that "an abundant supply of horses, cows, and donkeys is now entering the [Tientsin] market. . . . A small donkey fetches a price of only $20,000, with the result that private butchers are doing a flourishing business."

"In the spring," the writer of the letter comments, "the government issued an order prohibiting the slaughtering of cows needed for plowing. This fact reveals its concern for the rural population. . . . But cows, horses, mules, and donkeys are the 'speechless plowing friends' of us farming folk . . ." If, he continues, they are being sold today for butchering, it is only because of dire economic necessity. Therefore, could not the authorities help the farmers by arranging for the transport of animals from flooded areas and their care until autumn, when they could be restored to their original owners? "In this way the lives of our 'plowing friends' would be preserved and the difficulties of the farmers would be largely solved. . . . Otherwise, after the flood waters recede, with what will we till the ground and plant wheat?"

Today's *Progressive Daily* contains what is possibly an answer to this plea. "In order to preserve livestock and prevent interference with agricultural production," it says, the Tientsin municipality has ordered that the regulation issued this spring prohibiting the private slaughter of plowing cattle be recircularized, and that an educational campaign be launched on the subject. It has also instructed the Departments of Safety, Industry and Commerce, and Revenue, to maintain strict inspection of all slaughtering activities. No suggestion is given, however, as to how the farmers themselves are to obey these prohibitions and at the same time cope with their economic difficulties.

Special Service

Today I said farewell to a Chinese whom I know well. As I was leaving, I asked about his son, who has recently completed a training course at one of the new Communist universities.

"He is doing very well," my friend replied. Then, lowering his voice, "He has been given a position in the Bureau of Public Safety."

"The Peiping Bureau of Public Safety?" I asked.

"No," he replied, "The Central Bureau of Public Safety for all North China. It is dangerous work. He carries a pistol."

Through further questioning I learned that my friend's son, though working in an office at the moment, will probably later be appointed principal of a school, where he will perform the usual administrative duties, while at the same time maintaining a secret check upon political activities. For this work, like all young men who dedicate themselves to the service of the new regime, he will receive, over and above a bare living allowance (to cover himself alone, irrespective of dependents), a supplementary "salary" of twenty pounds of millet monthly—well under two American dollars at current prices. "But perhaps," my friend remarked somewhat wearily, "his income may be increased next year."

Thus the Communists, like the Kuomintang, are beginning the use of *t'e wu* or "special service" agents—men who will presumably be posted as they were under the old regime among students, teachers, office functionaries, factory workers, and the like. No doubt the existing conditions in China, plus the Communists' own ideology, make any other course hardly possible. Nonetheless it is sad to see this development. What is striking is that a young man like my friend's son, himself not a member of the Communist party, should have been chosen for such delicate work after only four or five months of intensive indoctrination. Granted that he is of more than average intelligence and that he has long been sympathetic to the Communist cause, his appointment shows nevertheless how short the Communists are in trained personnel.

Tangku, August 28 (Sunday)

Farewell

For more than two weeks we have been in the throes of preparing for departure—a night-and-day struggle against packing, red tape, farewell entertainments, and a steady stream of friendly but time-consuming visitors who have brought over one hundred letters for us to carry to the outside world. The result for us has been utter exhaustion. It was after one o'clock in the morning of August 24, the date of our departure, when we completed the last details of packing and could lie down for a few hours of uneasy sleep.

Nine hours later we made our way to the railroad station in a car provided by our ever-thoughtful friend the American consul.

There we spent a hectic three quarters of an hour passing ourselves and our baggage through the station inspectors, loading it into the railroad car, and in the last few moments exchanging hurried good-byes with the gallant little group of friends who had come to see us off. How different was this leave-taking from the last time we left Peking, in 1937. With what light hearts we left then.

This time the farewells were tense and painful, dominated by concern for the friends we leave behind, particularly those whose lives, for one reason or another, are tied to the fate of Peking; dominated also by the sense of making an irrevocable transit from one world to another, and that perhaps the two may never meet in our lifetime; dominated, finally, by the unspoken conviction that we may never again see this city which we have loved and known so well.

Hardest of all was the parting from our boy Chin. As the bell rang signaling the train's departure, he ran to the side of the car, gripped first Theo's and then my hand firmly through the window, cried in a broken voice, *"Yi-lu p'ing-an!"* "May your whole journey be peaceful!"; then retired behind the assembled leave-takers, tears welling from his reddened eyes. It seems incredible that we may never again hear the voice of this man who has served us so faithfully during the past year, and who during that time has become almost a member of the family. May the future China be good for him and for the other Chinese like him!

On the 90-mile journey to Tientsin we passed field after field of corn and kaoliang, stunted, withered, and yellowed, obviously capable of yielding only a fraction of the yield once expected from it. It looked as if it had been stricken by drought; in actual fact, the cause of this desolation was rain and flood. As we approached the city, many fields were standing deep in water. It had been a choice, we were told, either of inundating them or exposing Tientsin to flood. The fields had been sacrificed.

At last Tientsin itself, with its miles of monotonous stone streets and foreign houses, its wide-flung factories, its stagnant and foul-smelling canals, its all-pervading atmosphere (at least to us, who know Peking) of foreignized affluence amid physical ugliness and intellectual sterility. In spite of its evidences of past wealth—symbolized by mansions of foreign businessmen and the

Country Club—Tientsin seems today a dying city. Its streets are deserted as compared with the bustling traffic on Peking's avenues and *hutungs;* its offices are still and lifeless.

And yet the attitude of those foreign businessmen I have seen in Tientsin remains curiously optimistic compared with the pessimism that has gripped many in Peking's foreign colony during the past two months of intensified anti-imperialist propaganda. In Peking not a few foreigners appear ready to give up and pull out. In Tientsin, on the contrary, the attitude seems to be: Yes, conditions are very difficult. Business is bad. Perhaps it will become impossible. But for the time being we are willing to wait and see what we can do.

The words of one foreign businessman particularly struck me. "You know," he said, "many of the things the Communists do are not bad. They are inexperienced in foreign trade. They make mistakes. Many of their regulations give lots of trouble. But it is possible to reason with them, and if they are shown to be wrong, they are willing to change. Moreover, they are completely honest. None of the monkey business that went on under the Kuomintang. Suppose you are Dr. Bodde and I am Mr. Wang. When we go to the authorities, we receive exactly the same treatment. I happen to represent three firms. Under the Kuomintang I never paid any taxes. But now under the Communists I have had to pay the equivalent of US$600 for six months' taxes. Now, naturally I don't particularly enjoy this, yet figure it is reasonable, so have paid without question." He went on to explain how in the hooked-rug export business it was formerly possible, through over- or undervaluation and complicated exchange transactions, to make fantastic profits on a single deal. "People sometimes used to make thousands of American dollars overnight through speculation. Now that has become impossible. A lot of people of this sort are leaving Tientsin these days. It is they who say that the Communists have made business impossible. But I am content to do business if I can be assured of a ten per cent profit. Yes, conditions are not easy. You can wish me luck, I need it. But I'm prepared to stay and try and make a go of it."

After four days in Tientsin spent disentangling ourselves from the red tape necessary for departure, we showed up at the wharf at seven o'clock this morning, together with the hundred or more other passengers destined for the British steamer which is to take us to Hong Kong. Three hours later, having finished the immigration and customs inspection, we climbed aboard the primitive tug-drawn lighter which would carry us down the river to the steamer itself. It boasted of a far from adequate awning as protection against the blazing sun; no seats save those provided by the bundles of passengers' luggage; no food or water, save again what the passengers themselves provided; and no toilet save a hole in a swaying platform slung over the stern and surrounded by a waist-high canvas screen. The journey down the meandering yellow river between open fields and desolate mud flats lasted six hours. By its conclusion many faces had been turned by the sun into the color of boiled lobster. For all of this we paid the sum of PN$40,000 each, or, at the current exchange, about US$16. But a little after 4 P.M. we reached the little town of Tangku near the mouth of the river. There lay our steamer, rising white and cool above our dirty barge. We climbed her side. Our baggage followed. The almost incredible goal toward which we have been striving the past several weeks was achieved! Tomorrow at 6 A.M. we sail!

Apart from the uncertainty of securing steamer accommodation in these days of blockade and limited sailings, the greatest hazards confronting the foreigner who leaves North China are psychological. Violent anti-foreign propaganda, coupled with various restrictive regulations, has conditioned him to expectations of search, detention, and trouble of all kinds, so that he lends a ready ear to rumors of what happened to previous departing foreigners. In our own case I am happy to say that all these expectations proved unfounded.

True, the regulations of the suspicious People's Government cost us many weary hours, but once complied with, we passed through the red tape without hitch. Our exit visas were granted in Peking without question. Our meager supply of American dollars, deposited in the Bank of China months ago, was restored in actual American greenbacks upon request and accompanied by a document permitting us to take the money out of the country. At the Peking railroad station, our exit visas, though inspected three or four times, aroused no difficulty, and only two or three of our twelve pieces of baggage were examined. At the Tientsin station the checking of visas and baggage took even less time, while subsequent registration with the Tientsin Bureau of Public Safety was expeditious and simple.

The final customs inspection at the lighter jetty, though considerably longer, can only be described as cursory. Much of the baggage was barely looked at, so that we could have smuggled out any amount of clandestine American dollars had we been so inclined. Even our legitimate store from the Bank of China was neither discovered nor asked about. This was not true of everyone. I saw one Chinese, for example, whose every pocket was carefully searched, down to the emptying of a box of matches. But it was true of all the dozen foreign passengers on our ship.

The porters, both at the jetty and the Peking and Tientsin railroad stations, were well behaved and charged fixed prices for their services, in contrast with the extortion sometimes practiced in the past. Eight days before our departure, I had been upset by the news that my books—to be shipped to America by freighter since we ourselves are flying from Hong Kong—had been denied customs clearance as personal effects. This meant that I would have had to apply for a license to send them out as export merchandise, with all the complications this entailed. Much precious time during our last hectic days was spent in writing a letter of appeal in Chinese and securing supporting letters from Chinese scholars acquainted with my work. Yesterday, however, half an hour before the closing of offices for the week-end holiday, my Tientsin shipping agent phoned to say that the letters had achieved their purpose and that my precious books had been granted clearance.

In short, the only really unreasonable incident connected with our departure was the exorbitant price charged for the journey on the Tientsin municipal lighter—our British steamship company having been forbidden for some obscure reason to operate lighters of its own. This was a slight matter compared with all the dire stories we had heard.

At Sea, August 31 (Wednesday)

Imperialist Blockade

This afternoon our steamer has been sailing past the picturesque rocky tips of the Shantung Peninsula. By rights we should have passed them thirty-six hours ago. Here is what happened.

On the morning of the twenty-ninth, at six o'clock, we cast off as scheduled from the Tangku dock and with easy heart watched ourselves recede from the shore. But then we noticed with alarm that the steamer failed to pick up speed. Instead she circled until her bow lay where her stern had been. Lines were thrown out, and in a few minutes she was again tied to her former resting place. What had happened? Had the authorities decided to make another, really thoroughgoing customs examination? Or another check on passports? We soon learned. A Kuomintang gunboat had been sighted hovering on the horizon beyond the mouth of the river. How much delay would this mean? Perhaps three or four days, our captain told us.

All that day we remained at our moorings. Several climbs to the masthead by a man with binoculars yielded only negative results. The next day, the thirtieth, we missed the morning tide. But in the afternoon we heard electrifying news: we were going to make a run for it. At 5 P.M., with the high tide, the welcome figure of the pilot stepped aboard. Again the lines were cast off, and this time we really got under way.

As we steamed down the river and into the bay, huge British flags prominently painted on our hatch covers, everyone peered anxiously ahead. What we saw on the horizon were a freighter, two lightships, several fishing junks, and a small dark object which steamed rapidly away and, to our alarm, looked suspiciously as if it might be the dreaded gunboat. We remembered the story of the tug (or was it some other small craft) that had been stopped by a Kuomintang gunboat, shelled and sunk near this spot, only a few weeks ago. By the time we drew past the anchored freighter, the object had vanished. Shortly afterward, however, what was unmistakably a naval vessel appeared over the horizon and drew toward us. In the setting sun she presently engaged us in warm conversation by blinker. This is it, we thought dismally. We shall be stopped, searched, and perhaps escorted to Formosa.

As our spirits sank, the armed guard standing beside us (carried as a precaution against pirates) suddenly exclaimed in Chinese, "English ship! Not Chinese ship!" And indeed, she turned out to be a British destroyer which, as we learned the next day from our captain, just "happened" to be in the vicinity. Mistakenly identified as a Kuomintang vessel, she had unwittingly caused all our delay. That evening it was a comforting sight to see her following us, all lights ablaze. Then during the night she disappeared, and today we are alone. But that we are not completely out of danger is indicated by a notice on our bulletin board:

"Passengers wishing to send radio messages should do so today. After today no messages will be accepted until Saturday, as the ship will maintain radio silence."

Imperialist blockade? This phrase has not only appeared constantly in the Chinese press during the past weeks but has crept into the English-language press as well. Perhaps. But if so, our experience proves that it is costing at least one "imperialist" nation no little time and money to circumvent.*

* On December 29, 1949, however, our State Department, after protesting several times to the Kuomintang against the illegality of the "blockade," solemnly warned American ship captains that they faced revocation of their masters' licenses if they continued to run American vessels into Shanghai waters. Though this act may not technically constitute "imperialism," it surely seems to the average Chinese an excellent facsimile thereof.

September 1949

Hong Kong, September 8 (Thursday)

Capitalist Paradise

On Monday the fifth, at seven in the morning, we steamed into Hong Kong's ever-spectacular harbor. As we entered, its majestic encircling peaks were wrapped in clouds. What a difference, both physically and psychologically, between this lush haven and the drab grayness of the north! First to capture our attention, while we were still aboard ship, was the roar of planes rising in quick succession from the airfield across the bay. Next was the sight of a Kuomintang flag fluttering from one of Hong Kong's downtown buildings. It is almost five months since we saw our last plane; more than seven since we saw a Kuomintang flag.

In Peking nobody talks any longer about the Kuomintang. Here in Hong Kong it is strange to find the statements of its leaders still given prominence. Here, too, for the first time since the end of the Japanese war, I have heard the term "free China" used to designate the shrinking remnants of the Nationalist domain. We also find obvious evidence that Kuomintang propaganda is hard at work. An American lady, for example, asked me in all seriousness, "Is there any truth to the report about the nationalization of women in North China?" And an English missionary confirmed that in Chungking, from which he has recently arrived, the same rumor has caused alarm among segments of the population.*

The most overpowering impression of Hong Kong, however, is that of its seemingly inexhaustible affluence and luxury. All the wealth of China is being funneled through this port, brought by

* This Kuomintang fable is of long standing. See p. 132 for the way in which it continued to circulate in Tientsin during the early postliberation period.

the Kuomintang and its followers in their mad rush to save themselves and their dollars from the advancing red tide. The housing situation is fantastic, as much as US$10,000 being given as "key money" to insure occupation of a moderate-sized apartment. The air-conditioned restaurants are jammed with waiting patrons, and the shops overflow with luxury goods, both Chinese and American—the latter sometimes even cheaper than in the United States, owing to Hong Kong's unique status as a duty-free port. The streets are filled with latest-model American cars, mostly Chinese-owned. Yesterday, Galia and Theo spent five minutes counting those passing our hotel, and not a one contained a foreigner.

Most striking of all, however, are the shapely silhouettes of beautiful Chinese girls, swaying on high-heeled shoes, in their closely fitted silk gowns. We have seen more of them here these past three days than during our entire year in the North. As Galia remarked of one, "There goes China's 'war criminal' money on high heels." What a contrast to Peking, with its unpainted buildings, rickety pedicabs, battered wood-burning cars and trucks, and shapeless gray uniforms! How different this wanton prodigality from the Spartan earnestness of the North!

But there is poverty and despair, too, in this capitalist paradise. Yesterday, on one of the busiest street corners, I saw an unkempt man, a woman, and their girl, squatting with bowed heads upon the sidewalk. An inscription neatly written in Chinese characters upon a spread-out sheet of red paper, supplemented by a brief conversation, told me their story. Less than a year ago the man had been a soldier on the Tsinan front. Following the fall of that city he and his family, after many adventures, had managed to reach Formosa. While there, however, they were robbed of all their possessions. Then they drifted to Hong Kong, where they now are a homeless trio in a strange city in which few people speak their northern dialect. Though the man is jobless and the daughter ill, an appeal to the local branch of their native Shantung provincial guild has brought no help. How long will the occasional ten- and twenty-cent notes dropped by sympathetic passers-by keep this family alive, one of the innumerable bits of flotsam cast up by war?

October 1949

Philadelphia, October 10 (Monday)

Home Sweet Home

Today is China's national holiday, the "Double Tenth" as the Chinese call the tenth day of the tenth month. The Nationalists are celebrating by evacuating the remnants of their government from Canton to Chungking. The Communists started to celebrate some days ago by proclaiming a new Central People's Government for all China. Its capital will be Peking, the "Northern Capital"—this name officially replacing that of Peiping.

It is already a month since we flew from Hong Kong on September 9 and two days later dropped through the mist onto the San Francisco airport. On September 19 we were home again after an absence of more than fifteen months.

Our most striking first impression is the apparent sameness of everything since we went away. This absence of change amid a changing world gives to America, though for different reasons, that same quality of unreality we at first felt in Peking a year ago. Some of the little things we find it hard to get used to—a stable currency; the hurry and noise of an industrial civilization; the daily relegation to the trash can of innumerable boxes, bottles, paper bags, and wrapping paper which two months ago we would have carefully hoarded; the search in the daily papers for news which is sandwiched between an endless succession of advertisements, sports pages, comics, and columnists.

On a higher intellectual level, one of our dominant feelings is that of helplessness in trying to convey to our friends here a real impression of what we have seen in China. Another is the feeling of being ourselves irrevocably cut off from the events with which we have so long been in close contact. *The New York Times* dutifully prints a brief account of the formation of the new government in Peking, accompanying it with an editorial blast against "the nauseating farce" taking place in that city. Galia's grocer (who obviously does not read the *Times*) comments to her sympathetically, "It must have been horrible living there in China under them Russians."

Yet the attempt at communication must be made somehow. Here, then, are some of the salient points I would like to suggest to Americans:

The picture in China is neither as black as the *Times* would have us believe, nor as white as the *Daily Worker* paints it. It is a mixed picture, brighter in some spots, darker in others, and one in which the lights and shadows refuse to remain constant.

Economically, at least, what has happened in China to date cannot be called communism. The program of the New Democracy includes land redistribution, rationalization of commerce and industry through government controls, fostering of cooperatives, development of labor unions and peasant associations, and a system of social security (health insurance, old age pensions, etc.) that is only just beginning. It does not, so far, include collectivization of land (save to a very limited degree in Manchuria), suppression of private capital, or even such elementary devices as government-enforced food rationing or a graded income tax (tried in Peking some months ago and then abandoned).* No wonder that some of my British friends in Peking remarked that what they had seen thus far would seem mild in England. Mao Tse-tung himself has warned against the dangers of "Leftist deviation" (meaning overzealousness in speeding economic change) and has proclaimed the New Democracy as a transitional period that may last decades before the evolution of the full-fledged Socialist state.

Despite this economic gradualism, however, there is no doubt

---

* On January 2, 1950, however, *The New York Times* reported from Hong Kong that food rationing had been instituted in Tientsin (and presumably other North China cities).

that the Marxist view of life is, for the Chinese Communists, the one and final truth. Unquestioned faith in this truth, in fact, explains in part their willingness to move slowly: they rest secure in the conviction that sooner or later the forces of history will inevitably bring them to the final goal. This faith engenders in them certain striking qualities: enthusiasm, selfless devotion, concern for the submerged masses of China, idealism, incorruptibility, and willingness to accept untold hardships—qualities such as commonly characterize a major religious movement. The similarity to religion is heightened by the indoctrination techniques they employ—group discussion, self-criticism, public confession—by means of which they generate a fervor in their converts reminiscent of an oldtime revivalist meeting. All men save a handful of hopeless irreconcilables, the Chinese Communists seem to believe, can through patient education and moral suasion be led to see the truth and thus be saved. It is this conviction, to my mind, that makes of the present revolution in China, aside from its purely military aspects, one of the least bloody revolutions in history.

Morally, what have the Communists to contribute to China? A great deal, it seems to me, that was lacking before: discipline, constructive purpose, confidence in man's ability to improve his environment, cooperative effort toward a common goal, individual concern for communal welfare, awakening of political consciousness among the masses, instilling in the intellectual of awareness of and respect for the common man, incorruptibility in public office, stripping of special favors and privileges, to name only a few. I remember the starving man whom Galia saw a year ago lying for days uncared for in the Peking *hutungs*; the demoralized human rabble that for months camped in our compound and called itself "students"; the corruption, oppression, and rank stupidity under the Kuomintang; and then, by contrast, the People's Army privates who, on their own initiative, restored to their pedestals the bronze incense burners in the Pei Hai park. As I remember these things, I am convinced that there is much China can learn to advantage from the New Democracy.

But there is a darker side as well, and one which, because it is most immediately evident to the foreigner, will attract chief attention from the outside world. It is seen in the use of "special service" agents, now beginning to characterize Communist China, as it did Kuomintang China; the threat of force that underlies their moral blandishments; the effort to pigeonhole all individuals into occupational or social groups, partly, at least, in order to insure their easier control; the existence of a small inner group that "knows" and does the controlling, and a large outer mass that is told what to know and is the object of that control; the manipulation of the press, education, literature, and the arts for the advancement of a particular ideology.

Behind all these phenomena lies the one irreducible fact to which I have already alluded: the Communist conviction that Marx-Leninism is the only truth, that the Communists are the chosen instruments for leading mankind to this truth, and that all who cannot be won to their side must be automatically against them. In this last view they are abetted by the words and acts of conservatives themselves. It remains, in my opinion, the duty of every genuine believer in liberal thought to prove, if he can, that a third way does exist—a way consonant with economic security and well-being, intellectual integrity, and freedom from exploitation of man by man.

Irrespective of what happens to the Communists, one fact is certain, the Kuomintang is through. By its cupidity and corruption, cynicism and apathy, stupidity and inability to make contact with the common man, it has irrevocably forfeited that mass support it once enjoyed. And by the same token the Communists, displaying the reverse of these qualities, have succeeded in capturing that support. Their success in retaining it depends upon how well they handle the new problems confronting them now that they have entered the cities and become an organized state.

In the short run, can they cope with the dire food shortages that seem certain in the coming year? In the longer run, can they industrialize China without imposing too heavy an economic burden on the peasants? Can they keep the intellectuals satisfied on a steady Marxist diet which, fresh and exciting today, may become monotonous five or ten years hence? * Can they hold power and still retain their present idealism and mental flexibility? And behind all these questions lies another of fundamental importance: Can any government, in the face of China's overpopulation, scarcity of certain natural resources, and numerous other difficulties, raise her standard of living to a level comparable with that of other industrialized countries? It would be a rash person who would venture to answer these questions at this early date, other than to say that, on the evidence so far, it seems quite unlikely that the Chinese Communists will lose their present dominance for a considerable time to come.

The most vociferous supporters of the new order are the intellectuals, especially the students. It is easy to understand why Chinese who called themselves liberals should now suport the Communist program. The program to date has been a mild one; it has given China the only clear-cut alternative to Kuomintang misrule; the intellectuals, long ignored by the Kuomintang, are now made to feel that their specialized skills are needed in the new China; they long for security and stability after twelve unbelievably difficult years of mental and physical privation. Disappointing, nevertheless, is the failure of intellectuals to temper their enthusiasm with greater independence and objectivity. Overtly, at least, none of the "democratic personages" have ever ventured to disturb a unanimity of public opinion that to the outsider seems deadening. As pointed out by a Chinese lady who knew and admired the Communists in Yenan, and who returned to North China this August, "If the 'democratic personages' really talk in private the way they do in public, I am not interested in meeting them."

This phenomenon, it is worth repeating, is not the result of terror. Many intellectuals are sincere converts to Marxism; others have hopped on the band wagon; some undoubtedly see the dangers but accept them as necessary for China's salvation. This is the more unfortunate because the Communists themselves

* As a non-Chinese worker for the People's Government remarked to me this August when I commented on the drab monotony of the daily press, "The newspapers are not intended to function as purveyors of news but as organs of education for the masses." This may be fine for the politically illiterate masses of a country like China, but what remains for the intellectuals?

would, I think, have been ready to accept greater criticism if it had been offered in a constructive spirit. To do this in future will become more difficult as the patterns of the new China assume increasing rigidity. But whatever the reasons, events have shown that the liberal tradition was weaker in China than we had supposed and that American policy has erred in regarding the Chinese intellectuals as a "third group" capable of functioning effectively *outside of* prevailing political forces.

In view of the foregoing it is manifestly absurd to apply the word "democratic," as used by us, to the new Peking government. None of its members could have been admitted if deemed capable of seriously opposing basic Communist policy. On the other hand, the government as now constituted demonstrates the wide range of public opinion that has gone over to the Communist side, including as it does even that once implacable foe of Communism, General Fu Tso-yi himself. It is not unlikely that within certain limitations its non-Communist constituents can make their influence felt, even though all final decisions will doubtless be presented to the outside world as unanimous.

A basic American error, eagerly encouraged by Kuomintang spokesmen, is that the Chinese revolution has been "made in Moscow" and is proof paramount of foreign domination. Such a claim dangerously over-simplifies the issue by disregarding the long chain of social conditions and movements within China itself leading up to the present situation. Secretary Acheson, in his introduction to the State Department's White Paper on China, refers to the Chinese revolution as "the product of internal Chinese forces, forces which this country tried to influence but could not." That these forces gained inspiration from Soviet example cannot be doubted. But that they were directed or substantially aided by Russia remains unproved. Materially, indeed, whatever aid the Communists may have received from the Russians in Manchuria or elsewhere has been infinitesimal compared with the billions which we have vainly poured into the other side. That they should now proclaim themselves pro-Russian and not pro-American is inevitable in view of their own ideology and the world situation but does not suffice to prove Moscow dictation.

It is in foreign relations and propaganda, nevertheless, that the Chinese Communists have made their chief blunders. Their least successful task, psychologically, has been that of "selling" Russia to their people: trying to prove, for example, that Russia's invasion of Manchuria in the last week of war forced the Japanese surrender, and that the Russians removed industrial installations from Manchuria to prevent their acquisition by imperialists.

Similarly, Communist restrictions on foreigners in China, particularly diplomats and newspapermen, have robbed them of many foreign friends at a time when these would be most valuable. And in Peking, at least, their violent anti-imperialist propaganda has had little effect upon rank-and-file Chinese, even though it has admittedly made foreign contacts with Chinese intellectuals more difficult. Psychologically, these policies are understandable. The Communists have reason enough to dislike and distrust America, and they are determined to show their people that they are masters in their own house. Practically speaking, however, the price may be costly in view of China's desperate need for the sort of economic assistance that the United States is best able to provide.

In view of the foregoing, it is obvious that we too have blundered disastrously in our Chinese propaganda. American cries of "foreign yoke" come with ill grace from a country that has actively intervened on behalf of an increasingly unpopular government. If such a yoke exists, the best thing is to let the Chinese discover it for themselves. Similarly, as things now stand, promises of support to Chinese believers in "democratic individualism" or to any other Chinese groups do nothing but compromise these groups in the eyes of their own people. If we really want to have friends in China, we should not advertise who they are. In general, we would do well to avoid sermons about democracy, free elections, and free speech in China when for years we have actively supported a government that was the antithesis of these concepts.

No war of modern times has succeeded in really solving the issues for which it was ostensibly fought. Every war has brought increasing chaos and unrest. Today the world is split into two hostile blocs. The United States, as a major party in one of these blocs, owes it to itself and the world to try every decent means to reduce the tension. The communization of China represents an enormous potential accretion of strength to the other side. There are certain factors in the Chinese situation, however—China's economic structure, her vast size and overwhelmingly non-Communist population, her tradition and temperament, the strong cultural and commercial ties that have long linked her with the Western countries, her pressing need for continuing large-scale trade with the West, and the present marked divergence, on many points, of the Chinese Communists themselves from orthodox Communist theory and practice—that suggest a future evolution of communism in China somewhat different from that in Europe. With these factors in mind, the effort to reach a *modus vivendi* with the new forces in China is well worth trying. It will not be easy. Perhaps it will prove impossible. But it should be made, with honesty and good faith, before we turn to other alternatives.

Epilogue

Philadelphia, May 28 (Sunday), 1950

A Plea and a Warning

One evening some months ago, at the conclusion of a talk I had given on China, a lady came up from the audience and remarked, "You don't seem to realize that the so-called Kuomintang shellings of American blockade runners and bombings of Chinese cities are really all being done by the Chinese Communists themselves. They are simply a trick to divide us from the Chinese people and from their legitimate government." In vain I tried to disillusion her. She had been told so by a friend, who had been told by someone else, who had heard it from an American ship captain recently back from the Far East. Fortunately such fantastic beliefs are not found very frequently. Other misconceptions about China do exist, however, which, because seemingly more plausible, are therefore more widespread, even in high circles.

Perhaps the commonest is that Moscow is directly responsible for everything that has recently happened in China. A more sophisticated variant is that at any rate the Chinese Communists themselves are puppets of Moscow and therefore what has happened in Eastern Europe must now inevitably repeat itself in China.

The first assertion commits the methodological error of tearing recent Chinese events out of their whole historical context. It refuses to recognize these events as inextricably a part of a decades-old process of social, political, and economic revolution—a revolution whose ideological ingredients include not only Marxism, but such diverse ideas as those of Christianity, the French and American revolutions, the lectures given by Bertrand Russell and John Dewey to Peking students in 1919 and 1920, and Japan's slogan of "Asia for the Asiatics."

The other assertion similarly overlooks the indigenous factors —historical, geographical, economic and cultural—which make China vastly different from an Eastern Europe country, and by which the Chinese Communists have been and continue to be confronted at every step. This point is well put by John K. Fairbank at the beginning of his book, *The United States and China* (Harvard University Press, 1948), in which he writes:

China is only superficially a meeting point between the United States and the Soviet Union. Fundamentally it is a society alien to both Russia and America, which is developing according to its own tradition and circumstances. . . . To be sure, both America and Russia have exerted powerful influences on China. . . . But as Modern China responds to this Western impact we may be sure that she will develop ways of her own, under the influence of long millennia of her own history and cultural tradition. . . . It is incredible that Modern China, the greatest and oldest single mass of humanity, could be brought into the orbit of any foreign power—Russian, American, or any other— *except* in so far as China's own inner development *itself* conduced to such an orientation.

What he might have added, were he writing today, is that we ourselves, by refusing to deal with Communist China on the grounds that it is a Soviet satellite, thereby assist in a negative way precisely those inner Chinese forces that most conduce to a Russian orientation. The more we shout dire predictions, the more we make it probable that what we fear will come to pass.

Another misconception is that the situation could have been saved if only America had given more aid to the Kuomintang and we had not "betrayed" Chiang Kai-shek. It is abundantly clear today, even though it was less clear in 1945 and 1946, that at that time the Kuomintang had already reached a stage of inner decay from which no recovery was possible. Its fate was to be that eventually suffered by every ruling group when, in the words of Arnold Toynbee, it becomes a "dominant minority." Greater aid on our part could at best have postponed but not prevented that fate.

Still a third misconception is that the Chinese Communists owe their rise to no constructive qualities of their own, but solely to the mistakes and weaknesses of their adversaries. Capitalizing upon these mistakes, it is argued, they have now "enslaved" the Chinese people. The fallacy of this allegation should be evident to anyone who has taken seriously the facts narrated in this book.

Finally, many Americans like to argue that what we have done, after all, is merely to support the legitimate government of China, and it is no fault of ours if that government has proved unworthy. Hence it is unreasonable for politically-minded Chinese to feel bitter toward us today. This point of view—technically "correct" but psychologically naïve—is well expressed in the May 13 editorial of *The New York Times* commenting on the release of two American aviators from Tsingtao after nineteen months' captivity by the Communists as "prisoners of war." "We were not at war with anyone," the *Times* remarks plaintively, "except Japan and Germany in October, 1948, when these men made a forced landing in North China. . . . They were where they had every right to be under invitation of the legitimate Government of China."

This raises the question of what "legitimacy" means in a country like China, where the ballot has never been known. The Kuomintang gained its own "legitimacy" solely as the result of successful armed revolution, and in this respect is no different from any other government that has ruled China during the past three thousand years. To justify such changes of power, the Chinese long ago developed a politico-metaphysical doctrine known as that of *T'ien Ming,* the "Mandate of Heaven." When a new dynasty comes to power, they said, it is because heaven has conferred on it its mandate, and it continues to enjoy this mandate as long as it rules adequately. If, however, it should rule so badly as to provoke rebellion, in the course of which it is overthrown, heaven then transfers its mandate to the successful revolting group, which thereby becomes legitimate. This theory, repeatedly invoked in the past, still lives in Chinese minds today. It is succinctly expressed, in fact, in the very name for revolution, *ko ming,* which literally means "transferring the mandate."

From a Chinese point of view, therefore, it matters little today whether or not the Kuomintang still remains "legitimate" in the eyes of some foreign powers. As far as the Chinese themselves are concerned, it had already lost that legitimacy at the moment, impossible to date precisely but certainly as early as the capture of the two American fliers in October 1948, in which a majority of politically conscious Chinese decided they had enough of the *ancien régime* and were willing to try the Communists instead.

In summary, then, though there are excellent reasons why we as Americans should be opposed to communism ourselves, we should also realize, if we hope to correct our past mistakes, that there are valid reasons why communism (or more accurately, the Chinese version of communism) should have gained favor in China; that these reasons are primarily internal rather than external; and that by disregarding them and trying to oppose Chinese communism by force rather than ideas, we have in the long run merely promoted its growth. This view is an unpopular one in America today, running counter as it does to a Washington view of the world which regards Chinese events in quite a different light. How this Washington world view operates with regard to China might be illustrated by many quotations, but the two following are typical:

"Underground" agents of free, democratic trade unionism flourish in Communist China despite severe repression by the Communist regime. . . . No figures exist as to the number of former trade union leaders who have "disappeared." It is estimated that the number killed and missing runs into the thousands. (Special Washington dispatch to *The New York Times* of April 27, 1950, quoting an unnamed "authoritative source.")

Since the Chinese National Government disintegrated and the Chinese Communists seized control on the mainland, the plight of hundreds of millions of Chinese has been tragic. Their new taskmasters have been heartlessly indifferent to the worst famine which has occurred in China in 100 years. (Speech of President Truman at Laramie, Wyoming, May 9, 1950.)

It is instructive to compare these Washington statements on China with those of American educators and others who know present-day China at first hand. On February 12 of this year an

American teacher in one of Peking's universities—a man who when I knew him last summer was far from enamored with the new government—wrote me as follows:

We have come to know our students much better this year. It has been interesting to watch their progress under the terrific indoctrination they have been getting. They all have been most friendly, in spite of the fact that there is certainly little liking for America to be found anywhere. This business of the useless bombing of Shanghai has made them furious, especially since it is reportedly done by Japanese or American pilots [sic]. And this business of America not sending any more military aid to Formosa becomes a farce to them when, at the same time, they hear about tanks being loaded at Philadelphia for shipment there. The Chinese don't give a hang when they were bought, and you certainly can't blame them. . . .

The students all have a tremendous pride in the new government, and though things are definitely bad, the government is doing a fine job of controlling the situation. It is probably the first time in modern history that a Chinese government has really tried to do something about such a terrible famine. Moreover, in spite of definite shortages, they have managed to keep prices from going up too fast. Flour is now listed at PN$90,000, but with the U.S. rate at PN$29,000, it makes flour about US$3 for a 44-pound bag. And there has been no sign of famine in the cities this winter, as was predicted by many people. They have managed to stop speculation by taking over most of the flour mills and setting up state-owned companies to handle distribution.*

What about Chinese labor conditions? Some weeks ago, from a recently returned American whom I had last seen in Peking, I learned something about what has been happening in the large American-operated Peiping Union Medical College. "As you know," this American told me, "the P.U.M.C.'s workers were al-

---

* On May 24 the same American wrote me that since the beginning of 1950 there had actually been a slight *drop* in prices, and that "in Peking, at least, there seems to be a plentiful supply of everything, including cotton cloth which was so short before. With good crops predicted everywhere, the worst of the financial trouble seems to be over." On June 30, 1950 a French businessman, who the year before had been bitterly hostile to the new government, similarly wrote: "Since your departure conditions here have much improved owing to the stability of the currency and prices. It was obtained by terrific taxation which is now being slightly eased off."

ways well paid by Chinese standards. In the old days, however, they were unorganized and therefore had no direct means of informing the administration about any grievances they might have. Everything had to pass through an intermediate layer of Chinese foremen. But today all that has changed. The workers have formed a union, representatives of which sit down with the administration in weekly meetings. As a result, the administration has learned a lot of things which it never thought much about before. For example, the workers had no complaint to make about their wages, but they did say that they wanted a six- instead of a seven-day week. This has now been granted them, causing a rise in labor costs, while the meetings themselves take up considerable time. But on the other hand it is surprising how the morale of the workers has improved. They feel an increased sense of participation and responsibility, which has resulted in reduced operating costs such as more than make up for the larger payroll. A year or so ago, for example, the P.U.M.C. was burning forty-five tons of coal daily to keep its power plant going, but this winter it has been burning only thirty-five—this despite the fact that it has meanwhile opened several new wards. Furthermore, the return of peacetime conditions to North China has brought a sizable drop in coal prices."

On May 18 the two earlier-mentioned American fliers who had been released from Tsingtao by the Communists gave a press conference at Pearl Harbor which was reported as follows by the Associated Press:

Bender . . . and . . . Smith . . . said they were treated better "than we could possibly have expected." . . . "We ate as well as the Chinese did," Smith observed. He added that their captors "went out of their way to give us as much as they could of all that they had."

Bender said the Chinese people he saw "are getting a better deal under the Communists than they were under the Nationalist government."

They saw no Russian equipment of any kind. Smith said "the only foreign equipment we saw was American." . . .

Throughout their captivity, they said, they remained on friendly relations with their captors. "They wouldn't ask us questions we might refuse to answer," Smith said. "We left them last month the best of friends," Bender added. "There were no hard feelings on either side." . . .

Bender said the anti-American propaganda was aimed solely at the U.S. government and "they had nothing against the American people." Smith added that everyone they saw seemed sold on communism although only a few educated Chinese among them knew anything about Communist theory.

Such a dispatch has become exceptional in our press today. We are faced by a growing uniformity of public utterance which masks, but fails to conceal, similarly growing feelings of fear, uncertainty and inner contradiction on the part of many. On the one hand we know we are the world's richest and most powerful country, and miss no opportunity to belittle the achievements of the countries across the curtain. On the other, we gaze spellbound upon the doings of those countries with a curious mixture of bewilderment, fear and uneasy anticipation. On the one hand we exalt freedom of speech as the principle that has made our country great; on the other, we hound men who now seek to exercise it with cries of "Red!" and "Traitor!" On the one hand we protest quite rightly against violations of human rights in totalitarian countries; on the other, we seem content to see a small band of determined men in our own country year after year talk to death a bill for an F.E.P.C. On the one hand we proclaim that actions speak louder than words and that in all we do and say we must affirm the positive goals of free peoples; on the other, we commit ourselves to foreign policies which though worded in terms of idealism, smack too often of expediency and power politics. On the one hand we laud our government as a model for the world to follow; on the other, we elect to it certain men ready to drag it through dirt of their own making, if by so doing they can ruin the reputations of other men and thereby advance their own political fortunes.

In short, were we to behave as individuals in the way we are now beginning to behave as a nation, it is not unlikely that we would be advised to consult a psychiatrist. By "we" I mean, of course, only a small percentage of Americans, but it is precisely they who make the headlines these days, while most of the rest of us sit back in stunned silence.

On February 18 of this year the city council of San Diego, California, rescinded its decision to inscribe Roosevelt's Four Freedoms on a projected war memorial, arguing that " 'Freedom from want' is a Russian communistic slogan" and " 'Freedom from fear' is a political slogan."

On April 10 a story in *The New York Times* described how a young professor of mathematics who the year before had lost his university position because he had allowed a Negro family to occupy his New York apartment in a large housing development was about to lose his new position in another university for the same reason.

On May 1 thousands of men marched the streets of New York in a May Day "Loyalty Parade," naïvely believing that by so doing they were displaying loyalty to their country. On the same day the American Legion post at Mosinee, Wisconsin, staged a "May Day mock Communist invasion," in the excitement of which the town's mayor and a Methodist minister suffered heart attacks from which they subsequently died. The significance of this incident is not so much the childishness of grown men thus playing at cops and robbers as it is the psychological state of two respected townsmen that could lead to such a tragic denouement.

Perhaps these scattered incidents are trivial in the total stream of American life, yet we may be sure that they are noticed and commented on not only in China, Russia, and the rest of the Communist world, but in many non-Communist countries as well. They are symptomatic of an inner insecurity which ill equips us for our self-avowed battle for the minds of men. We have already lost that battle in China, and as I write these lines we seem to be beginning a similar campaign in Southeast Asia from which similar results may be predicted. Worst of all, we appear to be losing our own self-control and self-understanding.

More than two thousand years ago, an anonymous Confucian scholar wrote, "Know your deficiencies and then you can return to your true self. Know your difficulties and then you can strengthen yourself." And Mencius, the most famous follower of Confucius, remarked still earlier that "Men who are great, by correcting themselves, thereby cause others to become correct."

Appendix

Price Fluctuations in Tientsin
August 24, 1948 to August 23, 1949

The weekly index figures given below portray the fluctuations in wholesale prices and in the cost of living for laborers that occurred in Tientsin between August 24, 1948 and August 23, 1949. Were comparable statistics available for Peking, they would no doubt reveal a roughly similar pattern. These weekly figures (but not the over-all statistics and general deductions drawn from them) are the work of the Institute of Economic Research of Nankai University in Tientsin. Many were originally published week by week in the Tientsin *Progressive Daily*. Others are taken from the *Index Figures for North China Wholesale Prices* (Tientsin, April 1949), which is the first in the Institute's series of *Nankai Index Figure Monographs*. For making available to me the remaining data for weeks not covered in these two sources, I am deeply indebted to Professor Pao Chüeh-min, present director of the Institute.

In compiling these statistics (employing a simple geometric average), the base figure 1 represents average Tientsin price levels during the year July 1936-June 1937. It will be noted that prices for the weeks immediately following August 24, 1948 do not range very high above this 1936-37 figure in spite of eleven intervening years of inflation. The explanation lies in the currency reform of August 19, 1948, as the result of which the highly inflated fa pi currency was supplanted by a new unit, the gold yuan, theoretically stabilized at the rate of FP$3,000,000:GY$1. After the Communists took over Tientsin, calculations were continued on the basis of the new regime's people's notes.

The indices for wholesale prices have been calculated on the basis of over one hundred separate items, falling into two main classifications: (1) classification by industries (foods, textiles, metal products, building materials, fuels, chemicals, miscellaneous items); (2) classification by stages of production (agricultural food products, other agricultural products, animal products, forestry products, mineral products, industrially used commodities, consumer goods). The laborers' cost-of-living indices have been calculated on the basis of the prices of food, clothing, fuel and water, shelter, and miscellaneous items. Unfortunately, the Institute has published no comparable statistics for wage fluctuations during this same period. This is perhaps because of the difficulty of compiling such data in view of the wide spread in income existing between individual wage earners, in many cases even those belonging to the same occupational groups.

The absence of statistics for the period of January 11-18, 1949, is the result of the fighting that then took place, in the course of which Tientsin passed from Kuomintang to Communist control. A comparison of the total price rises, in percentages, that occurred during the preceding period of almost five months of Kuomintang control, with those that occurred during the subsequent seven-month period of Communist control, yields the following figures:

	Percentage of Increase	
	Wholesale Prices	*Laborers' Cost of living*
Kuomintang Period	546.64%	655.24%
(Aug. 24, 1948-Jan. 11, 1950)		
Communist Period	352.79%	294.98%
(Jan. 25-Aug. 23, 1949)		
Total Increase	899.43%	950.22%

Converting these figures into weekly averages for the two periods, we obtain the following results:

	Wholesale	*Cost of living*
Kuomintang average weekly increase:	26.03%	31.20%
Communist " " "	11.38%	9.51%

If we eliminate from consideration the admittedly abnormal four weeks when Tientsin was under siege, the Kuomintang averages become somewhat reduced, as follows:

	Wholesale	*Cost of living*
Kuomintang pre-siege average weekly increase:	25.52%	25.60%

These figures indicate that the Communists, on coming into power, succeeded in slowing the rate of inflation by considerably more than one half. This achievement, while striking, is not surprising in view of the wide over-all differences in the spirit, operation, degree of effective control and popular support of the Kuomintang and Communist regimes. What is interesting, however, is that under Kuomintang rule, wholesale prices rose somewhat less rapidly than did laborers' cost of living, whereas under the Communists the opposite was true.

This reversal is probably attributable to several factors. Of prime importance, no doubt, is the fact that the Communists, unlike the Kuomintang, controlled the countryside which produced several of the items—notably food—that bulk largest in the average worker's budget. It is evident that E.C.A. flour imports (operative under the Kuomintang, but halted by the Communists when they came to power) were not enough to overcome this Kuomintang handicap. By way of contrast, many items whose prices enter into the wholesale index figures consist of overseas imports, which could more readily be shipped to Tientsin by the Kuomintang than by the Communists, who were confronted by insufficient shipping, the Kuomintang naval blockade, and other wartime factors.

Still another factor exists, however, that should not be overlooked. This is the underlying difference in ideology and motivation between the two regimes. The Kuomintang bureaucracy (at least as a system, if not in all individual cases) was more interested in retaining power and wealth for itself than in taking really effective measures to alleviate the economic suffering of the ordinary man. The Communists, on the other hand, seriously tried to check the rising living costs of the poorer classes. For this purpose they fostered such organs as consumer cooperatives, brought large quantities of food into the cities by means of their North China Trading Corporation, and instituted other measures designed to insure economic stability—tasks made considerably more difficult by the disastrous drought and floods from which North China suffered in the spring and summer of 1949. That this policy was a fact seems indisputable, irrespective of whether it was animated by idealistic concern for mass welfare, by political expediency, or by a combination of the two. There is no doubt, however, that if figures were available for the months following August 1949, they would be far less favorable than those presented here, since the cumulative effects of drought, flood, pest, naval blockade, and civil war had by the winter of 1950 combined to produce one of the worst food shortages in Chinese history.

The following table gives a detailed week-by-week picture of what happened during the Kuomintang and Communist periods:

| Period | | Wholesale Prices | | Laborers' Cost of living | |
		Index Figure	Percentage Difference	Index Figure	Percentage Difference
1948					
Aug.	24	2.807	+19.49	1.729	+0.40
	31	2.596	—7.52	1.670	—3.41
Sept.	7	2.824	+8.78	1.735	+3.89
	14	3.024	+7.08	1.846	+6.39
	21	3.193	+5.58	1.907	+3.30
	28	3.289	+2.69	2.087	+9.44
Oct.	5	3.889	+18.18	2.393	+14.66
	12	7.732	+198.81	6.596	+175.64
	19	11.196	+44.80	13.947	+111.45
	26	11.852	+5.85	12.740	—8.65
Nov.	2	14.365	+21.20	13.757	+7.98
	9	15.962	+11.11	14.247	+3.56
	16	18.300	+14.64	16.174	+13.53
	23	18.961	+3.61	15.926	—1.53
	30	22.742	+19.95	20.180	+26.70
Dec.	7	30.887	+35.81	27.631	+36.92
	14	38.305	+24.01	37.288	+34.95
	21	33.955	—16.13	38.337	+2.81
	28	50.721	+49.38	61.535	+60.51
1949					
Jan.	4	86.903	+31.90	118.40	+92.41
	11	128.218	+47.54	194.52	+64.29
	18	lacking	lacking	lacking	lacking
	25	162.558	+26.70	134.48	—30.86
Feb.	1	185.772	+14.28	164.70	+22.97
	8	226.917	+22.14	172.09	+4.48
	15	261.172	+15.09	186.71	+8.49
	22	314.527	+20.42	230.71	+23.56

Period		Wholesale Prices Index Figure	Percentage Difference	Laborers' Cost of living Index Figure	Percentage Difference
1949					
March	1	335.316	+6.61	234.16	+1.50
	8	349.460	+4.22	240.44	+2.68
	15	374.080	+6.23	259.87	+8.08
	22	386.199	+3.24	271.76	+4.58
	29	381.470	−1.22	264.14	−2.80
April	5	384.960	+0.91	267.16	+1.14
	12	411.953	+7.01	280.85	+5.12
	19	444.099	+10.78	317.68	+13.11
	26	496.929	+11.99	357.34	+12.48
May	3	644.586	+29.71	516.61	+44.57
	10	786.679	+22.04	592.73	+14.86
	17	912.949	+15.38	695.32	+17.31
	24	971.564	+6.42	730.26	+5.03
	31	988.121	+0.88	730.49	+0.03
June	7	977.776	−1.05	709.13	−2.93
	14	988.875	+1.13	700.88	−1.16
	21	978.369	−1.35	699.32	−0.22
	28	981.902	+0.36	690.17	−1.31
July	5	1,093.604	+11.38	779.49	+12.94
	12	1,186.628	+8.51	862.61	+10.66
	19	1,450.461	+22.23	1,098.06	+27.30
	27	2,060.841	+42.08	1,679.65	+52.97
Aug.	2	2,607.690	+26.54	2,078.43	+23.74
	9	2,994.091	+14.83	2,444.90	+17.63
	16	3,128.365	+4.48	2,629.09	+7.53
	23	3,154.135	+0.82	2,668.26	+1.49

Index

Index

a

Acheson, Secretary of State Dean, 239, 263
air raid, 160, 170
airfields, 70-1, 73-4, 77, 79-80, 82, 88, 92, 97, 139, 142, 175
amah (maid), 34, 58, 75, 79, 112-13, 117, 243
America:
  Chinese concept of, 190
  Chinese policy of, 24, 39, 106, 109, 131, 161-3, 239-40, 263-4, 268
  democracy in, 39-40
  influence on China, 24, 192, 268
  psychological state of, 273-4
  return to, 258
American Consulate, 27, 43-4, 85, 194
Americans, evacuation of, xviii, 35, 43-4, 59
Amethyst, H.M.S., 164
Andrews, Dr., 47
anti-empiricism, 141, 146
art, 29-30, 227-8
  Communist view of, 103, 142, 225-7
  decline of Chinese, 10, 29-30, 183
  popular, 29, 182, 228
  see also drama; handicrafts; literature
Associated Press, 109, 120, 200, 272
austerity, 139, 147, 204

b

Bank of China, 153, 171, 186, 221, 252-3
barter trade, 128-9, 221; *see also* commerce

bean election, 228
beggars, 9, 80, 194
Belden, Jack, 168
birth control, 244
black market, 52, 153, 171, 177, 186, 194
blockade, Kuomintang naval, 6, 217, 232, 237, 252, 254-5, 267, 277-8
Bolshevik revolution, 45
Booth, General, 200
Boxer uprising, 71
Britain, Soviet attitude to, 62
British cemetery, 187
British Council, 219
British Yangtze incident, 164-5, 170
Buddhism, xvii, 36, 149, 245
business, *see* commerce; industry

c

capitalist in new China, 195-6
Catholic reports on Communists, 53
Catholic University, *see* Fu Jen University
CC Clique, 83, 97
Central Bank, 17, 55, 102
Central News Agency, 35, 98, 105, 200
Central Park, 14, 69, 92, 182, 205
Chang, Professor, 20, 110
Chang Pi-hsien, 241
Changchun, 33, 35, 69
Chao-kuan-ying, 123-4, 128
Chase National Bank, 219
Cheeloo University, 71
Chen, Mr. (landlord), 88, 111-13, 152
Ch'en Li-fu and Ch'en Kuo-fu, 83

Ch'en Po-ta, 225
Ch'en-t'ang-chuang, 125
Ch'en Yüan, President, 183
Ch'i Pai-shih, 183
Chiang Kai-shek, 32-3, 35, 87, 91, 94,
    104, 108, 110, 132, 160, 164, 188,
    205 209, 212, 216, 268
    Madame, 34, 36
Chieh-fang Pao, see Liberation News
Ch'ien Ch'un-jui, 226
Ch'ien Men (front city gate), 73
Ch'ien Tuan-sheng, Professor, 195
Chin (pedicab- and house-boy), 53-4,
    56, 67, 75, 80, 86-7, 100-2, 108, 110-11,
    179-80, 187, 197-9, 206, 231, 250
Chin-pu Jih-pao, see Progressive Daily
China and the World Press, 93
China Reconstruction (Chung Chien),
    41, 45, 60, 71, 157
China Shakes the World, 168
Chinese civilization, social outlook of,
    36-7, 94-5
    breakup of, 61
Chinese Eastern Railroad, 156
Chinese Revolution and Chinese Com-
    munist Party, 135, 168, 183
Chopin, 83
Chou En-lai, Foreign Minister, 199
Christianity, 244-5, 267
Christmas, 79, 82
ch'ü (district), 121
    and chieh (street), 213
Chu Teh, 101, 108, 160
Chung Chien, see China Reconstruction
Chung Hai, 13-14, 69
Classics, Hall of, 14, 60-1
Coal Hill, 69, 160
coalition government, 44, 201-2
Coalition Government, On, 135, 183
collectivization, 122, 127-8, 221, 224, 259
College of Chinese Studies, 7; see also
    Language School
College of Fine Arts, 227
commerce, 124-5, 189, 259
    foreign, 129, 159, 172, 177-9, 220-1,
        250-1
    see also industry
common man, cult of, 147; see also lao
    pai hsing

communications, restoration of, 107,
    114-15, 163, 179, 216, 225
communism, American and Chinese at-
    titude to, 24, 39, 270
    as a religion, 146-9
Communists (Chinese):
    and capitalism, 195-9, 212
    — Chinese psychology, 148-9, 216
    — class struggle, 71-2, 241
    — culture, 103, 142, 187-8, 225-7
    — intellectuals, 24, 121, 126, 131, 157-
        9, 262
    — labor, 195, 211
    — marriage, 132-3, 144-5
    — religion, 155, 244-6
    — U.S., 77, 106, 158-9, 209, 239-40
    — U.S.S.R., 156-7, 199, 210, 212, 237-8,
        263-4, 267-8
    arms of, 19-20, 104, 272
    army of, 181-2, 235
    as instrument of popular will, 106
    avoidance of terrorism, 132, 260
    designation of, 87
    drama under, 142-3, 165-9, 228-31
    economic program of, 259
    educational program of, 117-18, 140-1,
        242, 245-7
    factors in victory of, 162-3
    foreign policy of, 109, 158-9, 186-7,
        209-10, 263-4
    future of, 265
    ideology of, 127-8, 146-9, 260-1
    industrial and commercial program
        of, 124-5, 127, 139, 189, 202
    justice under, 112-13, 155-6, 215
    land program of, 91, 105, 121-5, 127,
        153-4, 221-4, 259
    moral consciousness of, 143, 216, 260
    nationalism of, 130, 226
    number of, 208
    popular attitude to, 26-7, 99, 104, 234
    press under, 108-10, 118-20, 130-1,
        143-4, 200, 202, 240-1, 262
    problems of, 261-2
    propaganda of, 21, 98, 104-6, 108-9,
        118, 191, 228, 267, 273
    strategy of, 21
    taxes of, 125, 172, 177-8, 194, 216-17,
        224, 259, 271

Communists (Chinese) (*continued*)
treatment of foreigners, 145, 148, 174-5, 186, 219-20, 264, 272-3
victory parade of, 103-4
see also soldiers, Communist
confession, public, 133-4, 147, 150, 223, 260
Confucianism, 36-7, 95, 216
and Marxism, 46-7, 184
conscription:
labor, 80-2, 92-3
military, 56-7, 63-4, 67-8, 75
cooperative effort, 136, 175-6, 206, 224, 243; *see also* individualism, democratic
cooperatives, 125-9, 137-8, 171-2, 189-90, 204, 235, 259, 277
correspondents, foreign, 109-10, 120, 131, 158, 264; *see also* press
cosmopolitanism, bourgeois, 226
Creative Society, 193
criticism and self-criticism, 41, 83-4, 121, 189-90, 212, 233, 260
culture, Communist attitude to, 187-8, 225-7
see also art; drama; handicrafts; literature
currency, Aug. 19 reform of, xvii, 21, 41, 47, 57, 100, 275
exchange of foreign, 32, 49, 52-3, 55, 63, 66, 153, 171, 177, 186-7, 194, 271

d

Daily News Release, 179, 181, 197, 217, 221
Daily Worker, 202, 259
democracy, in China, 201
Western and Soviet concepts of, 62-3
"Democratic Dictatorship, On the People's," 208-12
in action, 213-14
Democratic League, 116, 201-2, 208
Democratic National Construction Association, 201-2
Dewey, John, 268
Dick (Fulbright student), 75-6, 88-9, 147-8
disasters and anomalies, 28

Dix, Dorothy, 144
dogs, killing of, 85-6
drama, 142-3, 165-9, 228-31; *see also* art; literature
drought, 162, 171, 218, 234, 250, 277-8

e

E.C.A. (Economic Cooperation Administration), 22, 109, 152, 162, 277
economic conditions, 9, 21-2, 26-7, 32, 35, 41-3, 47, 63, 100, 107-8, 115-16, 128-9, 137-9, 171-2, 176-9, 194, 200, 204, 216-19, 232-3, 247-8, 259, 271
education, 117-18, 140-1, 173, 242, 245-7
Eighth Route Army (Pa Lu Chün), 76-7, 98, 166-8, 188, 222, 237; *see also* People's Liberation Army
Eimer, Father, 53
electricity, supply of, xvii, 60, 70, 73, 75, 79, 85, 87, 90, 97-8, 163
"emperor-countryism," 190-1
Engels, 212
enlightenment, instantaneous, 184, 245
ever-normal granary, 127
examinations, university entrance, 23

f

fa pi dollars, 21, 57-8, 275; *see also* currency
"face," 38
Fairbank, John K., 268
family, conflicts in, 241-3
Fang Chia Yuan, 7, 150-1
father image complex, 94
Fengtai, 54, 72
Fitzhugh, 15, 165
fliers:
American captured, 269, 272-3
Kuomintang, 44, 50
flood, 218-19, 232, 234, 248, 250, 277-8
Fogg Museum, 32
food, arrival in Peking, 102
Manchurian, 171, 176
shortage of, 162, 171-2, 176, 232, 234, 259, 261, 270-1, 278
Forbidden City, 13-14, 67, 69, 108, 151, 188, 191, 205

Foreign Policy Association, 106
foreigners:
　attitude to Communists, 145, 177, 187,
　　251
　attitude to students, 175
　Communist treatment of, 109, 145,
　　148, 174-5, 186, 219-20, 264, 272-3
　plight of, 18
　see also correspondents, foreign
Forke, 53
Formosa, 9, 164, 255, 257, 271
Fortune Magazine, 203
"fox story," 109-10
Fu, Professor, 157-9, 174
Fu Jen (Catholic) University, 28-9, 183
Fu Tso-yi, General, 51, 64-5, 68-70, 78,
　　82, 85, 98, 101, 105, 110-12, 116-17,
　　139, 175, 263
　confession of, 150
　surrender of, 96, 106, 113
Fulbright (Program and Fellows), xvii,
　　xx, 44, 49, 75, 85, 173
funerals, simplification of, 189

g

Galia (author's wife), xvi, 2, 14-16, 26,
　　34, 48-9, 54, 79, 83, 86, 100, 107,
　　110-12, 153, 175-6, 187, 198, 206-7,
　　220, 241-2, 257, 259-60
gasoline, shortage of, 116, 172, 191
glacis, 71, 77, 79-80, 97, 100, 103; see also
　　Tung-tan glacis
Gold Fish Hutung, 180
gold yuan, xvii, 21, 43, 57, 66, 102, 107-8,
　　115, 275; see also currency

h

Hals, Father, 53
handicrafts, 10, 30; see also art
Harbin, 53, 119
Harvard University, 32
Hatamen Street, 73, 100
Heaven, Altar and Temple of, 12-13,
　　34, 48, 51, 59, 61, 74, 79-80, 82, 88,
　　92, 188
Ho, Mr., 172

Ho Ssu-yüan, 97, 106
Ho Ying-ch'in, War Minister, 27
hoarding, 90-1
Hong Kong:
　arrival in, 4
　as capitalist paradise, 256-7
Hopei Medical College, 42
house, author's, 7-8, 150-3
Hill, Miss, 173, 192-3
Hitler, 238
Hsi Yuan, 66, 74; see also western air-
　　field
Hsia Kung Fu (Palace of Duke Hsia),
　　8
Hsin Min Hui (New People's Party),
　　67
Hsin-min Pao (New Citizen), 119
Hsing-t'ai, 173
Hu Shih, Dr., 57, 145, 183-4
Hu Yu-chih, 237
Hua-pei Jih-pao, see North China
　　Daily News
hutung (small street), 7-8, 73, 77, 205,
　　260

i

I Chose Freedom, 183
imperialism and "emperor-countryism,"
　　190-1
individualism, democratic, 240, 264; see
　　also cooperative effort
industry and industrialization, 114, 124-
　　5, 128, 216-17, 259, 262
inflation, 32, 47, 78, 91, 100, 153, 179,
　　194, 275, 277
　how to beat, 138
　see also prices
Institute of Economic Research, 128, 275
intellectuals:
　and Communists, 24, 121, 126, 131,
　　157-9, 262
　— manual labor, 13
　— Marxism, 184, 192, 262
　— other classes, 37
　— U.S., 23-5, 131
　— U.S.S.R., 23-5
　as a wavering class, 193
　mentality of, 46

International News, 105
Internationale, 140
internationalism, proletarian, 226

i

Jade Fountain, 75-6
James, Mr., 55
Jen Li Rug Co., 178
Jen-min Jih-pao, see *People's Daily*

k

k'o-t'ing (guest hall), 7, 50
Kravchenko, 183
Kremlin, 191
Kuan Ch'a, see *Observer*
Kuang-ming Jih-pao (Glorious Daily), 202
Kuo Mo-jo, 193, 225, 244
Kuomintang (Nationalist) party and government:
  cultural policy of, 27
  disintegration of, 84, 261
  economic policy of, 27
  ideology of, 95
  popular attitude to, 26-7
  press criticism of, 41, 83-4
  propaganda of, 11, 21, 33, 105, 256
  see also soldiers, Kuomintang
Kuomintang Revolutionary Committee, 116, 201, 208

l

labor, *see* conscription, labor; workers; unions
Lama Temple, 14, 58
land reform, 21, 91, 105, 121-5, 127, 153-4, 172-3, 221-4, 259
landlord:
  and servant, case of, 112-13
  oppression, 165-8
Language School, 7-8, 48, 64
lao pai hsing ("old hundred names" or common people), xx, 139, 147, 234
law, 112-13, 155-6, 203-4

Legation Quarter, 71
Lenin, 212
letters, *see* mail
Li Tao, General, 186
liberals, *see* intellectuals
Liberation Army, *see* People's Liberation Army
Liberation News (Chien-fang Pao), 130, 202
Life, 106
Lin Piao, General, 181
Lincoln, Abraham, 227
literature, New Democracy, 118, 202
  modern Chinese, 192-3
  theory of, 225-7
  see also art; drama
Liu-li-ho, 65
Locke, 36
Loehr, 75, 88
Loucks, Dr., 55
Lu Chih-wei, President, 150

m

Ma, Mr. (Chinese teacher), 26-7, 54, 63-4, 110, 152, 242-3
Ma Hung-kuei, 65
MacArthur, General, 110
mail, 58, 83, 129-30, 142, 161, 185, 193, 218
Malthus, 244
Manchuria:
  and Russia, 156-7, 174, 236-8, 263-4
  food of, 171, 176-7
  economic situation in, 161-2
Mandate of Heaven (*T'ien Ming*), 269
Mao Tse-tung, 87, 101, 108, 118, 120, 140, 146, 148, 161, 182-4, 195, 203-4, 214, 217, 226, 234, 259
  eight points of, 91, 103, 105, 150, 160
  policy statement of, 208-12
Marco Polo, description of Peking, xv
Marco Polo Bridge, 70
marriage, 132-3, 144-5, 154-5, 197-9, 231
Martin, 35
Marx, 36, 212, 244
Marx-Leninism, 202, 204, 261

Marxism, 118, 127, 222, 226-7, 242, 244, 260-2, 267
  and Confucianism, 46-7, 184
  intellectual reaction to, 184, 192, 262
May 4 and 30 movements, 171, 192
Mei Lan-fang, 225
Mencius, 274
Mo Tzu, 37, 149, 189
Mongolia, Outer, 163, 237
Morrison Street (Wang Fu Ching Ta-chieh), 65, 73, 100, 103, 107, 130, 151, 153, 180, 194, 200
movies, 118
mu (Chinese acre), 123-4, 172-3, 232
Mukden:
  conditions in, 33
  siege of, 69, 119
Mukden Medical College, 108
Muller, Professor, 19, 155-6
museums, Chinese attitude to, 31-2

n

Nan Ch'ih Tzu, 73
Nan Hai, 13-14, 69
Nan Yuan, 66, 74; *see also* southern airfield
Nankai University, 128, 137, 275
Nanking:
  capture of, 164
  rehabilitation of, 181
Nation, The, 46
National Library, Peking, 18, 188
National Youth Congress, 173, 175
nationalism, 130, 226
Negro problem, 39-40, 274
Nei-wu Pu-chieh (Avenue of the Ministry of Internal Affairs), 48-50, 52, 59, 86
new China, spirit of, 135-6
New China News Agency, 119, 143, 179, 185, 187, 239-41
New Democracy, 118, 131, 141, 245-7
  and socialism, 196, 204, 259
  religious qualities in, 146-9
New Democracy, 135, 183
New Democracy Youth Corps, 140, 146
New Life Movement, 11

New Republic, 106
New Times, 202
New Year, 83, 85
  Chinese, 99-101, 107, 110, 228
New York Herald-Tribune, 106
New York Times, 259, 269-70, 274
night soil, 80-1, 92, 182
Normal College, 35, 67, 174
North Atlantic Pact, 144, 240
North China Daily News (Hua-pei Jih-pao), 82, 100, 105
North China Liberation Army, 202
North China Military Administration University, 117-18
North China People's Government, 116; *see also* People's Government
North China People's Revolutionary University, 117
North China Trading Corporation, 115, 126, 129, 137, 171, 178, 277
North China University, 117, 140, 146-7, 165

o

Observer (Kuan Ch'a), 41
Olive, Vice-Consul, 219
Oxford Movement, 134

p

Pa Lu Chün, *see* Eighth Route Army
Palace Museum, 114
P'an T'ao Kung (Hall of Spiral Peaches), 143, 145
pao chia system, 64, 213
Pao Chüeh-min, Professor, 275
Paoting, loss of, 59
parade, Communist victory, 103-4, 164
peace moves, 83, 87, 96-7, 106-7, 116, 141-2, 150, 158, 160
pedicabs, 9
  union of, 108, 179-80
Pei Hai, 13-14, 69, 83, 97, 107, 163, 260
Peiping and Peking, names of, xv-xvi
Peiping Chronicle, 32-3, 35, 56, 58-9, 63-4, 72-3, 80, 83

Peiping Digest, 118, 124, 126, 153, 179

Peiping Union Medical College
(P.U.M.C.), 55, 271-2

Peita, 35, 38, 43, 60, 117-18, 157, 173-4,
179, 183, 195, 241; *see also* Peking
National University

Peking:
arrival in, 5, 7
departure from, 232, 249-50, 252
description of, xv-xvi
dreamlike quality of, 17-19
impoverishment of, 8-10
journey to, 1-6
military activity in, 17, 69-70, 80
morning sounds of, 16-17
name of, xv-xvi, 258
rehabilitation of, 107, 114
Russians in, 190
shelling of, 69, 91-2
siege of, xvii-xviii, 68-72, 78-9, 81-3, 89,
91, 96-7, 114, 118, 175-6
social life of, 18-19
surrender of, 96-8, 100-1, 103, 105-6,
120, 164

Peking American School, xviii, 7

Peking Hotel, 75, 102

Peking National University, 35, 57; *see
also* Peita

People's Bank, 102, 106, 116, 125, 138,
144

People's Court, 113, 155, 215

People's Daily (Jen-min Jih-pao), 105,
108-9, 117, 119, 137, 143, 160, 202

People's Government, 106-7, 117, 129,
131, 186, 194, 235, 252, 262

People's Liberation Army, 98, 100-2,
105-7, 109, 114, 118, 135, 181-2, 186,
225, 228, 234, 241, 260
victory parade of, 103-4
see also Eighth Route Army; soldiers, Communist

people's notes, 102, 107-8, 115, 275; *see
also* currency

Peters, 52

Pi Yün Ssu, 60

"planting songs," see *yang ko*

Po-ling Jih-pao, 240

police state, 132, 213

Political Consultative Conference, 201,
208
political developments, 116
political legitimacy, concept of, 269-70
population problem, 244, 262
Port Arthur, 156
posters, Communist, 98, 104-5, 118
press under Communists, 108-9, 118-20,
130-1, 143-4, 200, 202, 240-1, 262;
see also correspondents, foreign
prisoners:
reform of, 133-4
release of, 67, 75, 77-8
professors, economic status of, 18, 35,
116, 173, 200, 233
prices, 21-2, 32, 35, 42, 47, 63, 73, 100,
107, 115, 128, 137, 139, 171, 177-8,
194, 204, 218-19, 232-3, 271, 275-9;
see also inflation
Progressive Daily (Chin-pu Jih-pao),
119-20, 123, 128, 132-3, 137, 143-4,
147, 171-2, 176, 189, 195, 202-4, 208,
215, 231-3, 238, 245, 247-8, 275
letters in, 144, 154, 156, 237
propaganda:
Communist, 21, 98, 104-6, 118, 191,
228, 264, 273
Kuomintang, 11, 21, 33, 105, 256
Proust, 24
P'u-yü, 173
public mood, xvii-xviii, 205-6, 233-4
puritanism, 147, 216

r

radio, short-wave, 120, 234
Red Spear Society, 123
Red Star over China, 183
refugees, 60-1, 65-6, 73-4, 80-1, 92, 115,
180; *see also* students, refugee
rehabilitation, 107, 114, 175-6, 179
religion, 143, 155, 244-6
politics as a, 146-9, 260
Renaissance, Chinese literary, 45, 57, 192
republic, Chinese term for, 41
responsibility, Chinese sense of, 16
Reuter's, 200
revivalism, political, 134-5, 147, 229, 260

rice riots, 47
rich, how it feels to be, 89-91
Rites, Book of, 46-7
Roberts, 145
Roosevelt, Franklin D., 227, 274
Rotary Club, 220
Rousseau, 36
rumors, 44, 132-3, 154-5, 256
Russia:
    and Manchuria, 156-7, 174, 236-7, 263-4
    Chinese Communist attitude to, 156-7, 199, 210, 212, 237-8, 263-4, 267-8
    influence on China, 24-5, 192, 268
    views on, 62-3
    war against Japan, 237-8
Russian and English, teaching of, 237, 246
Russell, Bertrand, 268

S

salaries, 18, 35, 116, 173, 200, 233
Salvation Army, 15, 200
savings-unit plan, 138, 144
self-examination (*fan sheng*), 133-4
Shanghai:
    capture of, 185-6
    conditions in, 41-2, 47-8, 63, 181, 193-4, 219, 232-3
    through train from, 216
Shih Ch'a Hai (Lake of Ten Temples), 197
Shih-chieh Jih-pao, see *World Daily News*
Shih-ching-shan, 20, 70, 85
Shihchiachuang, 116, 119, 173
ship, breakdowns of, 2-5
siege, Peking, xvii-xviii, 68-72, 78-9, 81-3, 89, 91, 96-8, 114, 118, 175-6, 187
silver dollars, Chinese, 49, 63, 66, 116, 129; see also currency
Sinkiang, 163
Sino-Soviet Friendship Treaty, 156-7, 199, 238, 244
Snow, Edgar, xx, 183
society and individual, Chinese concept of, 15-16

Soil, Altar of, 14
soldiers:
    Communist, 72, 76, 101, 111, 135-6, 152-3, 163, 260; *see also* People's Liberation Army
    Kuomintang, 68, 76-7, 110-11, 116-17, 135, 187-8, 188
Song of the Red Flag, 228
southern airfield, 66, 73-4, 170; *see also* Nan Yuan
southern expedition, 117, 140, 152-3, 173, 181-2, 234, 236, 241
Soviet Consulate, 45
Soviet Union, *see* Russia
Soviet Woman, 202
"special service" (*t'e wu*), 23, 248-9, 261
Stalin, 105, 212
starving man, 14-16, 37, 260
State Department, U.S., 239, 255, 263
Stuart, Ambassador Leighton, 187
students:
    and America, 38-40, 174-5
    — Kuomintang, 22
    — manual labor, 13, 175
    arrests of, 22, 67
    Chinese attitude to, 96
    refugee, 12-14, 34, 48-52, 58-61, 64, 81, 85-8, 95-6, 98-9, 111-12, 141, 151, 174, 188
study groups, 133, 140-1, 260
Summer Palace, 18, 76, 175, 190
Sun (cook), 110-11
Sun Yat-sen, 50, 121, 148, 161, 188, 210, 214, 244
Sung, Mrs. (landlady), 8, 34, 44, 50, 57-8, 86-8, 111-13
superstition, *see* religion

†

Ta-chung Jih-pao (*Daily Masses*), 130
Ta Kung Pao, 41-2, 47, 58, 65, 119; see also *Progressive Daily*
T'ai Miao, 13, 51, 66, 69
Taiyuan, siege of, 35, 68-9, 112, 141, 164, 170, 177
Taku, 126

Tangku, 249, 252, 254
Taoism, 36
Tass News Agency, 109
taxation, 125, 172, 177-8, 194, 216-17, 224, 259, 271
Theo (author's son), xvi, xviii, 7, 14, 16, 26, 54, 60, 66, 79, 93, 99, 151-2, 250, 257
  operation of, 55
thought control, 118, 120, 142-3, 159, 261
Three People's Principles, 247
Three People's Principles Youth Corps, 126, 140
T'ien An Men (Gate of Heavenly Peace), 108
T'ien Chün, 199
Tientsin:
  departure from, 251-3
  foreign trade of, 177-8, 250-1
  occupation of, 91, 105-6
  prices in, 275-9
Tientsin Daily, 119
Tito, 109
Tolstoy, 45
Tong, Hollington K., 93-4
trade, see commerce
treaties, unequal, 156-7
Truman, President, 110, 120, 270
Tsinan:
  Communist treatment of, 33, 53, 71-2
  fall of, 20-1, 27, 257
Tsing-ho, 68
Tsinghua University, 23, 29-30, 35, 65, 68, 70, 74-6, 82, 107, 117, 145-8, 158, 172, 175, 183, 238
  bombing of, 81, 89
Tsingtao, capture of, 193-4
Tung An market, 22, 78, 151, 164, 194
Tung Hsing Lou restaurant, 172
Tung Pi-wu, 116
Tung-tan glacis, 71, 73, 79-80, 139, 175; see also glacis
Tung-tan market, 66
Tung Yüeh Miao (Temple of the Eastern Peak), 51, 59
Tungchow, 65, 72
turtle in Chinese folklore, 108, 216
Tz'u Hsi (Manchu empress dowager), 8

U

U.S.S.R., see Russia
U.S. Information Service (U.S.I.S.), 39, 49, 52, 61, 92, 120, 195, 219
Union at the Heavenly River, 230-1
unions, 108, 179-80, 197, 259, 270, 272; see also workers
United Press, 109, 120, 200
United States, see America
United States and China, 268

V

verbalism, 10-11
Versailles Treaty, 171
Victors, the, 145
Village in August, 199
Voice of America, 234
VOKS, 219

W

Wallace, Henry A., 39, 63
Wan Shou Ssu (Temple of Ten Thousand Years of Longevity), 74
Wang An-shih, 127
Wang Mang, 127
Wang Shou-jen, 37
war, three years of, 225
Water Classic Commentary, 183-4
water supply, xvii, 70, 73, 75, 79-80, 83, 87
western airfield, 66, 73, 142; see also Hsi Yuan
Western civilization, social outlook of, 36
Western Hills, xvi, 13, 60, 76, 97, 141, 145, 175
"white Chinese," 88
White-haired Girl, 165-9, 174, 181, 200, 228
White House, 190-1
White Paper on China, 239, 263
Wo Fo Ssu, 60
wo-t'ou (corn flour dumplings), 86, 242
women, 145; see also marriage
Women, All-China Federation of, 145

Wong Wen-hao, Premier, 42
Wong Yun-wu, Finance Minister, 32
workers, 211, 217, 228-9, 270-2; *see also*
  conscription, labor; unions
World Daily News (Shih-chieh Jih-pao),
  57, 83, 98, 119
Writers and Artists, All-China Confer-
  ence of, 225
Wu Han, Professor, 173
Wu Hua-wen, General, 72
Wusih, 245

Y

yang ko ("planting songs"), 103, 147,
  164, 194, 205, 214-16, 243
Yao and Shun (sage rulers), 47
Yeh Chien-ying, General, 102
Yen Hsi-shan, General, 68, 112
Yenan, 105, 109, 193, 262
Yenching University, 70, 74, 76, 89, 145,
  150, 172, 175, 200
Yunnan University, 43